Dribbling for Dawah

Advanced Praise

A welcome addition to the growing body of literature on sports and religion, this book discusses not only the contributions of Muslim athletes, but also the views of American Muslims on what it means to be both American and Muslim.
—Amir Hussain, professor of Theological Studies,
Loyola Marymount University, and author
of *Muslims and the Making of America*

Dribbling for Dawah is groundbreaking, rich, and compelling. Steven Fink reviews the emerging body of literature that explains the functions of sports and religion and defines the concepts and acts of piety in the context of sports, reminding readers what sports have done for other religious and racial minorities in American societies. He then introduces readers to Muslim Americans who relied on sports to bond with one another and build bridges with their neighbors. Fink writes beautifully, meticulously, skillfully, sensitively, and authoritatively. He has written an indispensable work that comparative and interdisciplinary scholars of religious studies will appreciate and all readers will enjoy.
—Ahmed E. Souaiaia, associate professor of Religious Studies,
International Studies, and College of Law, University of Iowa

If you are looking for an accessible, yet scholarly introduction to the role of sports in Muslim American communities, this is it. Covering famous professionals and youth athletes alike, Steven Fink explains the central role of sports in shaping Muslim communities, embodying Islamic values, and serving as a bridge to non-Muslims. A diverse group of Muslim Americans from across the country explains what sports mean to them, and Fink ably analyzes how Muslim American athletics reflect and shape the long history and contemporary role of religion and sports in the United States.
—Edward E. Curtis IV, Millennium Chair
of the Liberal Arts & professor of
Religious Studies, IU School of
Liberal Arts, Indianapolis

D1595650

SPORTS AND RELIGION

A SERIES EDITED
BY JOSEPH L. PRICE

Dribbling for Dawah

Sports Among Muslim Americans

Steven Fink

MERCER UNIVERSITY PRESS | *Macon, Georgia*

2016

MUP/ P536

© 2016 by Mercer University Press
Published by Mercer University Press
1501 Mercer University Drive
Macon, Georgia 31207

9 8 7 6 5 4 3 2 1

Books published by Mercer University Press are printed on acid-free paper
that meets the requirements of the American National Standard for
Information Sciences—Permanence of Paper for Printed Library Materials.

ISBN   978-0-88146-592-1
Cataloging-in-Publication Data is available from the Library of Congress

Contents

Acknowledgments

I would like to begin by thanking the eighty-five people whose insights made this book possible. Though far too many names to list here, each individual who generously gave his or her time to be interviewed shaped this book greatly. I came away from each conversation with invaluable material and thought-provoking ideas, not to mention pleasant memories of connecting and laughing with people I had never met before. I would particularly like to thank those interviewees who read and commented on portions of my draft pertaining to their insights, and special thanks go to Rizwan Butt for his extensive remarks on multiple chapters.

I am grateful to Mercer University Press Sports and Religion Series Editor Joe Price, both for his vision for the series and for his confidence that an examination of Muslim American athletic activities would make a significant contribution to the series. Price gave excellent editorial assistance; thank you for your helpful suggestions and attentiveness to detail.

I would like to express my gratitude for my 2014 spring sabbatical provided by the University of Wisconsin-Eau Claire, which propelled me to pursue a book-length project.

I am deeply appreciative of the influential role of family and friends on this book. My parents, Bob and Darlene, have been lifelong sources of support, and my parents-in-law, Bob and Alice, have enriched my life tremendously. Thanks to my sister Lori for modeling enjoyment of words early in my life, and I extend my appreciation to childhood friends Scott Oswald, Geoff Wright, and Kevin McCreight for countless hours of enjoying sports together. I would like to acknowledge my two great mentors who helped me find my way through graduate school, Ahmed Souaiaia and David Klemm. I also want to thank my colleague Charlene Burns, who encouraged me to pursue this book idea shortly after it crossed my mind. My sons, Nathan and Justin, have been a huge part of this project, giving me great companionship and fun times along the way. Finally, to my wife, Dorie, I feel like you have been with me every step of my research and writing. I cannot thank you enough for your encouragement and sacrifices that made this book possible.

Introduction

As the ref heaved the ball upward for the third overtime tip-off, I suspected I was not the only one excited to see the game continue. Muslim Sports Day participants were pouring into the gym, drawn by a drama that seemed like it might never end. After Connecticut's Finest finally finished the game on top, I was as struck by the mass of people who had gathered courtside for this men's basketball semifinal as I was by both teams' exhaustion and displays of mutual respect. I had been looking forward to Muslim Sports Day for months, anticipating that a day of observing over a thousand men, women, and youth take part in a panoply of athletic events would fill my mind and my notebook with abundant material. I was not expecting, though, to be riveted by the athletic activity as I was with the triple-overtime thriller. Not all Muslim Sports Day events mirrored this level of intensity; joviality filled much of the air, as it did during the baby crawling race or a preliminary-round cricket game in which players and fans chirped with banter and laughter. Yet, as events progressed to their quarterfinal, semifinal, and championship stages, there was no mistaking that competitiveness was coursing through participants' veins.

I had seen this competitive fire before while watching other Muslim American sports activities, and I had heard many Muslim Americans testify to their own athletic zeal. Whether through observation or interview, it became abundantly clear that many Muslim Americans love sports, enthralled by the chance to compete and by the pleasure that pervades play. Though hoping not to dim the lights on such enjoyment of sports' intrinsic delights,[1] my focus in this book is nonetheless on particular *results* experienced through Muslim American athletic activity. Amidst Muslim-organized basketball leagues, sports programs at

[1] Two authors who concentrate at length on sports' intrinsic pleasures are Johan Huizinga, *Homo Ludens: A Study of the Play-Element in Culture* (Boston: Beacon Press, 1955) and Michael Novak, *The Joy of Sports: End Zones, Bases, Baskets, Balls, and the Consecration of the American Spirit* (New York: Basic Books, 1976).

mosques and Islamic schools, events such as Muslim Sports Day, and the accomplishments of pro Muslim athletes, I identify two major functions of Muslim American sports, which I label "bonding" and "bridging." Having adopted these terms from Mike Collins's 2007 article "Leisure Studies and the Social Capital Discourse," I have tweaked his meanings to fit the context of sports among Muslim Americans.[2] In my usage, bonding focuses exclusively on Muslims and refers to a strengthening of both personal piety and Islamic fellowship. My use of the term "bridging," on the other hand, centers upon relations between Muslims and non-Muslims, addressing the overturning of non-Muslims' negative perceptions of Islam and the spanning of gaps between Muslims and non-Muslims in post-9/11 America.

Setting its sights on these bonding and bridging functions, this book situates sports within the trajectory of Muslim American dawah, a concept that connotes both drawing Muslims to deeper devotion and giving non-Muslims a favorable impression of Islam. As Zareena Grewal explains, although dawah may be translated as "missionizing," Muslim Americans commonly employ the term "to refer to the propagation of faith practices among Muslims themselves and to the labor of disabusing non-Muslims of stereotypes by giving them a more accurate, humanizing, and even beautiful picture of Islam."[3] In line with the word's etymological basis in an Arabic root containing the meaning "to invite," dawah in the athletic setting serves as an invitation for Muslims to pour themselves into pious practices alongside fellow Muslims as ardently as they might throw themselves onto the floor to grab a loose ball or grind it out in the training room in hopes of tasting victory in an upcoming game. At

---

[2] Mike Collins, "Leisure Studies and the Social Capital Discourse," in *Sport, Leisure Culture, and Social Capital: Discourse and Practice*, ed. Mike Collins, Kirsten Holmes, and Alix Slater, 155–66 (Eastbourne: Leisure Studies Association, 2007). For Collins bonding refers to the building and maintaining of relationships between those in similar life circumstances such as friends and family, whereas bridging refers to weaker connections across ethnic, geographical, or other social boundaries.

[3] Zareena Grewal, *Islam Is a Foreign Country: American Muslims and the Global Crisis of Authority* (New York: NYU Press, 2013) 49. Grewal goes on to say that the "idea of converting Americans operates as a distant, implicit, and abstract goal" in this common understanding of dawah (ibid.).

the same time, sports-based dawah invites non-Muslims to recognize Muslims as full-fledged American teammates, not as benchwarmers who lack the game to run with non-Muslims in improving American society or as opponents seeking to sink American success. As these invitational tasks are played out on playing fields and in gyms throughout the nation, Muslim American athletic activities enter the action of an Islamic "dawah movement," part of a worldwide revival with particular momentum for many Muslim Americans since 9/11.[4] While the local American context flavors each instance of bonding or bridging through Muslim American sports, a global revivalist emphasis on Islam as a complete way of life is an important ingredient in each localized recipe.

In addition to placing Muslim American athletic activity within the dawah movement, this book also puts Muslim American sports into the stream of American religious history. Setting my sights on the period 1850–1950, I consider other American religious groups' experiences with sports to promote bonding, discussing Protestants, Mormons, and Catholics, as well as to facilitate bridging, zooming in on Catholics and Jews. My selection to swim in this particular stream is drenched in desire to highlight Muslims' unequivocal belongingness in American waters. I aspire to demonstrate that for innumerable Muslim Americans a deep commitment to faith is paired with a deep commitment to country. While it is true that many Muslim Americans reject particular popular American practices such as consuming alcohol, it is also very much the case that Muslims frequently immerse themselves in efforts to enhance American communities and improve the well-being of American lives. Hoping to illuminate Muslim allegiance both to faith and to country and aiming to distance myself from notions of a cacophonous clashing between the two, I have chosen not to emphasize sports as a way for Muslims to assimilate into American society. As Kambiz GhaneaBassiri argues in *A History of Islam in America*, studies that investigate Muslim assimilation into American society often paint an essentialized picture of a one-size-fits-all Muslim bloc over against a uniform non-Muslim

---

[4] For the "dawah movement" and its relationship with international Islamic revival, see Saba Mahmood, *Politics of Piety: The Islamic Revival and the Feminist Subject* (Princeton: Princeton University Press, 2005).

American society and question how "successfully" the former has assimi-lated within the latter.[5] In this framework it is American society, not Muslim Americans, holding the cards to determine what "successful as-similation" entails, suggesting that "in order to be active participants in American society, Muslims had to make certain choices imposed on them by an 'external America' that was disembedded from their experi-ences in this country."[6] Scholars who employ this paradigm may illumi-nate important insights and may have no intention to harm Muslim Americans in any way, yet my concern is that an emphasis on assimila-tion lends itself too easily to an Islam vs. America clash mentality that can lead non-Muslims to conclude that Muslim Americans merit exclu-sion from rights in their own homeland. With this concern in view, I set an assimilationist framework aside and turn instead to the dynamic inter-

---

[5] Sunaina Maira provides further insight into this "successful assimilation" scholarship, identifying its connection to the theme of "Muslim immigrant youth straddling 'two worlds,' a trope which frames Muslim and American identities in binary opposition and that is pervasive in the academic literature on immigrant and second-generation youth and in general public discourse" (Sunaina Marr Maira, *Missing: Youth, Citizenship, and Empire after 9/11* (Durham NC: Duke University Press, 2009) 162). GhaneaBassiri writes that scholars "have inquired, for instance, into how Muslims in the United States deal with the mixing of sexes, liberal democ-racy, religious bigotry, and, of course, the wearing of the veil. These inquiries have commonly centered on the question of how Muslims identify themselves in this in-herently foreign society" (Kambiz GhaneaBassiri, *A History of Islam in America: From the New World to the New World Order* (New York: Cambridge University Press, 2010) 5).

[6] Ibid., 374. GhaneaBassiri criticizes Paul Barrett's *American Islam* as an exam-ple of this analytical framework. For example, Barrett writes, "Intolerance versus broad-mindedness. ...Reform versus reaction.... Integration with American society versus retreat into foreign antagonisms....Muslims face critical choices as they strug-gle for the soul of their faith in the United States" (Paul M. Barrett, *American Islam: The Struggle for the Soul of a Religion* (New York: Picador, 2008) 277). Elsewhere, suggesting that Muslims have passed the test of assimilation, he states, "Middle-class income, a college graduation rate on a par with that of the larger population, an in-clination to vote that is impressive for a mostly immigrant group—all of these are indications of a minority population [American Muslims] successfully integrating into the larger society" (Barrett, *American Islam*, 9–10).

4

relatedness between Muslim sports activities and the flow of American religious history.

Reflections on Interviews

In his *New Faiths, Old Fears,* Bruce Lawrence proclaims, "I want to explore how one can think differently—at once more subtly and more positively—about Asian communities and other non-Asian communities in twenty-first-century America."[7] I share such an ambition in terms of thinking about Muslim Americans, hoping that examining athletic activity can bring a new voice to the chorus of those who want to discuss Muslim Americans more subtly and more positively than often portrayed. Though not a Muslim, I grip this ambition tightly due to being deeply touched by countless expressions of Muslim kindness. Though not a great athlete, my lifelong love of sports made the prospect of exploring Muslim American lives through the lens of sports irresistible. A variety of sources ended up functioning as tour guides throughout this exploration. I would have lost my way without scholarly reflections on a spectrum of topics pertaining to sports and to American Islam, and my journey would have been unbearably bumpy without Muslim sports organization websites and Internet articles. Fueling my investigative drive forward more than any other set of sources, though, has been the insight I received in interviews with eighty-five individuals, including eighty-three Muslims encompassing a broad collection of connections to sports and two non-Muslim Islamic school physical education teachers, which I conducted from February through May 2014.[8]

Except for ten interviews by phone, these conversations took place face to face, in mosques, coffee shops, athletic clubs, homes, and sundry other settings, in the Mid-Atlantic, the Midwest, New England, and the

[7] Bruce B. Lawrence, *New Faiths, Old Fears: Muslims and Other Asian Immigrants in American Religious Life* (New York: Columbia University Press, 2002) 13.

[8] I conducted a total of seventy interviews, with thirteen involving two interviewees together and one simultaneously including three participants.

West Coast.[9] Interviews averaged twenty-five to thirty minutes in length, during which I asked some sort of variation on the following:

1. What is your personal connection to sports?
2. What benefits do sports have, for anyone at all or specifically for Muslims?
3. What negatives or challenges do sports have, for anyone at all or specifically for Muslims?
4. What are some ways in which sports bring Muslims closer together?
5. What are some ways in which sports bring Muslims and non-Muslims closer together?
6. What positives and negatives do you see in engaging in competition?

Posed within semi-structured interviews,[10] these questions provided a conversational backbone and were complemented by follow-up queries based on themes that germinated from these six questions' seeds. I made audio recordings and transcriptions of each interview,[11] and for the sake of boosting credibility of interview data I sent each transcription to the interviewee for verification and feedback.[12] I then analyzed transcriptions, along with any additions or corrections I received, by way of data-driven descriptive codes.[13] Finally, I requested that interviewees read por-

[9] States with the largest number of interviewees were New Jersey (seventeen), California (thirteen), Michigan (twelve), Massachusetts (ten), and Illinois (six).

[10] For characteristics of semi-structured interviews, see Mats Alvesson, *Interpreting Interviews* (Los Angeles: Sage, 2011) 53.

[11] Although time-intensive, I transcribed each interview myself, agreeing with Johnny Saldaña that doing so provides the researcher with "cognitive ownership of and potentially strong insights" into interview data (Johnny Saldaña, *Fundamentals of Qualitative Research* (New York: Oxford University Press, 2011) 44).

[12] See Martyn Hammersley and Paul Atkinson, *Ethnography: Principles in Practice*, 3rd ed. (London: Routledge, 2007) for helpful guidelines regarding verification and feedback from interviewees.

[13] As opposed to concept-driven codes, data-driven coding "implies that the researcher starts out without codes, and develops them upon reading the material" (Svend Brinkmann, *Qualitative Interviewing* (Oxford: Oxford University Press,

tions of my book draft pertaining to their comments (and to read as much of the entire draft as they desired) in order to elicit additional confirmation of accuracy and recommendation for revision.

To recruit interviewees I used both sampling and snowballing techniques. The former involved sending e-mails to a diverse set of potential participants, and for the latter I asked interviewees for additional participants to recommend. Aiming for "representativeness,"[14] I interviewed Muslim Americans not only from multiple geographical regions, but also spanning a large age range. The majority fell within the twenty-five to forty-year-old bracket, yet a significant percentage was in the eighteen to twenty-five range and a few above fifty.[15] I talked with sixty-nine men and sixteen women, with the sectarian breakdown ringing in at seventy-three Sunni and ten Shia. As for ethnicity or race, the stat sheet reads thirty-nine South Asian, twenty-nine Arab, seven African American, and ten Other.[16] Furthermore, the eighty-five individuals who generously gave me their time, insights, and laughter hold a wide range of relations

2013) 62). As for descriptive codes, Saldaña explains that they "are primarily nouns that simply summarize the topic of a datum. This coding approach is particularly useful when you have different types of data gathered for one study, such as interview transcripts, fieldnotes, and documents. ...For initial analysis, descriptive codes are clustered into similar categories to detect such patterns as frequency (i.e., categories with the largest number of codes) and interrelationship (i.e., categories that seem to connect in some way)" (Saldaña, *Fundamentals of Qualitative Research*, 104).

[14] Alvesson uses this term to refer to "breadth and variation among interviewees so that they allow the covering of the social category one aims to address" (Alvesson, *Interpreting Interviews*, 49–50).

[15] All participants were at least eighteen years of age due to my decision to obtain Institutional Review Board approval only to interview adults.

[16] The "Other" category mostly includes Europeans, Afghans, and a mixture of at least two categories. Also, among the thirty-nine South Asians and twenty-nine Arabs, slightly more than half were born in the United States. Confident that I received extremely valuable perspectives from my predominantly first-, second-, and third-generation immigrant pool, I nonetheless recognize a significant shortcoming in this pool with its small African-American Muslim representation, an unfortunate result of receiving minimal response from African-American mosques I attempted to contact as well as a product of extremely few Muslim American sports organizations being led by African Americans.

to Muslim American sports, as shown by the following list designating a primary role for each interviewee:[17]

- Sports organization (including basketball league) administrator: 16
- Islamic school administrator: 10
- Mosque leader: 10
- Muslim Students Association (MSA) leader or athlete: 9
- Islamic school physical education teacher: 8
- Mosque sports activity participant: 8
- Mosque sports director or sports committee member: 7
- Mosque youth director: 4
- Basketball league player: 3
- Martial arts instructor: 3
- Muslim Interscholastic Tournament (MIST) director: 3
- Public high school or college coach: 3
- Sports journalist: 1

Wrapping up this reflection on my interviews, I would like to point out that I asked participants if they were comfortable with my using their name of if they preferred anonymity.[18] Only one interviewee requested to remain anonymous, with five saying they would decide after viewing their comments in book draft form.[19] Wanting my readers to get to know these individuals and foreseeing no potential harm in doing so, I am using actual names throughout the book except in the lone case where anonymity was requested.

---

[17] Some of these individuals fit in more than one category, but in each case I selected just one primary category for that individual.

[18] Ian Parker argues that anonymity may be used by researchers to more easily skew interview data according to their own purposes, thereby denying interviewees' true voices from being heard. As a result, he advises open discussion with interviewees regarding whether or not they might prefer to be named in a book or article (Ian Parker, *Qualitative Psychology: Introducing Radical Research* [New York: Open University Press, 2005]).

[19] All five of these individuals ended up saying they are comfortable with my using their actual names.

Overview of the Book

Before handing the microphone to these interviewees, I travel back in time to the years 1850–1950. Chapter 1 looks at the role of sports in increasing religious piety and camaraderie within the YMCA, Mormon recreation movement, and Catholic Youth Organization. I delve into distinctively Protestant, Mormon, and Catholic textures of bonding, all of which feature the conviction that sports are a potent agent for promoting piety, especially among youth threatened with the perils of religious declension. Sticking with this same time period, the next chapter ponders the precedent of sports supplying a more positive view of an American religious minority. I look at the chipping away of anti-Catholic walls as the result of individual Catholic American athletes, especially Joe DiMaggio, and the gridiron greatness of the Notre Dame squad. Next up is anti-Semitism, which lost some of its sting thanks to the bridging promoted by Jewish-American sportsmen like boxer Benny Leonard and most significantly baseball slugger Hank Greenberg.

The book then turns its sights more specifically to Muslim Americans in chapter 3 by addressing Islamic revivalism and Islamophobia, major catalysts of Muslim American sports-based bonding and bridging, respectively. At the heart of a desire to bolster Islamic piety and Muslim brotherhood through sports is an Islamic revival that throughout the late twentieth and twenty-first centuries has emphasized Islam as a complete way of life, taking its cues from the Qur'an and the traditions of Muhammad. As for bridging via sports, much of its motivation lies in counteracting anti-Islamic thoughts and actions from American media, government officials, and others who contribute towards the creation of a climate in which Muslims are commonly cast as undesirable threats to American society. Chapter 4 continues to set the stage for in-depth discussion of Muslim American bonding and bridging through sports in later chapters. Drawing upon traditions of Muhammad, interview comments, and Internet articles about sports and Islam, I survey a spectrum of Muslim attitudes regarding sports, ranging from the belief that sports are an act of worship that cultivate Islamic values such as patience and brotherhood to the standpoint that sports' negatives outweigh their positives because they tend to come packaged with a culture in conflict with

Islamic principles. I wrap up my reflection on the relationship between sports and Islamic teachings by looking at a menu of options regarding how Muslims negotiate fasting during Ramadan in the thick of athletic activity. Providing additional groundwork before digging into bonding and bridging in the book's second half, chapter 5 focuses on two types of barriers to Muslim American athletic participation. I begin with a common first-generation immigrant parent prioritization of academics over athletics and then turn to an array of impediments to athletic activity among Muslim American females. The influence of both of these hindrances has been huge, but changing winds have started to blow; the chapter looks at female athletes such as weightlifter Kulsoom Abdullah and fencer Ibtihaj Muhammad as well as other signs of significant shifts in the Muslim American athletic opportunity air.

Chapter 6 kicks off my convergence upon bonding and bridging, beginning under the bright lights of professional sports, particularly boxing, basketball, and football. Luminaries in this chapter include arguably the best-known athlete of all time, Muhammad Ali, and two basketball behemoths, Kareem Abdul-Jabbar and Hakeem Olajuwon. Stepping onto the gridiron, I focus especially on Hamza and Husain Abdullah, brothers who put their football careers on hold to perform the Hajj pilgrimage to Mecca, and I draw the chapter to a close with Muslim NFLers who have formed charity organizations. At this point I make the move to the local, amateur scene, the territory I will continue to traverse until the book's conclusion. Chapter 7 concentrates on Muslim basketball leagues, where dribbling for dawah has affected a large number of Muslim and non-Muslim American lives. After tipping off with some theories as to why basketball is far and away the most popular sport among Muslim Americans, I enter the action of leagues in New Jersey, Southern California, and Boston. The next chapter turns to athletic activities affiliated with what I dub "revivalist organizations." From pick-up games with a handful of players to an annual athletic event involving over a thousand, sports activities in this chapter flow forth from the Muslim Students Association, Islamic Circle of North America, Muslim American Society, New Jersey's Muslim Youth Community Center, and a nationwide set of contests for high-schoolers known as the Muslim Interscholastic Tournament. Serving as the next installment of the local

Muslim American athletic bonding and bridging story, chapter 9 explores mosque-based athletic activities. After a general consideration of mosque sports programs' perks and problems, I look at martial arts in mosques and then discuss four mosques with exceptionally expansive sports programs. The chapter ends with attention upon Shia Khoja communities, all-stars among Muslim Americans in their integration of sports into mosque life. Finally, chapter 10 enters the doorways of Islamic schools, examining physical education and extracurricular sports programs. Though a variety of sports-related challenges severely test many Islamic schools, I look at some that offer "A+" athletic activities. Two of these schools participate in athletic leagues comprised mostly of Christian, Jewish, and non-religiously affiliated schools, thereby promoting opportunities for young Muslims to interact with non-Muslims and present a positive picture of Islam. As I emphasize in the book's conclusion, opportunities like these accentuate athletic activity's ability to accelerate Americans' acknowledgement that Muslims are undeniably and completely a part of their twenty-first-century pluralistic American homeland.

1

Athletic Bonding in American Religious History

The ultimate purpose of our being interested in this recreational work is to keep our young people safe, pure, and under the influence of the Church, and keep them in such environment that they ultimately will find their way into some one or other of the Church organizations, Priesthood quorums, Sunday schools, and other organizations—the end being to establish in their hearts faith in God, love for his work, desire to serve and keep themselves during their leisure period free from the vices and sins and contaminating influences of the world.[1]

Declared by Latter Day Saint Apostle Melvin J. Ballard in 1923, this proclamation pinpoints the purposes of his Mormon Church's athletic activities. Yearning to entice its young people away from worldly pitfalls and into the life of the Church, Latter Day Saints jumped on an American bandwagon crowded with Protestants and peppered with Catholics who believed sports could stem the tide of religious declension. This chapter explores this view from its mid-nineteenth-century genesis to its full flowering a century later, focusing specifically on the Young Men's Christian Association, Mormon recreation movement, and Catholic Youth Organization. In all three cases leaders were deeply distressed by the religious disengagement of youth, and in each case leaders portended that young people would drift away further without sports keeping them connected to their faith. This athletic activity, however, was regarded as more than a religious life preserver. Leaders concluded that sports would not only prevent youth from sinking into irreligious depths; athletic activity would also breathe life into young people's religious piety and bring them closer together in Christian fellowship. Well before athletic activi-

---

[1] Quoted in Richard Ian Kimball, *Sports in Zion: Mormon Recreation, 1890–1940* (Champaign IL: University of Illinois Press, 2003) 46.

ties began to promote the bonding functions of strengthening piety and solidifying fellowship among Muslim Americans, the roots of sports-related bonding were making a deep descent into American soil.

This soil lacked athletic nutrients during the nation's infancy. An attempt to situate sports-related bonding in Colonial or antebellum America would be marred by an anachronistic reconstruction of sports' role in American history. As stated in Elliott Gorn and Warren Goldstein's *A Brief History of American Sports*, "No one in the colonies ever claimed that athletics built character, or made men out of boys, or inculcated the ethic of fair play."[2] Donald Mrozek asserts that Americans continued to ascribe little, if any, instrumental function to sports throughout the first half of the nineteenth century. Describing a mentality that may seem unfathomable today,[3] Mrozek writes, "To Americans at the beginning of the nineteenth century, there was no obvious merit in sport—certainly no clear social value to it and no sense that it contributed to the improvement of the individual's character or the society's moral or even physical health."[4] Yet, little by little, nineteenth-century America experienced a sea change in its thinking about sports. Previously struggling for existence on societal margins and deemed to impart negligible individual and communal benefits, sports by century's end occupied a huge chunk of American life and was linked to physical, psychological, and social perks galore. This mental metamorphosis regarding sports was the fruit of multiple factors, including advances in medical knowledge about the

[2] Elliott J. Gorn and Warren Goldstein, *A Brief History of American Sports* (Champaign IL: University of Illinois Press, 2004) 45.

[3] This mentality does have its contemporary critics, however. Andrew Miracle and C. Roger Rees discuss what they call the American "sports myth," arguing that they "find little empirical evidence that sport builds character or has any positive effects on youth, even though the idea that it does has been around more than a century" (Andrew W. Miracle, Jr. and C. Roger Rees, *Lessons of the Locker Room* (Amherst NY: Prometheus Books, 1994) 8). While aware of studies claiming to corroborate the link between youth sports and character development, Miracle and Rees dismiss these studies, claiming they "either have examined small, special populations or they have used flawed methodologies. No studies capable of withstanding rigorous scientific scrutiny offer much support for any tenets of the myth" (ibid., 222).

[4] Donald J. Mrozek, *Sport and American Mentality, 1880–1910* (Knoxville: University of Tennessee Press, 1983) xiii.

value of exercise and the unity of mind and body, but no factor triggered this transformation with as much influence as industrialization. Entailing long, often sedentary work days coupled with cramped living quarters, industrialization mass produced physical inactivity in cities throughout the nation. Industrial capitalists realized they could capitalize on sports, since athletic activity could mold more effective laborers by fostering physical endurance and dexterity, just as it could inculcate other desirable labor traits such as dependability, obedience, and teamwork. Moreover, as hordes of immigrants heeded big industry's call, sports were frequently penciled into the lineup of attempts at Americanization. Industrialists and social reformers of the day associated team sports with teaching immigrants core American values. As stated by Joel Rosen, by the end of the century the notion that sports were "capable of instilling a solid moral grounding among America's diverse citizenry had become one of the nation's chief articles of faith."[5]

Like industrialists and social reformers, religious leaders espoused this article of faith with increasing fervency. Though a mere half century earlier a link between sports and their church's mission may have been completely alien to American clergy minds, by the twentieth century's dawning many considered sports a staple food to serve their religious flock, especially to its younger members imperiled by urbanization. From the perspective of these religious leaders, American cities teemed with corruptive pitfalls for youth of their church. Loitering on street corners, frequenting pool halls, gambling, and other degenerative amusements were pegged as pathways towards joining street gangs and leading lives of crime. With its sedentary lifestyle replacing vigorous existence in the open frontier, city life also carried the troubling prospect of an influx of lazy, unmanly youth lacking the physical strength and chutzpah of erstwhile American heroes such as Andrew Jackson or Davy Crockett. Additionally, religious leaders commonly connected urbanization with a lamentable loss of small-town values, causing the collapse of rock-solid family and community ties in which the local church played a dominant

[5] Joel Nathan Rosen, *The Erosion of the American Sporting Ethos: Shifting Attitudes Toward Competition* (Jefferson NC: McFarland, 2007) 63.

role in moral instruction.[6] Amidst all these concerns, whether to provide an attractive alternative to dabbling in debauchery, to help youth maximize their muscle mass, or to simulate small-town solidity, religious leaders frequently prescribed athletic activity as the antidote to the ailments of urbanized American youth. Many gladly dispensed this athletic medicine, upholding it as doubly potent since it could not only prevent degeneracy and religious declension, but also fortify piety and fellowship.

Protestants preceded Mormons and Catholics in dispensing this remedy, thanks to a mindset that originated across the Atlantic. "Muscular Christianity" emerged in English public schools and universities via the pen of Charles Kingsley, an Anglican clergyman and novelist. Kingsley's 1850 novel *Alton Locke*, as described by Gorn and Goldstein, valorized "the cult of heroic English gentlemen, tempered by manly sports, educated to a fine practical intellect, and consecrated with devotion to Church and country."[7] Kingsley developed his Muscular Christian amalgam of sports, religion, and morality further in non-fiction writings, articulating the tenet exemplified in his novels that sports are the premier pedagogical tool for the moral growth of boys and young men. Much more effectively and enduringly than instruction in the classroom or church pew, Kingsley asserted, sports taught "not merely daring and endurance, but, better still, temper, self-restraint, fairness, honour, unenvious approbation of another's success, and all that 'give and take' of life which stand a man in good stead when he goes forth into the world, and without which, his success is always maimed and partial."[8] As Kingsley's

---

[6] Steven Riess writes that late-nineteenth-century social reformers "saw sport as a substitute for the social life of small towns in which families had functioned as social and economic units, community ties were strong, and religion had played a dominant role in teaching sound moral values. While the small town was being displaced by the metropolis, sport would supposedly provide the same training for urban youth, especially children of the new immigrants, that daily country life had taught previous generations of Americans" (Steven A. Riess, *City Games: The Evolution of American Urban Society and the Rise of Sports* (Urbana: University of Illinois Press, 1989) 151).

[7] Gorn and Goldstein, *A Brief History of American Sports*, 88.

[8] This athletic character education found expression in another novel, Thomas Hughes's 1857 *Tom Brown's School Days*, which according to Gorn and Goldstein

ideas made their way onto American shores, Unitarian minister Thomas Wentworth Higginson drank them in and primed the pump for Muscular Christianity's popularity in the New World. In a series of *Atlantic Monthly* essays from 1858 to 1862, Higginson argued for the physical and moral benefits of athletic activity.[9] Rejecting an entrenched viewpoint within the Church that "athletic capacity" was "in inverse ratio to the sanctity expected of Christians," Higginson insisted upon the direct proportionality of "physical vigor and spiritual sanctity"[10] and urged churches to nurture this relationship by giving athletic activity a prominent position in their ministry, especially to youth. Not all Protestant clergy were convinced. Many evangelicals kept their distance from the Muscular Christian wave, with feet firmly planted inland due to a predisposition to view individuals as spiritual beings in need of eternal salvation rather than corporal beings with physical necessities. In plenty of liberal churches, on the other hand, Higginson's message prompted clergy to jump in and embrace sports as good news.

YMCA

With a growing number of converts, the gospel of sports bore a bounty of fruit first in the North and eventually throughout the United States, yet nowhere was the yield as great as the Young Men's Christian Association, or YMCA. Like Muscular Christianity itself, the YMCA was a British import to American soil. Unlike Muscular Christianity, it arrived in the United States without the emphasis on sports for which it would become best known. Athletic activities were few and far between in British YMCAs in their early years, prompting William Baker to pro-

---

"enjoyed instant popularity on both sides of the Atlantic. This romantic portrayal of life at Rugby School under headmaster Thomas Arnold idealized the sense of honor, fair play, and character development that English lads were said to imbibe with their strenuous games. Privileged young men who attended America's colleges after mid-century started emulating Tom Brown's muscular ways" (ibid.).

[9] William Baker states that Higginson's first essay, "Saints, and Their Bodies," marks "a definitive turning point in the long history of an uneasy relationship between religion and sport" (William J. Baker, *Playing with God: Religion and Modern Sport* (Cambridge MA: Harvard University Press, 2007) 40).

[10] Ibid.

fess that the YMCA "was born of Protestant piety, not playfulness"[11] during its inception in 1844. After arriving in its new American homeland in 1851, the YMCA's love affair with sports did not take place overnight. As the final Civil War shots were fired, no American YMCA housed a gymnasium, and New York YMCA Director Robert McBurney's clamoring for a gym met significant resistance from fellow New York YMCA overseers. McBurney responded to this opposition by organizing a committee that compiled a survey of moral and physical dangers faced by youth in the New York urban jungle, in hopes that survey results would cogently demonstrate a need for athletic activity at the YMCA. McBurney's wish came true. Construction of the New York YMCA gym kicked off a domino effect. By 1890 gyms could be found at approximately 400 American YMCAs, about half of which employed physical activity supervisors.

Thanks to McBurney, the New York YMCA initiated an additional trend in the national organization's relationship with sports, becoming the first YMCA to include the word "physical" in its constitution's description of its central goals. YMCAs followed suit across the nation, including in Springfield, Massachusetts, where Luther Gulick essentially expanded on McBurney's opening chapter of YMCA sports and made it into a tome.[12] Gulick championed Muscular Christianity's key precepts, building upon and propagating them as director of the YMCA Training School in Springfield. As Steven Overman puts it, Gulick believed that "the health and disposition of the muscles determined one's moral predispositions, that the right type of play had a greater influence over the character of a person than any other activity, and that morals rose no higher than they did in play."[13] Like other proponents of Muscular Christianity, Gulick contended that sports were in a league of their own at drawing youth away from licentious attractions while simultaneously

---

[11] Ibid., 42.

[12] In the words of Baker, Gulick "found the YMCA timidly stepping onto the playing field, uncertain of its right to be there; from the podium and with the pen, he removed the doubts" (ibid., 57).

[13] Steven J. Overman, *The Protestant Ethic and the Spirit of Sport: How Calvinism and Capitalism Shaped America's Games* (Macon GA: Mercer University Press, 2011) 160.

cultivating traits such as discipline, toughness, self-control, and leadership. Gulick embraced the notion of an inextricable link between sports and moral development, and by clearly integrating Christian theology into this nexus, he swayed YMCA leaders lukewarm towards sports to welcome athletic activity as an integral piece of the YMCA piety puzzle. Proclaiming Christ to be the savior of "the whole man, body, mind, and spirit,"[14] Gulick elevated Christian regard for the physical realm of life to a position of equality with the mental and spiritual. In 1895 the YMCA followed Gulick's lead and adopted the inverted triangle as its emblem, symbolizing mind, body, and spirit as the three components of the fully developed Christian man.

Besides formulating much of its theological underpinnings, Gulick's vast contribution to YMCA sports included designing training programs that became standard features of YMCAs throughout the nation and instructing future physical education directors who would implement these programs. One of Gulick's star YMCA Training School pupils stayed in town, where he responded to his teacher's call to create an indoor team sport that would provide young men at the Springfield YMCA with a recreational pursuit to satisfy their athletic appetites between football and baseball seasons. Most likely James Naismith had no clue that his response would provide the world with one of its most precious sporting treasures. As Springfield YMCA sportsmen tossed a soccer ball into peach baskets hung from the balcony railing at each end of the gym, basketball was born. Naismith's invention spread across the nation at fast break speed, accelerated by Springfield-trained disciples touting the game's physical and moral merits. Basketball soared to the top of YMCA athletic charts, though another sport forged in the crucible of YMCA athletic imagination was not too far behind. Encouraged by Gulick to design a game for urban businessmen who found basketball too strenuous for their tastes, W. G. Morgan served up volleyball. Gulick saw in Morgan's and Naismith's creations a goldmine for putting his Muscular Christian principles into practice; basketball and volleyball became the foundation of the YMCA Athletic League. Supplemented by YMCA swim meets and baseball and football teams, this league solidi-

---

[14] Quoted in Mrozek, *Sport and American Mentality*, 204.

fied a connection between Christianity and sports for innumerable Americans. While slow to penetrate bastions of evangelical resistance, Gulick's version of the Muscular Christian gospel gained zealous converts who regarded the YMCA gym as prime real estate for growth in Christian morality and camaraderie with fellow believers.

Amidst its proliferation, this gospel spilled forth outside of YMCA walls and made waves in local churches. Presaging a similar development in American mosques a century later, sports programs and leagues sprouted in Protestant churches in the late nineteenth and early twentieth centuries. One report pinpointed the number of church-based sports leagues in 1916 at an astounding 140.[15] Gulick and the YMCA cannot take exclusive credit for this ecclesial sporting boom. The road from the American introduction of Muscular Christianity to American church athletic activities did not always pass through Springfield. The social gospel laid down one well-trodden detour.[16] Nonetheless, YMCA influence was a highly significant cause of the rapid rise of sports at the local church level.[17] Gulick's footprints could be tracked in a church such as

---

[15] Baker, *Playing with God*, 82.

[16] Popular from 1870–1920 in many liberal Protestant churches, the social gospel called for the biblical principles of charity and justice to be put into practice for the sake of solving urbanized America's woes. Baker writes that largely because of the influence of the social gospel, "[d]uring the last two decades of the nineteenth century, a new kind of urban church emerged. ...It was an 'open' church, dispensing with old rented pews and quite literally opening its doors seven days and seven nights a week rather than the customary one or two. It built kitchens to provide sociable food and drink, rooms for domestic and industrial training, and a gymnasium for vigorous exercise and games. ...It sponsored basketball, baseball, and softball teams" (ibid., 74).

[17] Baker writes, "Taking a cue from the physical programs at the local YMCA, churches began building gyms and sponsoring sports teams and leagues" (ibid., 64). Rosen also cites Gulick's influence, declaring that churches "began hosting their own sporting events and various other sorts of competitions, subtly following Gulick's lead. ...[I]n addition to book learning and quiet contemplation, the church began to adopt the more modern suppositions regarding athleticism and physical exercise as a means to achieve a soundness of spirit while serving to reinvent the church as an instrument of vitality much in the manner that Gulick's triangle had reinvented aspects of the YMCA's charter" (Rosen, *The Erosion of the American Sporting Ethos*, 65).

the First Congregationalist Tabernacle Church in Jersey City, New Jersey, which at the turn of the century erected a YMCA-like structure dubbed the People's Palace. A gymnasium, swimming pool, bowling alley, and billiards room drew roughly 2,500 participants into its doors every month. Echoing the YMCA refrain that athletic activity would lure youth to pious gatherings instead of dens of sin, First Congregationalist minister John Scudder reportedly pointed from the People's Palace to his church building and proclaimed, "Play here or pray there, but keep away from the saloon and the gambling den."[18] Similar to Scudder, clergy at St. George's Episcopal Church in the Lower East Side of Manhattan were persuaded that sports belong in the ecclesial setting, fortifying more traditional elements like sermons or hymns. Croquet, tennis, and bicycling clubs constituted the St. George's sporting slate for older men and women, while younger men could enjoy baseball, basketball, and cricket, often going head to head against fellow New York churches in the Diocesan Union League and the Protestant Church League. Elsewhere in the Big Apple, forty Protestant churches formed the Sunday School Athletic League in 1904. Including baseball, basketball, track and field, and bowling, the league granted eligibility to players who attended a church Sunday School for at least four consecutive weeks and promised to eschew playing sports on Sundays.

Mormon Recreation Movement

With a pinch of YMCA-infused Muscular Christianity and a dash of rising concern over religious declension of urbanized youth, the recipe for sports-related bonding was doled out to churches beyond the Northeast, eventually reaching the Rocky Mountains. Forming what Richard Kimball designates the "Mormon recreation movement," the Church of Jesus Christ of Latter Day Saints, commonly known as the Mormon Church,[19] instituted sports as a vital part of its mission in the early twentieth centu-

---

[18] Quoted in Baker, *Playing with God*, 76.

[19] The term "Mormon" comes from the Book of Mormon, a sacred text viewed by Latter Day Saints as a supplemental testament to the Bible, written on golden plates unearthed by Joseph Smith. While the term was at first used against Latter Day Saints in a derogatory manner, they eventually adopted it for their own usage.

ry. LDS pioneers connected recreational activity with moral instruction from Mormonism's very beginning in the 1830s, yet this link remained predominantly in the background. It was brought out of the shadows in the following century by a new breed of Mormon leaders who organized a vast array of athletic activities and drew up a comprehensive LDS recreational philosophy. Reflecting their church's paradoxical relationship with the surrounding American society,[20] LDS leaders sought to relax yet maintain boundaries between Mormons and other Americans that had been firmly embedded before the granting of Utah's statehood in 1890. These leaders aspired to turn the page from the LDS Church's seminal era when Mormon theocracy and polygamy elicited aspersion from fellow Americans[21] to a new age when Mormons selectively opened up to the outside world while retaining a sense of distinctiveness apart from it.[22] Cautiously unlatching their gates to external influence, LDS overse-

---

[20] R. Laurence Moore argues that Mormons have regarded themselves "as good and typical Americans" while simultaneously not viewing themselves as "being like other Americans" (R. Laurence Moore, *Religious Outsiders and the Making of Americans* (New York: Oxford University Press, 1986) 45).

[21] Gordon and Gary Shepherd write, "The theocratic intervention of the Mormon Church in the worldly affairs of its members and in every aspect of territorial life was in distinct opposition to the capitalistic development of nineteenth-century American society. From the gentile perspective in Utah, the Mormon priesthood was perceived as an organization that violated American values of individualism and free enterprise and encouraged disloyalty to the United States. …Mormon beliefs and institutions—particularly the habit of block voting in political contests as counseled by their leaders—were denounced as un-American. Incensed by continued reports of Mormon disloyalty, theocratic intransigence, and immoralities in the name of religion, Congress repeatedly turned down church-sponsored bids for Utah statehood. Mormon polygamy was called a 'relic of barbarism,' and Congress began drafting legislation to put a stop to it" (Gordon Shepherd and Gary Shepherd, *A Kingdom Transformed: Themes in the Development of Mormonism* (Salt Lake City: University of Utah Press, 1984) 32–33).

[22] Kimball writes, "Mormons were caught between a past where plural marriage provided a strict border with the outside world and an uncertain future where boundaries would have to be carefully constructed to satisfy the mainstream world while maintaining the unique aspects—the 'specialness'—that the faithful had enjoyed throughout the nineteenth century. Boundaries had to be set that allowed the religious organization to maintain its integrity; however, those borders needed to be

ers embraced core Muscular Christian principles and a Protestant call to use sports to turn youth toward virtue in the Church rather than vice on the streets. Speaking at the annual LDS Mutual Improvement Association conference in 1910, Lyman Martineau professed that if LDS organizations "would take up athletics and make it one of the prominent features of their work, and invite the boys that were inclined to be wayward, that in due course of time these very boys would become enrolled members in the organizations. …Athletics, carried on in a proper manner, will do much to increase our attendance and bring about a general moral uplift."[23] On one level, Martineau's words could have come straight from Protestant clergy mouths, yet at the same time he and fellow LDS leaders spiced their church's athletic activities with a uniquely Mormon flavor. Kimball asserts that LDS sports "instructed adolescents in what it meant to *be* Mormon."[24] Like Protestant contemporaries, LDS leaders used sports to drown out the siren call of urban debauchery, but amidst doing so they distanced themselves from their contemporaries by seeking to replace this call with an enchanting melody of Mormon identity.

Muscular Mormonism took on a variety of forms, including a large number of "field days." At a three-day meet in 1910 in Holden, Utah, for example, 100 or so young athletes enjoyed running, high jump, pole vault, baseball, basketball, and wrestling competitions, capped off each evening by movies and chaperoned dances. The LDS field day granddaddy of them all was the annual Brigham Young University sports festival, which grew from humble 1911 beginnings to an assemblage of around 3,000 participants and even more spectators each year. These large-scale annual athletic events formed a conspicuous part of the Mormon recreation movement body, but it was basketball that made up its sporting backbone. Similar to what would materialize decades later among Muslim Americans, basketball became the most popular Mormon sport. Salt Lake City's Ensign Stake inaugurated a competitive

permeable enough to permit the passage of ideas and trends that would lead to acceptance by the world outside of the church community" (Kimball, *Sports in Zion*, 11).

[23] Ibid., 98.
[24] Ibid., 13.

league in 1908, marked by hundreds of spectators cheering on the team representing their ward.[25] In some wards there was simply too much enthusiasm for only one team, so top hoopsters played on a ward's "varsity" squad while others filled out its "junior varsity" roster. Basketball leagues continued to pop up across Mormon territory, and tournaments drew droves of zealous players and fans. A 1931 basketball tourney brought around 8,000 spectators to Salt Lake City to support their beloved church sides.

In order to accommodate the burgeoning basketball craze as well as other athletic activities, gym construction arose as a high LDS priority. Leaders maintained that this allocation of church resources was not just a matter of supplying growing athletic demand; far more importantly, the state of Mormon souls might be at stake. LDS President Joseph F. Smith proclaimed, "Gymnasiums have become apparently a very urgent necessity of late....We must not only provide places of worship for the youth of Zion, as well as for their fathers and mothers, but also find places for the rational amusement of our children, in order that they may be kept under proper influences, away from the contaminating, degrading practices too common in the world."[26] Spurred on by this view, gymnasiums became fixtures at meetinghouses throughout Mormon land, and the central LDS temple in Salt Lake City welcomed an impressive new neighbor. Built in 1910, the Deseret Gym was the largest athletic facility in the nation, a three-story edifice measuring in at 150 feet long and ninety feet wide. The gym's physical enormity was arguably surpassed by its symbolic magnitude, since its location a mere one block away from the central temple and advertising films christening it the "Temple of Health" testified strongly to sports' significance in the Mormon mentality. Kimball comments, "Just as attendance at the Temple of God promised spiritual blessings and renewal, participating in games at the Temple of Health brought physical renewal. One temple cared for the spirit, the other tended the body. Both were necessary appendages to a Mormon theology concerned with the spiritual, physical, and social welfare of hu-

---

[25] Akin to a diocese in the Roman Catholic Church, a stake is an administrative unit made up of multiple congregations, or wards.

[26] Quoted in Kimball, *Sports in Zion*, 60.

mankind."[27] Aiming to keep their youth in the fold and to put into practice the teaching that all realms of life belong under an LDS umbrella, the Deseret Gym spoke volumes about athletic activity's integral position within the mission of the Mormon Church.

Yet buildings alone, no matter how spectacular, would obviously not get this mission work done. LDS leaders recognized their intentions to promote bonding through sports would remain grounded without trained personnel to coordinate high-quality athletic activities and to ensure their Mormon distinctiveness. Thus Young Men's and Young Ladies' Mutual Improvement Association missionaries trekked across Mormon territory, planting athletic program seeds and instructing local community representatives how to cultivate them so their flowering might steadfastly reflect LDS standards and ideals. Additionally, as Kimball reports, during the first three decades of the twentieth century "hundreds of institutes and training sessions helped turn local lay leaders into recreational experts."[28] Much of this instruction was provided under Young Men's and Young Ladies' Mutual Improvement Association auspices, but an aspiring Mormon athletic program coordinator could also opt for a summer session recreational leadership course at Brigham Young University or Utah Agricultural College. Seats at these courses were in high demand. One edition of BYU's "Leadership Week," for instance, hosted 3,500 trainees from fifty stakes. Summer class students received tutelage not only from Mormons, but occasionally from non-Mormons as well. Instructors such as football coaching giants Knute Rockne and Glenn "Pop" Warner disclosed their pearls of athletic wisdom as guest faculty members during BYU and UAC summer sessions. The welcoming of these gridiron gurus exemplified a key Mormon recreation movement characteristic, its incorporation of input from individuals outside the LDS church. Thanks to newfound Mormon openness to surrounding society, ideas originating beyond church walls figured prominently in the development of an LDS recreation ideology that undergirded Mormon sports activities. LDS athletic vision was significantly shaped by Muscu-

---

[27] Ibid., 70.
[28] Ibid., 52.

lar Christian masculinity[29] and morality, especially as Mormon leaders deemed Muscular Christianity's moral principles to be akin to their own. LDS recreation ideology also drank heavily from the well of eminent play theorists and social reformers of the day. The 1914 LDS *Parents' Bulletin No. 1: Recreation and Play* was loaded with quotations from pioneering social reformer Jane Addams, child expert William Byron Forbush, Luther Gulick,[30] and plenty of other non-Mormon minds.

Straddling a fence between the larger American society and the particularities of the Mormon Church, early twentieth-century LDS leaders invited these outsiders to help build their sporting structure but also sought to prop it up with a share of distinctively Mormon emphases. These leaders deposited Mormon distinctiveness into LDS sports activities through means such as arguing for an inherent athletic advantage in upholding the Word of Wisdom, the doctrine enjoining abstention from alcohol, tobacco, and caffeinated beverages and encouraging consumption of herbs, fruits, and grains and avoidance of excessive eating of meat.[31] Direct correlations between sporting success and Word of Wis-

---

[29] Kimball writes, "An analysis of LDS athletic programs lays bare the male-centered nature of Mormon recreation. Although it is clear that young women participated in athletic events, they were not the primary focus of recreation leaders. Sports helped to resolve the 'boy problem'" (ibid., 97).

[30] Gulick became president of the Playground Association of America after his tenure with the YMCA.

[31] Believed by Mormons to have been revealed to Joseph Smith in 1833, the Word of Wisdom contains the promise that those who follow it will enjoy "health in their navel and marrow to their bones; And [they] shall find wisdom and great treasures of knowledge, even hidden treasures; And [they] shall run and not be weary, and shall walk and not faint" (Doctrine and Covenants 89:18–20). According to Douglas Davies, the Word of Wisdom expresses "the value that the Latter-day Saints place upon the human body as the arena of exercising agency and obedience to God and of preparing for the resurrection and the life to come. Given the food rules of ancient Israel and modern Jewry, the Word of Wisdom also marks out the Saints from others and provides an echo of their own sense of identity as God's own people" (Douglas J. Davies, *An Introduction to Mormonism* (New York: Cambridge University Press, 2003) 182). Coinciding with the highpoint of the Mormon recreation movement, the Word of Wisdom became a central LDS principle in the early twentieth century, and obedience to this regulation became a prerequisite for admission to the Temple beginning in 1921.

dom adherence became standard LDS lore. A 1928 article in the LDS periodical *Improvement Era* illustrates this motif, listing the accomplishments of Olympic high jump record holder Alma Richards, national broad jump champion Clinton Luke, and other Mormon athletes, and then identifying their faithfulness to the Word of Wisdom as central to their success. The panegyric proclaims, "It is interesting to note that every one of these unusual men is not only a member of the Latter-day Church, but each one has been a more or less rigid observer of the Word of Wisdom. Not a man among those who have won national honors has ever used regularly tea, coffee, tobacco, or strong drink."[32] The article turns to testimonials to further bolster its claims. High school mile record-holder Melvin Burke remarks, "I have not used regularly tea, coffee, tobacco, or liquor in any form. I am a firm believer in the Word of Wisdom. It is a great feeling to come to the end of a hard contest and still have a reserve for the sprint."[33] According to such accounts, the Mormon athlete who follows the Word of Wisdom sets himself up to earn both an athletic edge and the eternal reward accompanying obedience to LDS principles.

Catholic Youth Organization

As Muscular Christian ideas spread like wildfire in the Rockies, most evangelical churches continued to extinguish Muscular Christianity's flames,[34] advocating athletic teetotalism around the time of Prohibition.

---

[32] Quoted in Kimball, *Sports in Zion*, 116.

[33] Quoted in ibid., 117.

[34] A few early nineteenth-century evangelical churches were outliers, in some cases due to the influence of Billy Sunday, an ex-Major Leaguer who loaded his impassioned sermons with athletic allusions. Shirl Hoffman asserts that there may be "little question that Sunday's biography helped assuage the consciences of closet sports fans" among evangelicals (Shirl James Hoffman, "Harvesting Souls in the Stadium: The Rise of Sports Evangelism," in *Sports and Christianity: Historical and Contemporary Perspectives*, ed. Nick J. Watson and Andrew Parker, 131–49 (Hoboken: Taylor and Francis, 2012) 136), yet such assuaging was hardly widespread, deep-rooted evangelical endorsement. Evangelical closet sports fans, or maybe their children, would have to wait nearly a half century after Sunday hit the sawdust trail to see sports and evangelicalism mix in an enduring manner. This fusion gained trac-

Catholic churches of the early twentieth century tended to position themselves somewhere between these two poles, opting not to erect a firewall against Muscular Christianity but not fanning its conflagration. To an extent, ideological underpinnings of Muscular Christianity matched common Catholic Church emphases. Jay Coakley identifies the 1 Corinthians 6:19 reference to the body as a "temple of the Holy Spirit" as one such example, pointing out its frequent reference in both Muscular Christian and American Catholic church discourse.[35] On a deeper level, however, these apparent matches often contained dissimilar strains of thought. Coakley contends that whereas the Catholic conception of the body as a temple of the Holy Spirit typically carried the implication of keeping the body pure through sexual abstinence, the ultimate Muscular Christian upshot was maintaining bodily strength and vigor through athletic activity.[36] Nonetheless, a growing number of Catholic Americans followed in Muscular Protestants' footsteps. Little by little, a variety of local church athletic activities and interparish sports leagues arrived on the Catholic American scene, seeking to keep youth away from sinful enchantments of urbanized America and involve them in the practices and fellowship of the Church. The scope of Muscular Catholicism climbed throughout the early twentieth century, reaching its apogee in the Catholic Youth Organization (CYO). A mere decade after its 1930 Chicago birth, the CYO became a sports magnet for 150,000 youth in cities around the nation. Adding its own touches to groundwork laid by

tion with Billy Graham's crusades, as thousands of already committed and soon-to-be evangelicals packed stadiums and arenas and heard stirring salvation stories from famous evangelical athletes. Testimony from athletes was one of many features of the cement of the sports and evangelicalism amalgam, the Fellowship of Christian Athletes (FCA). Founded in 1954 by Oklahoma high school football coach Don McLanen, local FCA prayer and Bible study groups, or "huddles," as well as FCA summer sports camps and regional conferences, quickly emerged across the United States. FCA's ambit continued to expand; according to its 2009 "Annual Impact Report," for example, the organization reached 1,800,000 people that year, with 3,694 committing their lives to Christ thanks to FCA ministries.

[35] Jay Coakley, *Sports in Society: Issues and Controversies*, 10th ed. (New York: McGraw-Hill, 2008) 523.

[36] Ibid., 523–24.

Catholic athletic league forerunners, the CYO made the relationship between American Catholicism and sports appear to be a marriage arranged from above.

Officiating this marriage was Bishop Bernard Sheil, who bestowed the CYO with its initial vision and directed its course to nationwide prominence. In the words of Steven Riess, Sheil discerned that young Catholics "were being drawn away from the church by the competition of such exhilarating pleasures as drinking, fighting, and womanizing. The church, along with family and schools, apparently had lost its historic function as agent of socialization and had little relevance to the needs of young Catholic males in the 1920s and 1930s. Sheil wanted to find a way to bring the young men back into the fold."[37] Sheil recognized that bringing young wayward Catholics back to the Church was no easy task in the Chicago of his day. With the Depression leaving rampant unemployment in its wake, scads of young men in the Windy City had grown accustomed to filling up restless hours with activities that lured them away from Catholic devotion, and high-profile criminals like Al Capone served as role models to many Chicago youth. Especially in the Twentieth Ward of Chicago's West Side, nicknamed "The Bloody Twentieth Ward" and "Alcohol Avenue," young Chicagoans often venerated Capone, who would return to his Twentieth Ward boyhood stomping grounds and hand out dimes to children and distribute food baskets to hungry families. Sheil called upon sports to turn this tide, banking on the allure of athletic activity to pluck young Catholics off of Chicago's crime-infested streets and lead them to embrace core elements of Catholic piety. Seeking to galvanize support for this plan, Sheil exhorted fellow Chicago Catholic leaders to regard athletic activity as an excellent opportunity to reintegrate young Catholics into parish life and save those who had forsaken their faith roots. Sheil also persuaded Protestants to finance his fledgling organization, insisting that a structured athletic program would appreciably upgrade the Chicago community for residents of all creeds by curtailing juvenile delinquency and helping to Americanize immigrant youth. Considering the domestic and international climates of the age, Chicagoans of any religious persuasion got behind Sheil's goals of en-

---

[37] Riess, *City Games*, 101.

hancing the safety of the city's neighborhoods and promoting immigrant youth allegiance to their new country instead of loyalty to ancestral homelands that may be American enemies. Though the majority of CYO backing came from Catholics, non-Catholics contributed significantly to the CYO kitty as well.

These contributions funded more than athletic activities alone. They subsidized CYO vacation schools that inculcated Catholic values at churches in numerous Chicago neighborhoods, including the Twentieth Ward and the predominantly African-American South Side. These schools typified two CYO hallmarks, a commitment to embed itself right in the heart of Chicago's most dangerous and lascivious neighborhoods as well as an "open arms" policy to all youth regardless of religion, race, or gender.[38] Vacation schools and other religious education initiatives made up important spokes in Sheil's CYO master plan, but competitive sports programs were without question the CYO hub. From its inception, the CYO offered basketball leagues, softball games, swim meets, and bowling tournaments. Soon boxing tournaments, track meets, an ice hockey league, a flag football league, and golf outings were added to the docket. CYO intentions to promote piety as well as national allegiance were prominently on display before these sporting events, when young athletes proclaimed the CYO Pledge of Sportsmanship:

> I promise upon my honor to be loyal to my God, to my Country, and to my Church; to be faithful and true to my obligations as a Christian, a man, and a citizen. I pledge myself to live a clean, honest, and upright life—to avoid profane, obscene, and vulgar language, and to induce others to avoid it. I bind myself to promote, by word and example, clean, wholesome, and manly sport; I will strive earnestly to be a man of whom my Church and my Country may be justly proud.[39]

This oath rang out regularly in a prodigious, pricy CYO center that opened its doors at 31 East Congress Street in Chicago in 1932. Containing rooms for academic and religious instruction, the bulk of the center was gym space, where activities were coordinated by facility athletic

---

[38] Females were included in CYO education programs and in some CYO sports programs.

[39] Quoted in Baker, *Playing with God*, 179.

director and former Notre Dame football standout Jack Elder. The structure also boasted fifty-two bowling alleys in its basement and on its third and fourth floors, supplying a home to over a thousand registered bowling teams.

Sheil scored a strike with these bowling lanes, but in the diverse CYO athletic palette, neither bowling nor any other sport attracted as many individuals to the CYO as basketball and boxing. The CYO's inaugural boys' and girls' basketball tournaments in 1931 included 140 teams, jumping to 182 with about 2,200 players the following year. Over the course of the decade, CYO basketball leagues mushroomed in cities from the Atlantic to the Pacific. The CYO became the largest basketball association in the United States, making the CYO label synonymous with youth basketball for World War II-era Americans. Moving to the ring, 1,600 young men signed up to duke it out in eight weight divisions in the CYO's initial boxing tournament in 1931. Young Windy City residents poisoned by the Depression's bite likely found the CYO boxing call irresistible, as tournament registrants were provided with equipment and fighting instruction at high-quality gyms free of charge, and injuries they sustained were taken care of gratis by CYO doctors and dentists. Throwing in even more charm for potential participants, victors of each weight class's final bout, held at the spectacular new Chicago Stadium, received a four-year scholarship to attend any college of their choice. From Sheil's perspective, these enticements were well worth any chunk they took out of CYO coffers, since each young person drawn to the CYO ring might translate into the priceless treasure of one less lapsed Catholic living a life of degeneracy and crime.

Among CYO sports, Sheil considered boxing to pack a particularly powerful punch in getting young people off the street, due to its emphasis on toughness and tenacity that was right up poor, working-class young men's alley. Baker writes that for Sheil boxing was "a moral endeavor, a perfect antidote to urban youth gangs and violent crime. A well-regulated program was a potential savior for slum youths who grew up literally fighting for survival."[40] Sheil detected unrivaled ability in box-

[40] Ibid., 178.

ing to develop heroes who upheld Catholic values and could replace Capone and other gangster idols. The bishop proudly prognosticated,

> We'll knock the hoodlum off the pedestal out there, and we'll put another neighborhood boy in his place. He'll be dressed in CYO boxing shorts and a pair of leather mitts. He may have a shiner and a bloody nose, but he'll have a Championship medal. We'll make a new hero in Bloody Little Italy. Those kids out there love to fight. We'll let them fight. We'll make them fight. We'll find a lot of champions in that neighborhood.[41]

Sheil's Christianity was not about meekness and turning the other cheek. As CYO boxers ascended to national glory or to the 1936 Olympic gold medal podium in Berlin, the bishop believed the kingdom of God was increasing in glory with every knockout along the way.

[41] Quoted in Roger L. Treat, *Bishop Sheil and the CYO* (New York: Messner, 1951) 112.

2

Athletic Bridging in American Religious History

Though a time of economic scarcity, Depression-era America was an age of anti-Semitic plenty. As millions tuned their radios to catch the latest anti-Jewish sermon from Father Charles Coughlin, as Henry Ford plastered his newspapers with allegations of Jewish corruption of American society, as whispers of Jewish conspiracies to take over the world echoed across the nation, American plates were full of anti-Semitic fare. At the same time, baseball satiated countless American appetites. During the day of Ruth, Gehrig, and other Major League greats, slugger Hank Greenberg shook up deeply rooted Gentile conceptions of Jews. John Rosengren proclaims that the brawny ballplayer "became the face—and muscles—of Judaism in America. He single-handedly changed the way Gentiles viewed Jews."[1] Rosengren's assertion may be given to hyperbole, especially if taken to suggest that one man alone could completely counteract the damage done by anti-Semitic demagogues like Coughlin or Ford. Nonetheless, Greenberg's prominent platform as a Jewish star in a sport beloved by millions and intertwined with American values[2] prompted many to think differently about Jews, especially their stereotypes as weak and anti-American. Crushing baseballs over homerun fences for the Detroit Tigers, Hammerin' Hank connected on swings against anti-Semitism. Long before Muslim athletes began chipping

[1] John Rosengren, *Hank Greenberg: The Hero of Heroes* (New York: NAL Hardcover, 2013) 162.

[2] Former pitcher and sporting goods company founder Albert G. Spalding linked baseball to "American Courage, Confidence, Combativeness; American Dash, Discipline, Determinism; American Energy, Eagerness, Enthusiasm; American Pluck, Persistency, Performance; American Spirit, Sagacity, Success; American Vim, Vigor, Virility" (quoted in S. W. Pope, *Patriotic Games: Sporting Traditions in the American Imagination, 1876–1926* (New York: Oxford University Press, 1997) 72).

away at Islamophobic walls, Greenberg and other Jewish athletes did significant bridging work, just as Catholic athletes were playing their part in subverting anti-Catholic views. As in the previous chapter, I continue to focus on the period 1850–1950 in order to set a historical stage for Muslim American athletic activities' position within the flow of American religious history. Yet, unlike the previous chapter, this chapter's exhibitions of American athleticism are generally not grounded in intentionality. Whereas individuals like Luther Gulick and Bishop Sheil strongly intended to use sports for bonding purposes, many of the Catholic and Jewish athletes highlighted in this chapter may not have felt compelled to enter the stadium or arena due to bridging desires. Intended or not, though, their athletic achievements led to more than victory over sporting foes; they also played a significant part in vanquishing prejudice faced by Catholics and Jews throughout the United States.

American Anti-Catholicism

Anti-Catholic thoughts and actions arrived on American shores aboard Puritan ships, cargo packed during the English Reformation. American anti-Catholicism picked up steam amidst the smokestacks of late nineteenth-century industrialization, when Catholic immigrants streamed into American cities. The American Catholic population stood around 1.1 million in 1845. By 1880 it had grown to 6.3 million.[3] For many Americans, this influx signaled a serious threat to Protestant values and security, especially because of a widespread caricature of Catholics as disloyal Americans. As stated by Michael Isenberg, a large number of Protestants viewed Catholicism as "a political religion that sought to subvert the world by infiltration and coercion. Catholicism likewise was consistently pictured as cutting straight across the grain of American democracy. Catholics, it was believed, were held in thrall by the demanding hierarchy of the church; so bound in primary allegiance, they could make no contribution to a free society."[4] According to a Protestant tru-

---

[3] This 6.3 million figure constituted slightly over twelve percent of the 1880 American population.

[4] Michael T. Isenberg, *John L. Sullivan and His America* (Champaign IL: University of Illinois Press, 1994) 24. This view continued into the twentieth century,

ism of the day, American Catholic loyalty to the Pope trumped national allegiance and led Catholics to despise the very fabric of American society.[5] An 1854 listing of "Things Which Roman Catholic Priests and All True Roman Catholics Hate" proclaimed:

> They HATE our Republic, and are trying to overthrow it.
> They HATE the American Eagle, and it offends them beyond endurance to see it worn as an ornament by Americans.
> They HATE our Flag, as is manifest by their grossly insulting it.
> They HATE the liberty of conscience.
> They HATE the liberty of the Press.
> They HATE the liberty of speech.
> They HATE our Common School system.[6]

Among a variety of arenas in which such venom was spewed, the Know-Nothing Party offered an abundant share as it placed anti-Catholic candidates in a number of city and state government offices in the 1850s.[7]

Pouring fuel on the nineteenth-century anti-Catholic fire, highly esteemed Americans such as telegraph inventor Samuel Morse and Boston preacher Lyman Beecher spun tales of an international Catholic conspir-

---

rearing its head on multiple occasions including the Presidential candidacies of Catholics Al Smith and John F. Kennedy.

[5] Illustrating this common belief, Congregational minister Josiah Strong of Cincinnati declared in 1886, "We have seen that the commands of the Pope, instead of the constitution and laws of the land, demand the highest allegiance of Roman Catholics in the United States" (quoted in Diana Eck, *A New Religious America: How a "Christian Country" Has Now Become the World's Most Religiously Diverse Nation* (San Francisco: HarperSanFrancisco, 2001) 48–49).

[6] Quoted in Louise A. Cainkar, *Homeland Insecurity: The Arab American and Muslim American Experience after 9/11* (New York: Russell Sage Foundation, 2009) 237.

[7] The Know-Nothing Party called for restrictions on immigration, exclusion of foreign-born American residents from voting or holding public office, and a twenty-one-year residency requirement for citizenship. The party's name derives from the fact that when asked about their organization, members were to reply that they knew nothing about it. The group slowly shed its secretive nature and eventually adopted the official name American Party.

acy aimed at taking over the nation. These yarns described a plot, purportedly concocted at the Catholic Church's highest levels, to fill the expanding frontier with Catholic immigrants who would eventually bring America under the Pope's control. Along with this myth, scandalous stories of sexually starved Catholic priests ran rampantly across the nation, building on a trope that had become popular in Colonial America. Irene Whelan writes, "Nothing sold pamphlets and newspapers as successfully as the salacious and lurid accounts of the imagined goings-on behind convent walls."[8] The 1836 *Awful Disclosures of the Hotel Dieu Nunnery in Montreal* galvanized Protestant fury with claims supposedly based on revelations of a nun who escaped a hellish convent, in which lecherous priests executed nuns who refused their sexual advances and killed babies born to nuns they impregnated. Although an investigation revealed the baseless nature of these charges, it was impotent in stemming the tide of anti-Catholic fervor that ensued. Outcry over alleged priest immorality was a key factor in a spate of raids and burnings of convents, which, along with mob attacks on Catholic churches, demonstrated that American anti-Catholicism threatened not only Catholic psychological well-being, but also their property—and even their lives.[9]

Constituting approximately one half of all Catholic immigrants to the United States in the mid-nineteenth century, Irish Catholics were a major target of this scorn. Irish Catholics fled famine in their native land[10] and sought a new life in the New World, but old anti-Catholic

[8] Irene Whelan, "Religious Rivalry and the Making of Irish American Identity," in *Making the Irish American: History and Heritage of the Irish in the United States*, ed. J. J. Lee and Marion R. Casey, 271–85 (New York: New York University Press, 2006) 275.

[9] The most publicized of these attacks occurred in 1834, when a mob burned the Ursuline convent in Boston, largely due to the inspiration of anti-Catholic sermons by Beecher. Whelan remarks that this incident "revealed the level of danger attendant upon the combination of mob passion inflamed by sensationalist propaganda and conspiracy theories and backed by the most powerful voices of the evangelical world" (ibid.).

[10] The large majority of Irish immigrants from Colonial times until the early nineteenth century were Protestants, but an Irish population boom coupled with limited employment opportunity led to an influx of predominantly poor, illiterate, rural Catholics from Ireland onto American shores (Ralph C. Wilcox, "The Sham-

prejudices met them rudely and intensified as more of their countrymen settled in America. As Irish immigrant waves eventually subsided, boatloads of Catholic immigrants came to America from a Southern European land. Beginning in the 1880s and reaching a peak in the first two decades of the twentieth century,[11] Italian Catholic immigrants stepped onto American soil in immense numbers. In little time, they, too, became raw materials for the thriving American anti-Catholic industry. Due to general longstanding assumptions of Catholic national infidelity as well as particular associations made between Italians and organized crime,[12] Italian Catholics were regarded as unwanted threats to Protestant values and security.

rock and the Eagle: Irish Americans and Sport in the Nineteenth Century," in *Ethnicity and Sport in North American History and Culture*, ed. George Eisen and David K. Wiggins, 55–74 (Westport CT: Greenwood Press, 1995) 55). This Irish Catholic immigrant wave grew even larger with a series of famines, culminating in the Great Famine of 1845–1849. Nearly two million individuals left Ireland during the 1846–1855 time period, with millions more to follow from 1855–1921 due to falling wages and decreasing demand for agricultural labor in Ireland. Approximately ninety percent of these famine and post-famine Irish immigrants in America were Catholics (David Noel Doyle, "The Remaking of Irish America," in *Making the Irish American: History and Heritage of the Irish in the United States*, ed. J. J. Lee and Marion R. Casey, 213–52 (New York: New York University Press, 2006) 213).

[11] Nearly one million Italians arrived in America during the last two decades of the nineteenth century. From 1900–1920 over three million Italians emigrated to the United States, almost all of whom were Catholic (Jay P. Dolan, *The American Catholic Experience: A History from Colonial Times to the Present* (Garden City NY: Doubleday, 1985) 131). The vast majority of these immigrants were peasants from Southern Italy and Sicily, and as Carmelo Bazzano explains, many "were illiterate, unskilled laborers who did not possess the skills necessary to succeed and function in an emerging industrialized America" (Carmelo Bazzano, "The Italian American Sporting Experience," in *Ethnicity and Sport in North American History and Culture*, ed. George Eisen and David K. Wiggins, 103–16 (Westport CT: Greenwood Press, 1994) 106).

[12] Among the earliest articulations of these associations, in 1880 an American newspaper alleged the Italian government of regularly sending its criminals to the United States, an allegation that increased in popularity during the decades to follow (Luciano J. Iorizzo and Salvatore Mondello, *The Italian Americans*, rev. ed. (Boston: Twayne Publishers, 1980) 52).

Catholic American Athletic Activity

The story I tell of Catholic American athletic activity is an abridged version. With Irish and Italian Catholics as its key characters before heading to a Notre Dame football denouement, it fails to capture the athletic exploits of Germans, Poles, and members of other Catholic immigrant groupings.[13] Furthermore, my focus upon Catholic American athletes encompasses just three sports: boxing, baseball, and football. In this regard, too, accounts of significant Catholic American athletic accomplishments are muted. Members of America's Irish Catholic population, for example, were turn-of-the-century track and field titans. New York's Irish American Athletic Club runners regularly broke the victory tape in national and international meets, and a group nicknamed the "Irish Whales," many of whom were New York policemen, smashed the competition in the Olympic hammer throw from 1896 to 1924.[14] Acknowledging that these and scores of other Catholic American athletic feats would be intriguing to explore, I nonetheless focus on three of America's most popular sports and on two of its largest Catholic ethnic groups in order to serve up selective yet substantial slices of the late nineteenth- and early twentieth-century Catholic American sporting pie. At first, my discussions will dish out slices without consideration of bridging, focusing simply on Catholic American athletic accomplishments with no attempt to link them to the overturning of anti-Catholicism. Eventually, though, I serve up slices à la mode, bringing bridging into my exploration of the athletic exploits of Joe DiMaggio and Notre Dame football.

Irish Catholic boxers were turn-of-the-century kings of the ring. The 1890s saw the pinnacle of this success, as nine world champions were Americans whose ancestors hailed from Catholic regions of the Emerald Isle. One of these titleholders, John L. Sullivan, possessed the heavyweight crown from 1882 to 1892 and was likely the most recognizable athlete in America during the nineteenth century. Credited with

---

[13] Irish, Germans, Italians, Poles, French Canadians, and Mexicans were the most numerous Catholic ethnicities in early twentieth-century America.

[14] John F. Flanagan, an Irish-born New York policeman, became the first modern Olympian to win three successive gold medals, winning the hammer throw event in 1900, 1904, and 1908.

anywhere from seventy-five to 200 victories in the ring, the "Boston Strong Boy" smoothed boxing's transition from the bareknuckle era to the Marquis of Queensbury Rules, which feature the donning of gloves. Michael Isenberg labels Sullivan "the first significant mass cultural hero in American life"[15] and notes that, from his fights and public appearances, Sullivan probably earned over one million dollars, a sum "unheard of for one of his origins and occupation."[16] Isenberg goes on to say that Sullivan's admirers included "not only the underside of society," but also "political leaders, middle-class professionals, literary figures, and even clergymen."[17] No other Irish American pugilist matched Sullivan in garnering such appeal, yet Jack Dempsey came close in the 1920s. The "Manassa Mauler" became a megastar by piling up victories in the ring and by featuring a tough-man image and a relentless fighting style that pummeled overmatched foes. Dempsey's popularity, as well as that of his sport, was sky high when he went toe to toe with fellow Irish American Gene Tunney in 1926 and again the following year. The first Dempsey-Tunney bout drew a record crowd in excess of 120,000 to Sesquicentennial Stadium in Philadelphia. The rematch brought 102,000 boxing buffs to Chicago's Soldier Field and attracted 50 million radio listeners. Tunney's arm was raised in victory both times, serving as crowning jewels in his undefeated professional career, but his stardom never rose to Dempsey's heights, held down by his introverted nature and predilection to outsmart opponents rather than maul them in the ring.

As Dempsey and Tunney grabbed headlines, dozens of other fighters with Irish names were knocking out adversaries to much less fanfare. Unknown to many spectators, a significant percentage were not of Irish descent; they were Italian Americans with Irish pseudonyms. In light of Irish American dominance of the early twentieth-century boxing world as well as pervasive anti-Italian sentiments of the day, promoters regard-

[15] Isenberg, *John L. Sullivan and His America*, 13. Isenberg adds that Sullivan's "picture adorned countless barrooms from coast to coast, as did he himself with considerable frequency. His name was constantly before the public in newspapers and magazines, and even his handshake was famous. People would go to a theater simply to see him pose" (ibid.).

[16] Ibid., 14.

[17] Ibid.

ed fight cards with names of Irish boxers as paths to financial windfall and those listing Italian boxers as roads to pecuniary ruin. A few world champs with Irish monikers were actually Italian Americans. The world welterweight and middleweight titleholders known as Joe and Vince Dundee, for instance, were in reality Italian American brothers Sam and Vince Lazzaro. Gradually this pugilistic pseudonymity dropped to the canvas, felled by a few Italian American fighters winning titles while called by their names they carried since birth. Heralding Rocky Marciano, Tony Galento, and other members of future Italian American boxing royalty, these earlier champs who held on to their Italian-sounding names trumpeted the message that Italian Americans had arrived on the boxing scene, even if anti-Catholic Americans did not extend an invitation.

Like the boxing ring, the baseball diamond was home to an outpouring of Irish American athletic adeptness. An 1872 *Sporting News* article reported that Irish Americans composed one-third of all pro baseball rosters, and a turn-of-the-century Major League scribe stated that "all the prominent clubs of last year were captained by Irish Americans."[18] A few teams in particular were packed with a potent Irish presence. Five Irish American future Hall of Famers powered the Baltimore Orioles to a National League title three-peat from 1894 to 1896.[19] Irish eyes smiled especially broadly upon Mike "King" Kelly, a linchpin of his Chicago squad's run toward five National League pennants in the 1880s. Kelly performed well at the plate, leading the league twice in batting average, but he took the nation by storm on the base paths, where he racked up eighty-four steals in 1887 and inspired the hit song "Slide,

[18] Quoted in Ralph Wilcox, "Irish Americans in Sports: The Nineteenth Century," in *Making the Irish American: History and Heritage of the Irish in the United States*, ed. J. J. Lee and Marion R. Casey, 443–56 (New York: New York University Press, 2006) 447. Similar to boxing, some players not of Irish ancestry took on Irish names in order to further their baseball careers, a testament to the high esteem that Irish players came to enjoy.

[19] These Orioles were infielders Big Dan Brouthers, Hugh Jennings, and John McGraw; and outfielders Joe Kelley and Wee Willie Keeler.

Kelly, Slide."[20] Moving into the twentieth century, Irish Americans continued to place a strong stamp upon Major League Baseball, but more from the dugout than the diamond. Managers Connie Mack, Joe McCarthy, and John McGraw are enshrined in Cooperstown, thanks among numerous other distinctions to Mack spending a total of fifty years as manager and owner of the Philadelphia Athletics, McCarthy skippering the Yankees to seven World Series titles, and McGraw racking up a total of 2,763 victories with the Baltimore Orioles and New York Giants, second in Major League history only to Mack's 3,731.

At the same time these Irish Americans managed their way into baseball immortality, Italian American ballplayers added a deeper Catholic presence into the Major Leagues. The first star in the Italian American baseball firmament shone on a team loaded with luminaries, the 1927 "Murderer's Row" Yankees. Tony Lazzeri's fourteen-year career included a lofty batting average of .354 in 1929, and baseball historian Lawrence Baldassaro declares, "Both as a productive player and as an ethnic hero, Lazzeri was everything Yankee officials could have hoped for. He was idolized by Italian fans."[21] Ernie Lombardi further represented Italian Americans on the baseball field with great aplomb, hitting over .300 in seven of his ten seasons with the Cincinnati Reds. Lombardi's standout season came in 1938, when his .342 average made him the first catcher to grab a league batting title and the first Italian American to be selected league MVP. Excelling in the national pastime, Lazzeri and Lombardi were a source of great pride for fellow Italian Americans,

---

[20] Richard Peterson writes that "when baseball historians portray Kelly, their accounts draw far more attention to his heavy drinking, his flaunting of baseball rules, and his troublesome and often unmanageable behavior than to his accomplishments" (Richard F. Peterson, "'Slide, Kelly, Slide': The Irish in American Baseball," in *The American Game: Baseball and Ethnicity*, ed. Lawrence Baldassaro and Richard A. Johnson, 55–67 (Carbondale IL: Southern Illinois University Press, 2002) 60).

[21] Lawrence Baldassaro, "Before Joe D: Early Italian Americans in the Major Leagues," in *The American Game: Baseball and Ethnicity*, ed. Lawrence Baldassaro and Richard A. Johnson, 92–115 (Carbondale IL: Southern Illinois University Press, 2002) 105.

helping them feel more firmly established in their new land.[22] As for bridging, however, the effect of their sporting success was minimal. Ethnic heroes for Italian Americans they were. Turners of prejudicial tide they were not. With walls of American prejudice toward Italian Americans doubly reinforced, both by longstanding anti-Catholicism and by prevailing generalizations of Italians as lawless criminals, a new breed of Italian American athlete was required. An Italian American megastar who could transcend religious and ethnic difference, who could conjure up for all Americans images of what they deemed best about their nation, was needed to chisel through these thick walls. This athlete arrived in the form of Joe DiMaggio, who Baldassaro proclaims "became not only the most famous athlete of his time, but one of the most admired men in America."[23] On the field as a New York Yankee and off the field as an all-American celebrity of mythic proportions, DiMaggio captured hearts and minds of both Catholic and Protestant Americans.

DiMaggio's ascension to heroic stature began in the batter's box. He hit .381 in 1939 and .352 in 1940, winning the batting title both years. A three-time league MVP and member of nine World Series-winning Yankees teams, DiMaggio stood at the center of the sporting world in 1941 when his fifty-six-game hitting streak riveted the attention of baseball fans and non-fans alike. Lew Freedman writes, "Joe DiMaggio was a New York baseball hero by 1941. After 1941, he was a major league baseball god. The streak did it."[24] Public awareness of the streak was

---

[22] Baldassaro argues, "Especially for second-generation Italian Americans, baseball provided one avenue of entry to mainstream society, either as fans or as participants. Italians came to America at a time when baseball was already well established as the national pastime, and when journalists and social workers were touting the game as a means of acculturating the new immigrants to American values" (ibid., 93). As an example of such a claim, sportswriter Hugh Fullerton penned in a 1919 edition of the *Atlanta Constitution* that baseball "is the greatest single force working for Americanization. No other game appeals so much to the foreign born youngsters and nothing, not even the schools, teaches the American spirit so quickly, or inculcates the idea of sportsmanship or fair play so thoroughly" (quoted in Pope, *Patriotic Games*, 73).

[23] Baldassaro, "Before Joe D," 112.

[24] Lew Freedman, *DiMaggio's Yankees: A History of the 1936–1944 Dynasty* (Jefferson NC: McFarland, 2011) 162.

augmented by the Yankee Clipper playing for America's best-known team, in the nation's media capital, and DiMaggio strung together his streak during a tenuous time when American appetites were famished for good news instead of talk about impending war. Stepping into an anxious America, the streak not only created a pleasant diversion; it raised confidence in American ability. Michael Seidel asserts that the streak "helped buoy a nation forging a new and necessary myth of its own potential."[25] Seidel points out that on the day the *Washington Post* proudly proclaimed that American plane production was on the verge of surpassing German output of 2,000 aircraft per month, these same front pages strengthened American spirits further by announcing that DiMaggio was on the cusp of surpassing George Sisler's modern-day forty-one-game hit streak record. Such bulletins lifted the spirits of an array of Americans, not just those of Italian descent. Freedman comments that by means of his fifty-six-game journey, DiMaggio was "a personal unifier of people who loved the game. One thing everyone had in common that summer was rooting for DiMaggio to get another hit, to extend the streak one game longer."[26]

With Italy's wartime enemy status adding to already acrimonious American attitudes towards Italians living in the United States, DiMaggio's capacity to effect any kind of unity between Italian Americans and their compatriots was a feat of Hall of Fame proportions. Heightened suspicion of Italian American disloyalty sprouted in World War II-era America. In DiMaggio's home state of California, for example, all forty-seven Italian language schools were shut down, feared to be fascist propaganda propagators straight from the mouth of Mussolini. Complementing his streak and countless other on-field accomplishments, wartime military service helped the Yankee clip the wings of caricatures placing Italian Americans in antithesis to the United States. DiMaggio's army enlistment to take down America's Axis foes, including his parents' birthplace of Italy, functioned as a resounding pledge of Italian American national allegiance for a closely watching American populace. Yet, argua-

[25] Michael Seidel, *Streak: Joe DiMaggio and the Summer of '41* (Lincoln: University of Nebraska Press, 2002) 6.
[26] Freedman, *DiMaggio's Yankees*, 163.

bly even more so than disarming assumptions of Italian American war-time treason, DiMaggio's exploits on and off the field did significant damage to the stereotype of the violent, lawless Italian American. Instilled by dastardly depictions of Mafia deeds, this stereotype was affixed in the American consciousness, and its entrenchment was dug deeper by derogatory claims from so-called experts. The Dillingham Commission congressional report portrayed Italians as morally deficient, and eminent sociologist E. A. Ross pigeonholed Sicilians as prone to commit "ferocious crimes that go with the primitive stage of civilization."[27] With such views permeating American air, the all-American figure of DiMaggio dispersed many anti-Italian pollutants. Luciano Iorizzo and Salvatore Mondello argue that DiMaggio represented "a glamorized, positive image of Italian Americans, one which replaced the Capone era of the twenties and early thirties."[28] Undeniably, well-worn stereotypes die hard. One man alone could not completely drain the life out of deep-seated convictions that Italian Americans were disloyal Americans prone to criminal behavior. Nonetheless, by virtue of the stature he had attained among Americans of all stripes, DiMaggio dealt these convictions a stunning, if not fatal, blow for many of his fellow Americans.

With Italian immigrants making up a significant portion of Catholic America, DiMaggio's dismantling of negative conceptions of Italian Americans meant a reduction in the stereotyping of a large number of Catholics in the United States. Quite possibly, though, benefits of DiMaggio's bridging bonanza did not cross ethnic lines. Because caricatures he helped defuse may have been first and foremost considered purported ethnic traits of Italian Americans regardless of the religion they practiced, and since DiMaggio rarely emphasized his personal Catholic faith,[29] it may go too far to extrapolate from overturning caricatures of Italian Americans in particular to that of Catholic Americans in general.

---

[27] Quoted in Iorizzo and Mondello, *The Italian Americans*, 189.

[28] Ibid., 276. Iorizzo and Mondello similarly identify Frank Sinatra as an Italian American who popularized a positive image of Italian Americans during DiMaggio's era.

[29] Though DiMaggio frequently attended Mass at St. Patrick's Cathedral in Manhattan, he was rarely vocal about his Catholic faith.

Thus I sew up my sampling of sports-related bridging by Catholic athletes by turning to a more salient example for Catholic Americans of any ethnicity. I head from the Big Apple to the big soybean fields of Northern Indiana, home of the football team described by Kathryn Jay as "perhaps the most visible cultural representation of Catholic power in American society."[30] For Catholic Americans of any ancestry, this power source electrified the way in which they regarded their position within American society, instilling a greater sense of pride and belongingness in their American homeland. At the same time, it jumpstarted bridging by draining energy from American anti-Catholicism. As Notre Dame established itself as a gridiron juggernaut in the 1920s, hordes of Protestant Americans came to see the relationship between Catholic faith and American society in a new light.

Dubbing the Notre Dame football squad of the era a "Catholic team" asks for an asterisk. Many of its players were Protestants, as was legendary coach Knute Rockne prior to his conversion to Catholicism five years into heading the team. This Protestant presence prompted the jocular suggestion that Notre Dame's nickname should be the "Fighting Scandinavians," not the "Fighting Irish." Nevertheless, a squad from a Catholic university made up mostly of Catholic players, who participated in team visits to the on-campus Grotto of Our Lady before home games and attended Mass before away games, became stamped in the minds of countless Catholic and Protestant fans as a Catholic team. Moreover, as this squad enjoyed a meteoric rise to national powerhouse heights, it became cemented in many of these minds as *America's* Catholic team. As the story often goes, Notre Dame's climb to the college football mountaintop began with one huge step that stunned the football world. The year was 1913, and the consensus was that the chances of a virtually unknown team from a Midwestern Catholic school beating an East Coast behemoth such as Army were slim to none. Notre Dame head coach Jesse Harper might have agreed with this prognosis if his team were forced to outduel Army in a battle of running games, but fortunately, at his disposal was a freshly minted, rarely used addition to the rules of the game,

---

[30] Kathryn Jay, *More than Just a Game: Sports in American Life Since 1945* (New York: Columbia University Press, 2004) 25.

the forward pass.[31] Harper surmised that this secret weapon could lead to a shocking upset over Army. His estimation proved correct, manifested by a 35–13 Notre Dame victory that threw the popularity of the passing game forward throughout America and put Notre Dame on the national football map.

Getting on the map was one thing. Redrawing it to make South Bend, Indiana stand out in bold was another, made possible not by one upset victory but by sustained gridiron greatness. An obvious fount of this flowing success was a stream of outstanding players such as running back George Gipp. Immortalized by Ronald Reagan on the silver screen,[32] Gipp continues to hold the Notre Dame season record for rushing yards per carry and boasted the school career rushing mark until 1978.[33] Directing Gipp and friends to perennial power was one of the greatest ever to stroll the sidelines. During Knute Rockne's head coaching tenure from 1918 to 1931, the Fighting Irish celebrated five national championships and won 105 games, while losing only twelve and tying five. Thanks in large part to his wide-open offensive style, Rockne's winning percentage of .881 stands above that of any other coach in football history, college or pro. Jack Cavanaugh contends that in an age of outstanding coaches,[34] Rockne, "more than any other coach, put his school

---

[31] The legalization of the forward pass came about after President Theodore Roosevelt called representatives from Harvard, Princeton, and Yale to the White House in 1905 to address the plague of football-related deaths, estimated at 325 from 1880–1905. This White House meeting led to the establishment of a rules committee, which developed the forward pass and moreover served as a forerunner of the National Collegiate Athletic Association (NCAA).

[32] Gipp died of pneumonia and a severe streptococcal infection in 1920, following a deathbed conversation with Rockne that was featured in the 1940 film *Knute Rockne: All American*. Perhaps setting historical veracity aside, the film's version of the story has Rockne saving a message from Gipp for eight years and then incorporating it into a halftime speech to rally his squad to a come-from-behind victory over Army in 1928.

[33] Gipp's record is 8.1 yards per carry in 1920, and his Notre Dame career rushing total was 2,341 yards.

[34] Cavanaugh writes that Rockne's "college counterparts included such coaching immortals as Pop Warner at Pittsburgh, Amos Alonzo Stagg at Chicago, Fielding Yost at Michigan, Bob Zuppke at Illinois, and Tad Jones at Yale" (Jack

on the map, as bent on making Notre Dame famous as he was on winning football games."[35] Rockne gained glory for Notre Dame by marching to victory after victory on the field and also via a shrewd ability to spread the good news of his team and its university. Writing his own syndicated column and hiring Babe Ruth's publicist to disseminate his message, Rockne made sure that Notre Dame hype came hot off the press across the nation.

With this media blitz trumpeting triumphs piled up on the field, Notre Dame football's Roaring Twenties popularity rivaled that of the Charleston or talking pictures. Beano Cook claims that the Notre Dame "Victory March" became one of the four best-known songs in America, along with the "Star-Spangled Banner," "God Bless America," and "White Christmas."[36] Huge crowds made a sporting pilgrimage to watch the Fighting Irish in action, whether in their holy Northern Indiana abode or in stadiums such as Chicago's Soldier Field, where over 110,000 witnessed Notre Dame take on the University of Southern California in 1929. Standing alongside Rockne in loving every second of this Notre Dame fame, University Prefect John O'Hara took particular pleasure in seeing this prestige take a toll on anti-Catholicism. As he celebrated a Fighting Irish national title in 1924, O'Hara proclaimed, "Notre Dame football is a new crusade: it kills prejudice."[37] Much of the prejudice at which Notre Dame football took aim was of an extremely blatant variety, propagated by the Ku Klux Klan. Drawing an estimated one of every three Indiana men in the 1920s into its ranks,[38] the Klan's hatred of Catholicism in general was occasionally directed at Notre Dame in particular, most conspicuously at a series of South Bend clashes between robed Klansmen and Notre Dame students. Other forms of prejudice tackled by Notre Dame football may not have been as eye-catching as KKK rallies and skirmishes, but the trope of Catholic allegiance to their Pope

Cavanaugh, *The Gipper: George Gipp, Knute Rockne, and the Dramatic Rise of Notre Dame Football* (New York: Skyhorse Publishing, 2010) 4).

[35] Ibid.

[36] Murray A. Sperber, *Shake Down the Thunder: The Creation of Notre Dame Football* (Bloomington: University of Indiana Press, 2002) 24.

[37] Quoted in Baker, *Playing with God*, 133.

[38] Ibid., 132.

instead of their nation ubiquitously undermined their acceptance as Americans. As William Baker writes about Notre Dame, "Their patriotism called into question by Hoosier rednecks and white-collar politicians alike, they excelled at the All-American game of football. Knute Rockne was Notre Dame's answer to the Ku Klux Klan."[39] Shining brightly in this all-American sport, America's Catholic team built a bridge spanning an alleged chasm between Catholicism and American society. After stymying Stanford on New Year's Day 1925 to capture yet another national title, the Fighting Irish enjoyed what functioned as a twelve-day victory tour returning from the Rose Bowl in California back home to Indiana. Todd Tucker describes that in speeches at every stop of the tour, Prefect O'Hara held forth the national title as "proof that the University of Notre Dame and Catholic institutions of learning in general could mold successful Americans."[40] Certainly not all Protestants agreed. The Ku Klux Klan did not collapse due to Notre Dame gridiron greatness, and anti-Catholicism's rearing of its ugly head in John F. Kennedy's presidential campaign decades after the 1920s shows that Fighting Irish football of O'Hara's era did not defeat all vestiges of anti-Catholic prejudice. Yet, for innumerable Protestants in Roaring Twenties America, Notre Dame football cast serious doubts upon the presumed clash between Catholic faith and American values, suggesting the two might be triumphant teammates rather than forever foes.

American Anti-Semitism

"Give me your tired, your poor, your huddled masses yearning to breathe free." Settling into their new lives in the New World, Catholic immigrants quickly realized that many Americans disagreed with this Statue of Liberty inscription. Jewish immigrants met a similar fate, hearing exasperated ejaculations along the lines of "Go back where you came from!" instead of Lady Liberty's words of welcome. Roughly 675,000 Jews emigrated to the United States from 1881 to 1900, with the figure climbing to 1,364,000 from 1901 to 1914. Almost three-quarters of these immi-

---

[39] Ibid., 132–33.

[40] Todd Tucker, *Notre Dame vs. the Klan: How the Fighting Irish Defeated the Ku Klux Klan* (Chicago: Loyola Press, 2004) 188.

grants came from the Russian Empire,[41] many of whom made their transatlantic exodus due to the institution of legal restrictions that forced them to abandon long established ways of life and migrate to cities that offered paltry employment opportunity. Further fueling this exodus, intense pogroms against Russian Jews followed the assassination of Tsar Alexander II in 1881 and reappeared sporadically until World War I.[42] After they fled these tribulations in the frigid climes of Russia, Jews were often given the cold shoulder by fellow Jews who had come to America from Central Europe decades earlier.[43] Largely assimilated into American society and frequently prosperous in their New World homeland,[44] these so-called German Jews tended to regard their impoverished, more religiously conservative Eastern European co-religionists as stuck in the medieval mud. Though some German Jews were eager to lend a helping hand, many opposed Russian Jews' immigration, viewing them as a source of embarrassment and fearing they would kindle American anti-Semitic fires.[45]

[41] More specifically, these immigrants came from the fifteen western provinces of European Russia and the ten provinces of Russian-controlled Poland.

[42] Russian Jews especially poured out of their homeland following the 1881 pogroms, the 1903 Kishinev massacre, and pogroms due to the unsuccessful revolution of 1905 (Deborah Dwork, "Immigrant Jews on the Lower East Side of New York: 1880–1914," in *The American Jewish Experience*, ed. Jonathan D. Sarna, 102–17 (New York: Holmes & Meier, 1986) 102).

[43] In 1880, before the arrival of masses from Eastern Europe, the number of Jews in the United States stood at about a quarter of a million, only one-sixth of whom hailed from Eastern Europe. More than two hundred thousand were so-called German Jews who arrived primarily in the 1830s and 1840s (Gerald Sorin, *A Time for Building: The Third Migration 1880–1920* (Baltimore: Johns Hopkins University Press, 1992) 2).

[44] Sorin writes that German Jews "managed to carve out of their immigrant experience a distinctly attractive, and at least temporarily successful, cultural synthesis: Jewish, German, and American. German Jews had also managed to fulfill the immigrant ambition for a better life and more material comfort. Some even had made fortunes" (ibid.).

[45] Jonathan D. Sarna, *The American Jewish Experience*, ed. Jonathan D. Sarna, 102–17 (New York: Holmes & Meier, 1986) 118.

These fears were realized. As unwanted as they may have felt from German Jews, Russian Jews faced even greater hostility from Gentiles in America. This anti-Semitism soon became an equal-opportunity hater, not only directing its antipathy toward Jews from Eastern Europe, but also turning up its heat against German Jews. At least one German Jew paid for American anti-Semitism with his life, when Leo Frank was lynched in 1915 by a Georgia mob,[46] and Jews of any ancestral background faced widespread discrimination such as denial of access to clubs, resorts, and universities. Harvard President Abbott Lawrence Lowell proposed a quota system to rectify what he called the "Jewish problem," namely the rising enrollment of Jewish men at his university from six percent in 1908 to twenty-two percent in 1922. Though faculty officially rejected the proposal, it was tacitly accepted and implemented.[47] Strident voices in the media and in Congress associated Jewish Americans with radical anti-American ideologies, basing their claims on dubious evidence, chiefly *The Protocols of the Learned Elders of Zion*. The *Protocols* described a supposed plot to destroy Christian civilization, which allegedly was cooked up by a clandestine Jewish world government and had been taking its toll on unsuspecting Christian societies for nearly two thousand years. Countless Americans were hoodwinked by the *Protocols'* fabricated claims of Jewish manipulation of economic and political power, said to involve promotion of Marxism and Darwinism, corruption of churches and governments, and control over mechanisms of capitalism in its early twentieth-century manifestation. Americans were fed this fabrication by multiple hands, but no one ladled out *Protocols* excerpts as readily as Henry Ford in his newspaper the *Independent*. Stories about "the international Jew as the world's foremost problem" and "aspects of Jewish power in the United States"[48] filled *Independent* pages, which sought to convince readers that Jews were "the conscious enemies of all that Anglo-

---

[46] After Mary Phagen, a thirteen-year-old employee of Frank's factory, was found brutally murdered, Frank was convicted on dubious evidence and contradictory testimony and sentenced to death. This sentence was commuted to life imprisonment by Georgia's governor, angering a mob that took Frank from an Atlanta penitentiary to Phagen's hometown of Marietta and lynched him.

[47] Eck, *A New Religious America*, 302.

[48] Quoted in Sorin, *A Time for Building*, 238.

Saxons mean by civilization."[49] Seemingly no segment of Jewish involvement in American society escaped the *Independent's* calumny, and a particular favorite target was Jewish involvement in the national pastime. Publishing articles with headlines like "Jewish Gamblers Corrupt American Baseball" and "The Jewish Degradation of American Baseball," Ford spotlighted his anti-Semitism by declaring in one piece, "If fans wish to know the trouble with American baseball, they have it in three words—too much Jew."[50] Adding to Ford's assembly line of anti-Semitism, another Motor City-area resident sent his incendiary rhetoric across Midwestern and East Coast radio waves. Ten million listeners typically tuned in to Father Charles Coughlin's sermons, in which, like Ford, he blamed Jews for nearly every American malady. Coughlin's anti-Jewish jabs achieved their greatest reach over the airwaves, but they also filled stadiums and arenas holding huge assemblages. A 1939 gathering for Coughlin's Christian Front at Madison Square Garden in New York, for example, boasted a crowd in excess of 19,000. As Coughlin's condemnation comingled with brazen banners reading "Wake Up America! Smash Jewish Communism!" and "Stop Jewish Domination of Christian America!", there was no mistaking that anti-Semitism was booming within American borders.

Coming from Ford, Coughlin, and dozens of other anti-Semitic sources, one of the most commonly recycled stereotypes of the era was the caricature of the weak, athletically inept Jew. Academics including the well-regarded sociologist E. A. Ross contended that research proved the physical inferiority of Jewish immigrants compared to White Protestant Americans. Ross maintained, "On the physical side, the Hebrews are the polar opposites of our pioneer breed. Not only are they undersized and weak-muscled, but they shun bodily activity and are exceedingly sensitive to pain."[51] Ford built onto this pseudoscience by manufacturing his own claims. He asserted that "Jews are not sportsmen.... Whether this is due to their physical lethargy, their dislike of

---

[49] Quoted in Peter Levine, *Ellis Island to Ebbets Field: Sport and the American Jewish Experience* (New York: Oxford University Press, 1992) 106.
[50] Quoted in ibid., 107.
[51] Quoted in ibid., 11.

unnecessary physical action, or their serious cast of mind, others may decide.... It may be a defect in their character, or it may not; it is nevertheless a fact which discriminating Jews unhesitatingly acknowledge."[52] As demonstrated by Jewish sports historian Peter Levine, grains of truth could be sifted from these words. Levine declares that writings of Jewish intellectuals "contributed to popular images of Jews as people of the book rather than as people of the hook, right cross, or homerun,"[53] and Eastern European Jewish immigrants often opposed their children's athletic ardor, judging sports to be foolish wastes of time. Levine also displays at great depth, however, that Ford's generalization occludes the lucid reality that sports formed a significant part of thousands of early twentieth-century Jewish American lives. Critically, the upshot of veiling this reality was not simply a matter of promoting misunderstanding of Jewish Americans' athletic ability and interest. Considering the pride of place to which sports had climbed in America, the stereotype of Jews as athletically incompetent and averse to sports contributed greatly to conceptions of Jewishness and American society perpetually clashing in antithetical terms.

Jewish American Athletic Activity

Contrary to what this stereotype suggested, Jewish jocks excelled on college campuses. Citing the *American Hebrew* and other Jewish publications that regularly valorized the feats of Jewish college athletes, Levine writes:

> The purpose of such coverage remained consistent. Jewish athletic success challenged anti-Semitic claims that Jews were too intellectual and too debilitated physically to become fully assimilated Americans. The large numbers involved, their displays of physical prowess and excellence in a variety of sports, and their election as team captains all became evidence for arguments that Jewish college students and, by implication, Jews in general, if given a chance, were as eager and capable as Gentiles to participate in all that college and American life offered.[54]

[52] Quoted in ibid., 4.
[53] Ibid.
[54] Ibid., 200–201.

Many of these Jews represented their college and their religion on the gridiron. Over 500 Jews played college football in 1928, according to the *American Hebrew*, and college standouts Benny Friedman, Marshall Goldberg, and Sid Luckman became household names in both Jewish and Gentile living rooms.[55] Friedman and Luckman continued to grab headlines as they followed their campus glory days with outstanding professional careers. As quarterback for the New York Giants, Friedman led the NFL in both passing and rushing during the same season, a mark that no other player has accomplished, and quarterback Luckman propelled the Chicago Bears to four NFL championships. It was no small gain for Friedman, Luckman, and other Jews to achieve greatness on the college or pro gridiron. Due especially to the rough and tough nature of the game, their football prowess moved the chains downfield against the caricature of the feeble, athletically awkward Jew.

In addition to the football field, Jewish big men on campus stood tall on the basketball floor. Jewish court presence was particularly sizable in the hoops hotbed of New York, where Jewish players formed significant portions of squads that competed before huge Madison Square Garden crowds. The team with the strongest Jewish stamp was the City College of New York, whose roster during its heyday was typically about eighty percent Jewish. Eight CCNY Jews were named All-Americans, and CCNY captured the national championship in 1950 under Jewish coaching icon Nat Holman.[56] This Jewish mark on the college game was one of many manifestations of a Jewish love affair with basketball. Newly arrived Jewish immigrants flocked to basketball hoops shortly after James Naismith affixed peach baskets to his Springfield YMCA balcony in 1891, prompting Baker to declare, "Basketball and the American Jew were born of the same womb and of the same era."[57] Multiple factors may have accounted for this sibling relationship, but the most significant

[55] Friedman was a two-time All-American quarterback at the University of Michigan, Goldberg led the University of Pittsburgh to a national championship, and Luckman starred as quarterback at Columbia University.

[56] During much of Holman's coaching tenure at CCNY, he played professional basketball on the weekends, leading his New York Celtics to a 531–28 record over eight seasons.

[57] Baker, *Playing with God*, 184.

was basketball's rapid development as a city game. Needing little space and less equipment than most other sports, basketball was a natural fit for the densely populated urban jungles that recently arrived Jewish immigrants called home. The first Jewish basketball league was founded in 1902 in Philadelphia, composed of teams from synagogues, Young Men's Hebrew Associations, community centers, and settlement houses. Foreshadowing a similar trend in American Islam many decades later, Jewish leagues soon sprung up elsewhere across the nation. For a large number of Jews, the B'nai B'rith[58] was the basketball venue of choice. Local B'nai B'rith teams battled it out against one another in tournaments and occasionally tipped off against non-Jewish teams. A widely anticipated annual contest in Chicago pitted the B'nai B'rith All-Stars against a CYO all-star squad. Jewish teams also took the floor against Gentile sides at the semipro level. While not attracting the amount of attention to Jewish athleticism as stars at a college powerhouse such as CCNY, semiprofessional teams played a supportive sixth-man role in challenging the caricature of the non-athletic Jew. The best known of these teams was the SPHA, short for South Philadelphia Hebrew All-Stars,[59] who faced an array of Jewish and Gentile opponents while proudly proclaiming their Jewish identity. Donning shirts displaying the Star of David and Hebrew script, the team used the nicknames "Wandering Jews" and "Philadelphia Hebrews" during its barnstorming tours. Other semipro basketball monikers placed Jewish identity at the forefront, such as the "Fighting Rabbis" of Minneapolis's Talmud Torah Athletic Club.

Joining basketball's full-court press against the stereotype of Jewish athletic ineptitude, Jewish deftness in boxing dealt this caricature damaging blows. Levine highlights boxing's bridging significance for Jewish Americans, stating that because of its association with toughness and

[58] The B'nai B'rith (meaning "children of the covenant") emerged in 1843 from meetings of German Jews in New York's Lower East Side to confront what co-founder Isaac Rosenbourg called "the deplorable condition of Jews in this, our newly adopted country." These meetings led to humanitarian aid and service promoted by a system of fraternal lodges and chapters that grew across the nation and internationally ("B'nai B'rith International: About Us," B'nai B'rith International, http://www.bnaibrith.org/about-us.html (accessed 14 March 2015)).

[59] The original name was the South Philadelphia Hebrew Association.

courage, "no other activity provided such a clear way to refute stereotypes of the weak, cowardly Jew that anti-Semites employed to deny Jewish immigrants and their children full access to American opportunities."[60] While up until World War I a Jewish boxing champ was an anomaly, shortly afterward title belts were clasped around many Jewish waists. By 1928 the majority of titleholders and contenders in all eight weight classes were Jewish Americans. Like their bent for basketball, Jewish renown in the ring was a byproduct of life in urban America, where Jews honed their pugilistic craft at Young Men's Hebrew Associations and settlement houses and where fighting was one way to put the kibosh on anti-Semitic slurs on the streets. Boxing provided a promising path from daily struggles in Jewish American ghettos to fame and its accompanying fruit, a journey enjoyed by champions such as Barney Ross and Max Baer. Ross won the world lightweight and junior welterweight titles in 1933 and the welterweight crown in 1934, the same year Baer captured the world heavyweight championship. Baer's reach against anti-Semitism stretched across the Atlantic when he defeated German heavyweight and Hitler poster boy Max Schmeling. Baer took down the German Goliath while wearing trunks displaying the Star of David, a sartorial statement of identity also adopted by the most famous Jewish champ, Benny Leonard. Holder of the world lightweight crown from 1917 to 1925, Leonard tasted victory in eighty-eight consecutive fights, including sixty-eight by knockout. Sports historian Steven Riess dubs Leonard "the outstanding Jewish American athlete of the first third of the twentieth century,"[61] due not only to his boxing triumphs, but also to the praise he received from both Jews and Gentiles. A scribe for the New York publication *New Wahrheit* proclaimed in 1925 that Leonard "is, perhaps, even greater than Einstein, for when Einstein was in America only thousands knew him but Benny is known by millions."[62] Leonard's ability to garner Gentile acclamation in anti-Semitic America strengthened sagging Jewish spirits.

[60] Levine, *Ellis Island to Ebbets Field*, 162.

[61] Steven A. Riess, "Tough Jews: The Jewish American Boxing Experience, 1890–1950," in *Sports and the American Jew*, ed. Steven A. Riess, 60–104 (Syracuse NY: Syracuse University Press, 1998) 75.

[62] Quoted in Levine, *Ellis Island to Ebbets Field*, 154.

After Leonard's tragic death from a massive heart attack while refereeing a fight in 1947, reporter Al Lurie wrote, "When a people is beaten, persecuted and frustrated, it finds more than mere solace in its champions.... When Leonard was accepted and admired by the entire fair-minded American community, the Jews of America felt they, themselves, were being accepted and admired."[63] Like Lurie's posthumous assessment, columns written in the midst of Leonard's career avowed that the Great Bennah was lionized by Americans regardless of their faith, and pundits occasionally connected the veneration Leonard received from non-Jews with the overturning of anti-Semitism. Citing Leonard's gritty reputation in the ring as well as his appearances in exhibition fights to benefit Catholic charities, Arthur Brisbane claimed that Leonard did "more to conquer anti-Semitism than 1,000 textbooks."[64] Brisbane continued to say that the champ has "done more to evoke the respect of the non-Jew for the Jew than all the brilliant Jewish writers combined."[65] Some may disagree that the boxing glove could be mightier than the pen, yet through his direct assault on the stereotype of the frail, athletically incompetent Jew, Leonard did more than go the distance with anti-Semitism. For Americans who came to see Jews through a new lens thanks to his pugilistic prowess, Leonard knocked anti-Semitism down for the count.

A decade after Leonard hung up his trunks to conclude Riess's selection as the greatest Jewish American athletic career in the first third of the twentieth century, the athlete widely regarded as the greatest Jewish American sports hero of all time stepped up to the plate against anti-Semitism. Although not the first Jewish major leaguer,[66] Hank Greenberg was the first Jewish baseball star. The Hall of Famer, two-time American League MVP, and five-time All-Star batted a lifetime .313 in

[63] Ibid., 153–54.

[64] Quoted in ibid., 159.

[65] Quoted in ibid.

[66] The two most accomplished Jewish Major Leaguers before Greenberg were Buddy Myer and Andy Cohen. An infielder with the Washington Senators and Boston Red Sox in the 1920s, Myer was a consistent .300 hitter and respected stolen-base threat. Cohen batted .281 during his three seasons with the New York Giants in the 1920s.

twelve seasons with the Detroit Tigers plus one with the Pittsburgh Pirates, a career which included a four-year hiatus for World War II Air Force service. As impressive as his career batting average may be, it was Greenberg's power figures that punched his ticket to fame. Four times the first baseman led the American League in homeruns and runs batted in, and in 1938 Greenberg's name was on countless lips when his home-run pace threatened to surpass Babe Ruth's single-season record of sixty. Ending up with a total of fifty-eight round-trippers, Greenberg fell just short of the mark, but he was right on target in solidifying his status as a supreme slugger.

As a Jewish player in an almost exclusively Gentile baseball world, Greenberg faced a plethora of anti-Semitic epithets from opposing players and fans, especially early in his career. Looking back on playing with Greenberg, Tigers catcher Birdie Tebbetts suggested he "was abused more than any other white ballplayer or any other ethnic player except Jackie Robinson."[67] Multiple players have corroborated the claim that during the final days of the 1938 season, a few pitchers refused to give Greenberg good pitches to hit, seeking to ensure that a Jew would not break the single-season homerun record. While a target of anti-Jewish prejudice himself, however, Greenberg's importance in diminishing American anti-Semitism and its effects on fellow Jews was immense. Greenberg was much more than a wellspring of Jewish American pride; Gentiles, too, adulated Hammerin' Hank for his displays of power in the all-American sport of baseball. John Rosengren proclaims that Greenberg "had given his co-religionists a retort to every charge of weakness and timidity or ineptness. A single word that could stand up to any form of prejudice: Greenberg."[68] Like the scrappy Benny Leonard giving a black eye to stereotypes of spineless Jews, Greenberg's booming bat formed the backbone of an athletic assault on anti-Semitism in America. Pounding baseballs over homerun fences throughout the American League, standing at 6'4" and tipping the scales at 210 pounds, Greenberg

[67] Quoted in Robert C. Cottrell, *Two Pioneers: How Jackie Robinson and Hank Greenberg Transformed Baseball—and America* (Dulles VA: Potomac Books, 2012) 39.

[68] Rosengren, *Hank Greenberg*, 177.

was one of the Major League's biggest and strongest players of his era, poles apart from the caricature of the puny, punchless Jew. As Detroit-area residents Henry Ford and Father Coughlin propagated this caricature in hopes of marginalizing Jews further from American society, the Detroit slugger countered with a resounding reply. Though resonating throughout the nation, it was no small matter that this reply was heard loudest by hometown fans in the anti-Semitic hotbed of Detroit. The Motor City metro area of Greenberg's day was the breeding grounds not only of damning denigrations from Ford and Coughlin, but also of an active branch of the Black Legion, whose Michigan commander cooked up a plan to kill one million Jews by detonating bombs in every American synagogue on Yom Kippur. Moreover, it was no small matter that Greenberg powered his way to baseball stardom just as Hitler's anti-Semitism devastated Jews around the world. Reflecting on his career decades after retirement, Greenberg stated, "I was representing a couple of million Jews among a hundred million gentiles and I was always in the spotlight. ...As time went by I came to feel that if I, as a Jew, hit a homerun I was hitting one against Hitler."[69] The all too obvious and tragic reality is that what Greenberg accomplished on American baseball diamonds had no effect on preventing the unspeakable horrors that occurred in concentration camps across the Atlantic. What Greenberg came to realize, though, was that his athletic accomplishments could boost the spirits of Jewish Americans demoralized by these atrocities and could directly counter Hitler's mendacious portrayals of Jews. According to Jewish American civil liberties lawyer Alan Dershowitz, Greenberg "was what *they* all said we could never be. He defied Hitler's stereotype. For that very reason, I think he may have been the single most important Jew to live in the 1930s."[70]

Such importance was the product of sustained prowess displayed year after year, yet one particular series of events had an especially significant effect in prompting many non-Jews to reconsider prevailing notions casting Jews in opposition to American values. With the Tigers' pen-

[69] Quoted in Levine, *Ellis Island to Ebbets Field*, 138.
[70] Robert C. Cottrell, *Icons of American Popular Culture: From P. T. Barnum to Jennifer Lopez* (New York: Routledge, 2009) 136.

nant-winning 1934 season nearing its regular season conclusion, the Jewish High Holidays coincided with games against the Red Sox and Yankees, posing Greenberg with an apparent question of loyalty pitting religion against team. Shortly before Rosh Hashanah, the first of the High Holy Days, Greenberg commented that he might spend the day in prayer instead of on the diamond. Greenberg's remark sent fans and scribes abuzz, perturbing many that he might place his Jewish faith above his team amidst its tight pennant race with the Yankees. Anger abated when Greenberg chose to play, and it turned to elation for Detroit fans at game's end. The Tigers defeated the Red Sox 2–1 thanks to two Greenberg homeruns, one of which seemed to come straight out of a Hollywood script as he welcomed in the Jewish New Year with a bottom-of-the-ninth walk-off wallop. In the days ahead, Greenberg reignited quite a few fans' fury, choosing not to play on the holiest of all days for Jews, Yom Kippur. Positioning himself in prayer at a Detroit synagogue instead of at first base against the Yankees, from the perspective of some baseball buffs Greenberg was confirming the claim that Jewish faith and an all-American pursuit such as baseball are like oil and water. A number of Motor City residents, on the other hand, viewed Greenberg's decision positively and in some cases linked it to a favorable appraisal of his religion. Bud Shaver of the *Detroit News* declared that "the qualities which make [Greenberg] an appealing figure are the direct heritage of race and creed. His fine intelligence, independence of thought, courage, and his driving ambition have won him the respect and admiration of his teammates, baseball writers, and the fans at large."[71] According to Shaver, the "Jewish people could find no better representative"[72] than Greenberg as they sought to establish themselves within American society. Along with this glowing prose, Greenberg's handling of his High Holy Days dilemma was celebrated in verse. *Detroit Free Press* readers were treated the day after Game 1 of the World Series to Edgar Guest's poem "Speaking of Greenberg," which ended with the following stanzas:

[71] Quoted in Levine, *Ellis Island to Ebbets Field*, 135.
[72] Ibid.

In July the Irish wondered where he'd ever learned to play.
"He makes me think of Casey!" Old Man Murphy dared to say;
And with fifty-seven doubles and a score of homers made
The respect they had for Greenberg was being openly displayed.
But on the Jewish New Year when Hank Greenberg came to bat
And made two homeruns off pitcher Rhodes—they cheered like mad for
    that.
Came Yom Kippur—holy fast day worldwide over to the Jew—
And Hank Greenberg to his teaching and the old tradition true
Spent the day among his people and he didn't come to play.
Said Murphy to Mulrooney, "We shall lose the game today!
We shall miss him on the infield and shall miss him at the bat,
But he's true to his religion—and I honor him for that!"[73]

Perhaps Mulrooney did not share Murphy's sentiments. He may have been too entrenched in the anti-Semitic environment of his day to honor Greenberg for his commitment to his Jewish faith. In Detroit and across America, though, there were plenty of "Murphys" who highly esteemed Greenberg for his decision, and due to Greenberg playing on one Jewish holiday but not on the other, they came to see Jewish faith and American values as capable of cohabitation instead of locked at loggerheads.

[73] Quoted in Ron Kaplan, "Jewish Athletes and the 'Yom Kippur Dilemma,'" *New Jersey Jewish News*, http://njjewishnews.com/njjn.com/092806/sptsJewish AthletesYomKippr.html (published 28 September 2006; accessed 14 March 2015).

3

Catalysts of Muslim American
Athletic Bonding and Bridging

Catholic or American? Jewish or American? The previous chapter's sojourn in ardently anti-Catholic and anti-Semitic surroundings showed that, according to many Americans, Catholics and Jews living in their land needed to choose between two contradictory identities. From a common American perspective, it was inconceivable that an individual could inhabit both Catholic and American, or Jewish and American, modes of being. Especially since September 2001, Muslim Americans have been cast as characters in this same old story that featured Catholic and Jewish Americans in the past. Sometimes subtly and sometimes screaming at ear-splitting volume, many Americans have delivered the message that Muslims must choose between purportedly clashing religious and national allegiances. Providing background for my exploration of Muslim American athletic activities' role in challenging this view, the second part of this chapter scopes out the lay of the anti-Islamic land that sports-based bridging aspires to overturn. First, though, this chapter's ambition to set the stage for detailed discussion of Muslim American athletic activity has background matters regarding sports-based bonding in its sights. Before future chapters plumb the depths of strengthening Muslim piety and fellowship through athletic activities, I skim the surface of Islamic revivalism, a movement that stands at the heart of calls to boost Islamic devotion and camaraderie.

Islamic Revivalism in America

The Islamic revivalist label should be acknowledged as malleable, functioning as a ductile descriptor that defies being viewed in intractable terms. Muslims who have been categorized by this designation are by no means monolithic in their understanding of Islam.[1] Acknowledging that throughout the world and in America, Muslims identified as revivalists have manifested significant variety on many issues,[2] I nonetheless use this label as an umbrella term covering two common characteristics, a conviction that Islam is a complete way of life and an emphasis on the Qur'an and Hadith (a record of the life of Muhammad and his companions) in providing this comprehensive way of life with its direction. Revivalist Muslim American voices contain a variety of timbres, but a belief that Islam suffuses all realms of human existence, guided meticulously by the Qur'an and Hadith, undergirds these diverse tones.

Islamic revivalism made its mark on American soil beginning in the 1960s, arriving with immigrants who benefited from changing Civil Rights-era winds. As an increasing number of Americans came to grips with their nation's injustices towards Blacks, awareness grew regarding discriminatory black marks on American immigration law. The Johnson-Reed Act of 1924 welcomed Northern and Western Europeans but closed American doors to inhabitants of numerous other regions.[3]

---

[1] Nazli Kibria notes that revivalist Islam has also been described by the labels "fundamentalist Islam," "reformist Islam," "resurgent Islam," and the "new Islam" (Nazli Kibria, *Muslims in Motion: Islam and National Identity in the Bangladeshi Diaspora* (New Brunswick NJ: Rutgers University Press, 2011) 3).

[2] Revivalists may disagree, for example, on whether Muslims should become actively involved in the American political system or distance themselves from it. Edward Curtis writes that some American Muslims, such as members of the organizations Tabligh Jama'at and Hizb Tahrir, regard the American government and society as immoral and therefore avoid American political involvement. On the other hand, Curtis claims, "Most American Muslims...want to be fully Muslim and fully American, and they argue for the compatibility and complementary nature of American and Islamic values. They may wish to change certain elements of U.S. foreign and domestic policies, but they intend to do so using the same means that every other mainstream group uses. Like other Americans, American Muslims attempt to make their voices heard in American politics and the public sphere by supporting a variety of national public interest groups" (Edward E. Curtis IV, *The Columbia Sourcebook of Muslims in the United States*, ed. Edward E. Curtis IV (New York: Columbia University Press, 2008) 265–66).

[3] The Johnson-Reed Act based its quotas on what it claimed to be the origins of America's population in 1890, going back to a time when America was far more Northern and Western European than what it had become (David R. Roediger,

Thanks to the Immigration and Naturalization Act of 1965, these doors were flung open, precipitating an influx of Muslim immigration,[4] estimated at over one million during the next three decades.[5] Some of these newcomers staked out revivalist turf within the landscape of American Islam and stimulated revivalist awakenings across their new homeland. Shortly after their American arrival, revivalists formed the Muslim Students Association, while others took leadership positions in mosques. Edward Curtis documents that at the Islamic Center of New England, for example, immigrants and foreign students exercised their newly acquired leadership capacities to ban gambling, alcohol, and other practices they deemed incompatible with the Qur'an and Hadith. Similar to what was taking place at mosques across America, these new leaders gave lectures about traditional religious practices, translated Islamic literature into English, and taught Muslims who had been living in America for decades how to recite prayers in Arabic, a language that many second- and third-generation immigrants did not know but was considered by revivalists to be essential to Islamic piety.[6] Curtis asserts that whereas Muslims who came to America in the first half of the twentieth century frequently "stressed their ethnic and national origins as a primary source of identity," the post-1965 cohort "increasingly turned to religion to define their identity."[7] Many in this cohort would likely have looked askance at developments in a primarily second- and third-generation

Working Toward Whiteness: How America's Immigrants Became White: The Strange Journey from Ellis Island to the Suburbs (New York: Basic Books, 2005) 139).

[4] The Immigration and Naturalization Act emphasized two criteria, "family reunification" and "occupational preference." The latter was intended to shore up the American workforce in occupations struggling with a shallow labor supply (Lawrence, *New Faiths, Old Fears,* 79–80).

[5] Due to the Immigration and Naturalization Act, from 1966–1997 approximately 2,780,000 immigrants came to the United States from majority Muslim areas of the world. While religious affiliation was not asked about or recorded, one demographer estimates that about 1.1 million of these immigrants were Muslim, with 327,000 from North Africa and the Middle East and 316,000 from South Asia (Edward E. Curtis IV, *Muslims in America: A Short History* (New York: Oxford University Press, 2009) 73).

[6] Ibid., 68.

[7] Ibid., 68–69.

immigrant community such as that in Toledo, Ohio, which Egyptian sociologist Abdo Elkholy described as highly Americanized and liberal. As noted in Elkholy's 1959 ethnographic study,[8] though they personally abstained from alcohol, Muslims owned thirty percent of Toledo's bars, and their practice of Islam did not include a number of traditional elements including washings before prayer. Elkholy also reported that Toledo youth engaged in dating and mixed dancing at the mosque and that women provided social and religious leadership in the community.

Elkholy's portrayal of Muslim life in Toledo contrasts sharply with everyday affairs within mosques marked by a revivalist stamp, on which could have been found the faces of Sayyid Qutb or Mawlana al-Mawdudi.[9] Teachings of the Egyptian Qutb and Pakistani Mawdudi stressed the need for a complete implementation of the Qur'an and example of the Prophet within every sphere of social and personal life. Qutb and Mawdudi further emphasized the importance of the worldwide community of Muslims, or ummah, urging Muslims to regard themselves as inextricably linked with fellow followers of Islam around the globe. Consistent with this view, events involving Muslims overseas often profoundly influenced Muslim lives in America. Even before the Ayatollah Khomeini appeared regularly on American television screens, a number of revivalist Muslim Americans dipped their feet in the pool of political engagement, led to the water by American foreign policy. The

---

[8] Comparing this Toledo community with a Muslim cohort in Detroit, Elkholy argued that he found a strong correlation between Muslim religious practice and "Americanization." Curtis explains that Elkholy's research "showed that those Muslims who participated actively in the life of their mosques were more likely to assimilate into mainstream (white) American culture than those who did not participate in mosque life. Such findings challenged the assumptions of some social scientists, who believed that identification with a 'foreign' religion might prevent strong identification with American values and beliefs" (ibid., 57–58).

[9] Qutb was a leading figure in the Egyptian Muslim Brotherhood until his 1966 execution, having been convicted of plotting an assassination attempt against president Gamal Abdel Nasser. Qutb has influenced innumerable Muslims with his *Social Justice in Islam* and *Milestones* as well as other works emphasizing the social and political roles of Islam. Mawdudi was the founder of Jamaat-e-Islami, a Pakistani-based social and political organization. Mawdudi was a leading voice in calls for the creation of an Islamic state in Pakistan.

pool became more crowded after the Islamic Revolution in Iran, which held particular clout in shaping revivalism's course in the United States in the late 1970s. Kambiz GhaneaBassiri explains that this revolution "helped further an Islamic revival already on the way. Many American Muslims became more religious in this period. The revolution rejuvenated a sense of Islamic solidarity among average American Muslims and led to their greater politicization."[10] Shortly after the revolution, revivalism received an additional boost in America through the formation of the Islamic Society of North America (ISNA) in 1982. Spawned by the Muslim Students Association, ISNA quickly took on a life of its own as an overseeing body for a spectrum of organizations offering Islamic instruction, interfaith workshops, financial counseling, and sundry other services. ISNA's annual convention constitutes the largest gathering of Muslims in America, and its periodical *Islamic Horizons* keeps readers abreast of political events regarded through a revivalist lens. ISNA's vision of personal piety fueling political and social reform is shared by other major players on the American revivalist scene, including the Islamic Circle of North America, Muslim American Society, Muslim Public Affairs Council, and Council on American-Islamic Relations.[11]

Whether a result of being touched by the long arms of ISNA, a residual effect of the spiritual resurgence sparked by the Islamic Revolution in Iran, or due to some other factor, many Muslim Americans at the close of the twentieth century espoused a revivalist understanding of Is-

---

[10] GhaneaBassiri, *A History of Islam in America*, 325.

[11] Chapter 8 will provide more information about ICNA and MAS. Established in 1988, MPAC "is a public service agency working for the civil rights of American Muslims, for the integration of Islam into American pluralism, and for a positive, constructive relationship between American Muslims and their representatives" ("About MPAC," http://www.mpac.org/about.php (accessed 14 March 2015)). CAIR was originally established as a political advocacy organization in Washington, D.C. in 1994 and proclaims that its mission is "to enhance understanding of Islam, encourage dialogue, protect civil liberties, empower American Muslims, and build coalitions that promote justice and mutual understanding" ("CAIR: Vision, Mission, Core Principles," Council on American-Islamic Relations, http://www.cair.com/about-us/vision-mission-core-principles.html [accessed 14 March 2015]).

lam. In the present century, the topography of American Islam has contained even more revivalist features, especially as the fallout of 9/11 included an increase in revivalism in both breadth and depth. For Muslim Americans who, before the fall of the Twin Towers, made Islamic knowledge and piety a low personal priority, an eagerness often emerged to learn the ins and outs of their religion and practice it more staunchly. Frequently this eagerness was kick-started by a yearning to counteract the kicking down of their religion. Wanting to disabuse neighbors and co-workers of misunderstandings about Islam, these Muslims who had previously placed Islam on the margins of their lives recognized a need to educate themselves about their own religion before they could educate others. These Muslims tended to turn to revivalism, concluding that, with its emphases on the Qur'an and Prophetic tradition, it had just what their inquiring minds wanted to know. Moreover, for these Muslim Americans as well as those who had already been walking in step with revivalism before 9/11, negative stereotypes they faced often elicited more robust affirmation of Islamic identity and membership in the Muslim ummah. Writing about post-9/11 America, Nazli Kibria states that, "faced with intensive and largely negative scrutiny, Muslims have come together in a dynamic of reactive solidarity. They have responded to stigmatization by developing a stronger and more self-conscious collective identity."[12] Kibria's generalized claim finds its particularized proof in the pudding of post-9/11 studies of local Muslim American communities, including Jennifer Bryan's 2005 exploration of Muslim life in Jersey City, New Jersey. Bryan's findings connected these Muslims' exposure to anti-Islamic sentiments and actions after 9/11 with a "renewed and intensified interest in the Qur'an," as well as an escalated adoption of traditional Islamic practices such as donning of hijab by female members of the community.[13]

Thumbing their noses at classic models of assimilation that assume an inevitable shedding of "tradition" in response to the irresistible call of

---

[12] Kibria, *Muslims in Motion*, 2.

[13] Quoted in Anny P. Bakalian and Mehdi Bozorgmehr, *Backlash 9/11: Middle Eastern and Muslim Americans Respond* (Berkeley: University of California Press, 2009) 226.

"Americanization,"[14] the results of post-9/11 explorations by Bryan and other analysts disclose a power surge in Islamic piety, especially among young Muslim Americans. Geneive Abdo declares, "After the attacks, a generation of believers who were already becoming more spiritual than their parents rose up to defend their faith."[15] Abdo goes on to say that this desire to defend has manifested itself on multiple levels, from internalized longings for deeper devoutness to outward exhibitions of Islamic symbols such as the hijab and kufi (prayer cap). Drawing upon interviews with South Asian Muslim youth in North Carolina, Katherine Ewing and Marguerite Hoyler argue that for young Muslim Americans in the new post-9/11 milieu, "the significance of being a Muslim was dramatically redefined. Islam, which before 9/11 had been for many simply a part of their cultural heritage associated with their family's country of origin, came to be sharply distinguished from the concept of culture and detached from an association with any particular place."[16] Conceptualizations of an Islam freed of particular ethnic trappings had been around the American Islamic block before 9/11. Calls for a "cultureless Islam"

[14] Bryan writes, "The observation that most Arab Muslims in Jersey City did not attempt to blend in or downplay their Arab or Muslim appearance presents a challenge to the classic model of assimilation" (quoted in ibid., 227). Richard Alba and Victor Nee explain that "the old assimilation concept assumed that the minority group would change almost completely in order to assimilate (except for areas where it already resembled the majority group), while the majority culture would remain unaffected" (Richard Alba and Victor Nee, *Remaking the American Mainstream: Assimilation and Contemporary Immigration* (Cambridge MA: Harvard University Press, 2003) 4–5). According to Nadine Naber, "Dominant U.S. notions of Americanization often rely upon Eurocentric ideas that assume that religiously constituted identities—particularly identities constituted through Islam—are in opposition to Americanization, assimilation, and modernity" (Nadine Naber, *Arab America: Gender, Cultural Politics, and Activism* (New York: New York University Press, 2012) 124).
[15] Geneive Abdo, *Mecca and Main Street: Muslim Life in America after 9/11* (New York: Oxford University Press, 2006) 5.
[16] Katherine Pratt Ewing and Marguerite Hoyler, "Being Muslim and American: South Asian Muslim Youth and the War on Terror," in *Being and Belonging: Muslims in the United States since 9/11*, ed. Katherine Pratt Ewing, 80–103 (New York: Russell Sage Foundation, 2008) 81–82.

picked up plenty of fans at Muslim Students Association gatherings and other revivalist venues in the late twentieth century, persuading many that the dictates of an eternal God transcend the norms of transient cultures.[17] Yet, as Ewing and Hoyler affirm, these calls have been issued and embraced with greater frequency by young Muslims since 9/11,[18] along with the closely related revivalist emphasis on the interconnectedness of the global ummah, standing above any one particular ethnic or national grouping. The united ummah ideal has loomed large in young twenty-first-century revivalist Muslim Americans' understanding of the nuts and bolts of their faith. According to this understanding, acts of ritualistic piety such as praying the salat five times a day and fasting during Ramadan are essential but not enough. Without pieces aimed at strengthening Muslim fellowship on both the local and global levels, Islam would be judged by revivalists to contain a gaping hole.

Lest the previous paragraphs have created an impression that revivalism teems throughout Muslim American territory, however, it is important to point out that many Muslim Americans do not arrange the rhythms of their lives to a revivalist beat. Even after 9/11, for many Muslims in the United States, young and old alike, Islam is part of their cultural heritage but not a drive to religious devotion seen as applying to every aspect of their lives. Ihsan Bagby writes, "There are a large number of Muslims that hold on to their identity as Muslims, but choose not to practice, not to act out their beliefs in everyday life... Most of them would not view the world through the lens of religion and basically have put religion to the side to a certain extent to function in the world. A large portion of the American Muslim community are in this group."[19]

---

[17] Focusing on Chicago area MSAs, Garbi Schmidt asserts that for many young Muslims "Islam offered an ideology and a community (the *umma*) that claimed to transcend national borders and come from divine decree. Such an identification, therefore, undoubtedly looked and felt stronger to these young Muslims than an ethnic definition based on a national state or zone that might disappear tomorrow" (Garbi Schmidt, *Islam in Urban America: Sunni Muslims in Chicago* (Philadelphia: Temple University Press, 2004) 129).

[18] Ewing and Hoyler, "Being Muslim and American," 82.

[19] Quoted in Laurie Goodstein, "Stereotyping Rankles Silent, Secular Majority of American Muslims," *New York Times*, http://www.nytimes.com/2001/12/23/us/

Michael Merry addresses this issue by stating that in America "Islam does not play a central role in the lives of a large percentage of the individuals with a Muslim background... Many have the same material pursuits as other, nonreligious individuals. Others attach only minimal importance to their Islamic faith, preferring instead to participate in ethnically based voluntary associations."[20] Seeking to quantify approximately how many Muslim Americans might match these descriptions, one measure that might be considered is mosque attendance. In a 2006 nationwide poll of Muslim voters conducted by the Council on American-Islamic Relations,[21] only thirty-one percent reported attending a mosque weekly, and fifty-four percent indicated they seldom or never participate in any type of activity at a mosque. A 2011 study indicates a much higher percentage of Muslim Americans choosing not to enter mosque doors. The American Mosque 2011 report claims that a mere ten percent of all Muslims in America attend the nation's approximately 2,000 mosques.

These numbers deserve consideration but should also be taken with a grain of salt. Similar to the potential of ideological agenda to trump methodological rigor in counts of the total Muslim American population, which has spanned a gargantuan gamut from one million to eight million,[22] mosque attendance figures may possibly reveal more about re-

stereotyping-rankles-silent-secular-majority-of-american-muslims.html (published 23 December 2001; accessed 14 March 2015).

[20] Michael S. Merry, *Culture, Identity, and Islamic Schooling: A Philosophical Approach* (New York: Palgrave Macmillan, 2007) 95.

[21] "American Muslim Voters: A Demographic Profile and Survey of Attitudes," Council on American-Islamic Relations, http://pa.cair.com/annreport/AmericanMuslimVoters.pdf (released 24 October 2006; accessed 14 March 2015).

[22] Many authors address the notorious difficulty of quantifying Muslim Americans, a task complicated by practical matters, such as the United States Bureau of the Census not being permitted by law to gather information about religious affiliation, and by ideological matters, as agendas may skew surveys to report low or high figures for the Muslim American population "depending on how much you like or fear Muslims" (Shabana Mir, *Muslim American Women on Campus: Undergraduate Social Life and Identity* (Chapel Hill: University of North Carolina Press, 2014) 10). As Selcuk Sirin and Michelle Fine explain, "Those groups who would like to minimize and perhaps marginalize Muslims in the United States claim that the number is

port designers' aims to draw attention to a particular state of Muslim American piety than the actual state of mosque attendance in America. Furthermore, some important caveats should be mentioned if mosque attendance is used as a measuring stick of a Muslim's level of devotion. Rizwan Butt of the Easton Phillipsburg Muslim Association in Pennsylvania points out that most mosques "are volunteer-run institutions and it can be difficult for people to attend regularly, especially if they live or work far away from the mosque."[23] Nonetheless, even though suggested connections between low rates of mosque attendance and low levels of piety should be handled with care, from the perspective of many revivalist Muslim Americans the overall state of devotion among Muslim Americans falls woefully short of ideal. Citing the American Mosque 2011 report's ten percent figure, the 2013 documentary *UnMosqued* refers to "the dire situation we find ourselves in," declaring that major changes need to be made "in order that we not lose the future generations of Muslims in America."[24] From this standpoint, American Islam faces a

close to one million, whereas the groups who want to maximize the political clout of Muslims claim that the numbers are as high as eight million" (Selcuk R. Sirin and Michelle Fine, *Muslim American Youth: Understanding Hyphenated Identities through Multiple Methods* (New York: New York University Press, 2008) 37–38).

[23] Rizwan Butt, personal e-mail to author, 16 February 2015. Butt added, "In fact, if a person lives outside a specifically defined radius of a mosque, he is not even required to attend for the regular prayers. Women are always exempt from attending the mosque but have the right to do so. When it comes to non-worship activities within a mosque, it is completely up to the individual as to whether they wish to attend or not. This means that a 'practicing Muslim' may choose to remain away from the mosque (due to personal commitments, work schedule, or for any reason whatsoever) without being judged with regards to religiosity" (ibid.).

[24] "About *UnMosqued*," http://www.unmosquedfilm.com/about/ (accessed 14 March 2015). Much of the film's claim of culpability falls squarely upon older first-generation Muslim immigrant shoulders, holding these elders responsible for a tendency of Muslim youth to feel judged or unwelcome at the mosque, where they receive little friendliness and feel little personal ownership. Further diagnosis uncovers what the film presents as a failure in many American mosques to dissociate Islam from a specific cultural interpretation, which results in neglecting consideration of the mosque's American context. The primary producers of this particular carcinogen are identified as mosques populated mostly by one ethnic group, which, according to the film's citation of the American Mosque 2011 report, characterizes seventy-five

pandemic that requires serious response. The remedy must curb infectious attitudes that drive Muslims from the mosque, making it instead an attractive destination where all Muslims feel welcome and a part of its lifeblood. The medicine must impress upon Muslim minds that mosque attendance is just one, albeit an important, component of integrating Islam into every facet of life. The antidote must bring Muslims together across ethnic, racial, and generational lines, forming a microcosm of the united global ummah. Across the nation, numerous Muslims have prescribed sports to fit this billing, playing a bonding role that will be detailed in upcoming chapters.

Islamophobia in America

Anti-Islamic rhetoric has had a long run in America, predating the dawning of the nation. Colonial theological bigwigs such as Cotton Mather and Jonathan Edwards denounced Islam as a false religion and path to moral downfall, and Harvard President Samuel Langdon labeled Muhammad a counterfeit prophet and "emissary of Satan."[25] Fast-

---

percent of all mosques in the United States. Addressing this issue, the website declares, "As Muslims become integrated within American society and grow up in a diverse multi-racial environment, it becomes increasingly uncomfortable to enter a mosque that is predominated by a certain culture. Millennials and Generation Xers do not have as strong of a relationship with their parents' country of origin which exacerbates the discomfort they feel when entering ethnic-based masajid [mosques]" (ibid.). From *UnMosqued's* revivalist perspective, ethnically based mosques should carry a warning label not only because they deter mosque attendance of Muslim youth; they also foster further fragmentation among Muslim Americans, thereby ripping apart the cherished unity of the ummah.

[25] Michael B. Oren, *Power, Faith, and Fantasy: America in the Middle East 1776 to the Present* (New York: W.W. Norton & Co., 2008) 42. Oren goes on to write, "The jaundiced impression of Islam was reinforced by tendentious translations of the Quran. The 'newly Englished' *Alcoran* of Alexander Ross, published in 1649, set out to expose the 'contradictions, blasphemies, obscene speeches, and ridiculous fables' in the book, so that the Christian 'so viewing thine enemies in their full body...maist the better...overcome them.' Similarly, the 1734 version by the lawyer George Sales, a copy of which was found in Thomas Jefferson's library, aimed at enabling Protestants to 'attack the Koran with success' and hoped that 'for them...Providence has reserved the glory of its overthrow.' The purpose of the most popular Colonial-

forwarding to the twentieth century, anti-Islamic views intensified in America on the heels of the 1967 Arab-Israeli War and again during the Islamic Revolution in Iran, when television viewers devoured a steady diet of images of angry mobs shouting anti-American slogans along with updates on the ongoing plight of American hostages in Teheran. In the 1990s the Gulf War added more fuel to an American anti-Islamic fire, as did media coverage of the bombing of the Murrah Federal Building in Oklahoma City, initially attributed to Middle Eastern malevolence. As Edward Said demonstrates in *Covering Islam*, this early Oklahoma City reportage was part of a larger media trend. News outlets tended to shine their camera lights on actions of a violent Muslim minority who threatened American interests instead of on everyday affairs of Muslims highlighting their shared humanity with non-Muslim Americans.[26] By dint of this trend, monolithic caricatures of Muslims as anti-American fanatics of an inherently violent religion had become ossified in innumerable American minds even before American Airlines Flight 11 smashed into the World Trade Center's North Tower.

These caricatures did their share of damage to twentieth-century Muslim American lives. Directly following the Oklahoma City bombing, for instance, the Council on American-Islamic Relations reported over 200 incidents of anti-Muslim harassment, threats, and property damage. Spilling over into the next century, these stereotypes constituted the lens through which hordes of Americans viewed the 9/11 attacks. Louise Cainkar argues that anti-Islamic actions after 9/11 were to a large degree a result of "preexisting social constructions that configured them as people who would readily conduct and approve of such attacks."[27] The

era book on Muhammad, written by Humphrey Prideaux in 1697, was unambiguously announced by its title, *The True Nature of the Imposture Fully Displayed*" (ibid., 42–43).

[26] Edward W. Said, *Covering Islam: How the Media and the Experts Determine How We See the Rest of the World*, rev. ed. (New York: Vintage Books, 1997).

[27] Louise A. Cainkar, *Homeland Insecurity: The Arab American and Muslim American Experience after 9/11* (New York: Russell Sage Foundation, 2009) 2. Cainkar argues that these constructions "set the stage for Arab and Muslim American communities to be held collectively culpable for the 9/11 attacks by the government, the media, and the citizenry" (ibid.).

Council on American Islamic Relations received over 1,700 complaints of hate crimes and harassment during the two months after 9/11, and the Federal Bureau of Investigation's Hate Crimes Unit recorded an enormous uptick in attacks on Muslims, from twenty-eight in 2000 to 481 in 2001. Though these numbers declined, anti-Islamic attitudes and actions in the United States have continued to abound. A spate of exhibitions of Islamophobia were on display as America turned its page to the twenty-first century's second decade, prompting some analysts to declare that in comparison to the last few years of the previous decade,[28] American Islamophobia was growing once again. In her 2012 work *The New Religious Intolerance*, Martha Nussbaum asserts that "there is solid evidence that prejudice against Muslims is on the rise in the United States. Complaints of employment discrimination against Muslims to the Equal Employment Opportunity Commission (EEOC) have surged in recent times. Gallup, Pew, and ABC polls confirm a new upswing in anti-Muslim views."[29]

One sign of this upswing was a string of physical attacks on mosques and vociferous protests against planned constructions of new ones. During a five-month span in 2010, thirty existing or proposed mosques were the object of vandalism or strong opposition, according to the American Civil Liberties Union. Fortunately, some intended attacks never saw the light of day. A bombing plot against the largest mosque in the United States, the Islamic Center of America in Dearborn, was sniffed out by police, who in January 2011 arrested a sixty-three-year-old army veteran from California after he had amassed a stockpile of explosives to destroy the Michigan mosque. In other instances, plans to wreak havoc on mosques materialized. Fifty-two-year-old Randolph Linn testified that a thirst to avenge American military casualties in Islamic lands sparked his act of arson at the Islamic Center of Toledo, which forced

[28] One strong example of Islamophobia in the latter half of the 21st century's first decade involved fearful assertions that, as the biological son of a Muslim father, presidential hopeful Barack Obama was a Muslim himself, despite his statements to the contrary.

[29] Martha C. Nussbaum, *The New Religious Intolerance: Overcoming the Politics of Fear in an Anxious Age* (Cambridge MA: Belknap Press of Harvard University Press, 2012) 12–13.

this large community to find alternative locations to assemble for nearly a year. Another 2010 arson attack targeted the enlargement of a Murfreesboro, Tennessee mosque shortly after hundreds of opponents packed a county commission meeting in hopes of foiling this expansion plan. Among a cacophony of voices opposing mosque construction and expansion across the nation, none reached the decibel level as those protesting the establishment of Park51, the pejoratively labeled "Ground Zero Mosque," in Manhattan in 2010. Conceived by developer Sharif El-Gamal to hold much more than just space for prayer and religious instruction, the former Burlington Coat Factory building was slated to be open to adherents of all faiths and to include a gamut of services ranging from a performing arts center to a swimming pool to a culinary school. Yet, despite El-Gamal's peaceful interfaith intentions, over a thousand protesters rallied against Park51, holding signs with slogans such as "No 9/11 Mega Mosque." The fundamental fomenter of this fuss was Pamela Geller, leader of the organization Stop the Islamicization of America. Geller griped that Park51 would be a breeding ground of 9/11-like terror attacks and that, due to its proposed location, three blocks from the former World Trade Center site, it would rub salt in the wounds of 9/11 victims' families. Geller's all-out assault included blog postings with headlines such as "Monster Mosque Pushes Ahead in Shadow of World Trade Center Islamic Death and Destruction" as well as posters on New York buses that depicted the proposed Islamic center standing alongside the Twin Towers, impaled by airplanes and pluming with smoke.[30]

Concurrently to these mosque attacks and protests, Islamophobia surfaced further in the form of fear over so-called "Shariah Creep." This phrase entered the national lexicon after the passing of Oklahoma's Save Our State amendment, which boldly prohibited Oklahoma courts from drawing upon "the legal precepts of other nations or cultures," pointing to "Sharia law" as a particular object of concern. The amendment was concocted by state representative Rex Duncan, who framed it as a necessary weapon in a cultural "war for the survival of America."[31] Although

---

[30] After the Metropolitan Transportation Authority initially refused to use the posters, Geller sued and the MTA allowed the posters to be displayed.

[31] Quoted in Nussbaum, *The New Religious Intolerance*, 11.

eventually struck down by a federal district judge in response to Muslim arguments of First Amendment violation,[32] the drafting and especially passing of the Save Our State measure put Islamophobia's entrenchment within certain American necks of the woods on parade for all to see. Soon other states marched in step with Oklahoma. "Shariah bans" were proposed in over thirty states in 2011.[33] Some of these states put particularly curious twists on their measures, such as a Tennessee proposal to make following Shariah a felony carrying the punishment of fifteen years in jail. Such a proposal reveals a striking degree of ignorance about Islam, since Shariah's comprehensive applicability includes rules for prayer, dietary regulations, and countless other matters that in almost every context would never enter the conversation of felonious offenses. Ignorance hung in the air surrounding Gerald Allen, an Alabama state senator who introduced legislation to prohibit his state's courts from basing judgments on Islamic law. Asked by a reporter to define the word "shariah," Allen admitted he could not, demurely declaring, "I don't have my file in front of me. I wish I could answer you better."[34]

For many Muslim Americans, the result of such ignorance is not bliss. Faced with the misunderstanding that they strive to sneak a harsh interpretation of Shariah into their land, Muslims are seen through suspicious eyes by numerous fellow Americans. Feeding this sense of suspicion is a common trope found in a variety of Islamophobic iterations, namely that hordes of violent Muslims are hiding in America, abetted by the ability to blend in as amicable Americans and to dupe compatriots to believe the mantra that Islam is a religion of peace. This trope trains non-Muslims to beware, as from its fear-based perspective, the daily friendly greeting from your Muslim neighbor could very well be a smokescreen to prevent detection of the next Muslim terror attack on American soil.[35] This trepidation-invoking trope is old hat in America,

[32] The judge determined that the law did not have a secular purpose, it inhibited religious practice, and it promoted excessive state entanglement with religion.

[33] Zareena Grewal states that these measures were offered as a "wedge issue" in the 2011 election cycle (Grewal, *Islam Is a Foreign Country*, 300).

[34] Ibid.

[35] Louise Cainkar writes, "Since terrorists were alleged to be inconspicuously residing in 'our communities,' the message was apparent: Arabs and Muslims in the

including claims of clandestine Catholic conspiracy to infiltrate the American frontier and allegations of backroom Jewish backing of *Protocols of the Elders of Zion*'s aims. It has also made its rounds in American literature and on the silver screen. Nussbaum writes, "Most good horror stories involve a clear adversary who lies low, only to reveal his true nature when it is too late for the innocent victim to seek safety. ...[F]ear thrives on the idea of hiddenness, of danger lurking beneath the façade of normalcy."[36] This theme reared its head in the Park51 protest, in which developer El-Gamal's statement of intention to enhance the local community and promote interfaith harmony was dismissed as a trick to conceal his purportedly actual purpose of fostering Islamic violence. It rose again in a campaign against *All-American Muslim*, a reality show that aired for the 2011–2012 season on the cable network TLC. According to the Florida Family Association,[37] the series' portrayal of Michigan Muslims as regular Americans was an attempt "to manipulate Americans into ignoring the threat of jihad."[38] The trope has also popped up in the pulpit, particularly from the tongues of preachers who emphasize Christians' need to unequivocally support the nation of Israel.[39] One of these Chris-

---

United States should be closely observed and their seemingly normal activities should be treated as suspect. Arabs and Muslims, who understood their position as subjects of watchdogs in a panoptical world, were to be placed under a microscope by their non-Arab or non-Muslim neighbors" (Cainkar, *Homeland Insecurity*, 110).

[36] Nussbaum, *The New Religious Intolerance*, 23–24.

[37] The Florida Family Association describes itself as "a national organization that is made up of thousands of online subscribers across America who share in the same goal of defending American values. These supporters send more than one million e-mails every month to Corporate America officials associated with issues posted on this web site" ("Florida Family Association: About Us," Florida Family Association, http://floridafamily.org/full_article.php?article_no=94 (accessed 14 March 2015)). The organization is classified as a hate group by the Southern Poverty Law Center.

[38] Quoted in Sheila Musaji, "American Companies Accused of Joining the All-American Anti-Muslim Bandwagon," *The American Muslim*, http://theamericanmuslim.org/tam.php/features/articles/all-american-muslim/0018896 (posted 20 December 2011; accessed 14 March 2015).

[39] A fundamental Christian Zionist belief is that Jesus will take his true believers into heaven during the rapture and will subsequently return to earth, but only

tian Zionist pastors, John Hagee, shepherds a 19,000-member Texas flock and has established himself as a media maven with messages reaching millions through his personal television network. Hagee warns readers of his *Jerusalem Countdown* that they "must rise up out of spiritual fog and religious deception, and focus with laser-beam intensity on the absolute truth concerning the issue of Islam."[40] Contained within this "absolute truth" as spun by Hagee is the damning declaration that "Islam not only *condones* violence; it *commands* it,"[41] contrary to the veneer of peacefulness Muslims have applied to their everyday lives. As noisily as Christian Zionist warning bells have clanged, the theme of violent Muslims hiding behind a peaceful façade has reached arguably even more ears coming from the mouths of American government officials. With America struggling to find its footing in a dramatically redefined post-9/11 world, Attorney General John Ashcroft declared in 2002, "In this new war our enemy's platoons infiltrate our borders, quietly blending in with visiting tourists, students, and workers. They move unnoticed through our cities, neighborhoods, and public spaces."[42] United States Congressman Peter King has ascended to the throne of politicians who popularize this view. The New York legislator made his sentiments crystal clear during a national radio broadcast in 2004, asserting that eighty-five percent of Muslim American religious leaders are "an enemy living amongst us."[43] Seven years later, King again wore these feelings on his sleeve during a congressional inquiry into radical Islam that he initiated as chair of

---

after Israel, especially Jerusalem, is completely under Jewish control and contains a majority Jewish population (Steven Fink, "Fear Under Construction: Islamophobia Within American Christian Zionism," *Islamophobia Studies Journal* 2/1 (2014): 26–43).

[40] John Hagee, *Jerusalem Countdown: A Warning to the World* (Lake Mary FL: Frontline, 2006) 29.

[41] John Hagee, *In Defense of Israel* (Lake Mary FL: Frontline, 2007) 68.

[42] Quoted in Nadine Naber, "'Look, Mohammed the Terrorist Is Coming!': Cultural Racism, Nation-Based Racism, and the Intersectionality of Oppressions after 9/11," in *Race and Arab Americans Before and After 9/11: From Invisible Citizens to Visible Subjects*, ed. Amaney Jamal and Nadine Naber, 276–304 (Syracuse NY: Syracuse University Press, 2008) 284.

[43] Quoted in Cainkar, *Homeland Insecurity*, 271.

the House Homeland Security Committee. Casting suspicion upon the entire Muslim American community, King insisted that Muslim Americans uniformly refrained from "sufficient cooperation"[44] with law enforcement officials in rooting out Islamic terror.

Proclaimed from the pulpit, halls of Congress, or any other setting, the trope of malevolent Muslims cloaked in deceptively nonviolent garb has had baleful consequences for Muslim Americans. Constant scrutiny from suspicious eyes has pulled a welcome mat out from under Muslim feet in their own American homeland, and damage done to Muslims in this milieu of mistrust has gone far beyond psychological harm. Large numbers of Muslim lives were significantly altered after 9/11 by an assortment of government actions that have been criticized as legally dubious by many, both non-Muslims and Muslims. Adding to mass arrests, preventive detentions, FBI interviews, wiretapping, reviews of private communication, and closing of charities,[45] one measure that hit Muslim lives hard was special registration. This program required non-resident students, visitors, and individuals doing business in the United States from twenty-four Islamic nations and North Korea to be fingerprinted, photographed, and interviewed. Over 13,000 individuals were deported due to special registration, yet not a single terrorist suspect was discovered. The ostensible legality of special registration and its cronies crafted in the name of homeland security found much of its basis in the USA PATRIOT Act, a direct and quick response to 9/11. Among its many provisions, this act expanded government power to employ surveillance and wiretapping without first demonstrating probable cause, allowed secret searches and access to private records with no oversight, and authorized the detention of immigrants and denial of admission into the nation based simply on suspicion and guilt by association. Muslims and non-Muslim Arabs overwhelmingly felt the brunt of the PATRIOT Act's

---

[44] Quoted in Nahid Afrose Kabir, *Young American Muslims: Dynamics of Identity* (Edinburgh: Edinburgh University Press, 2012) 215.

[45] These measures were enforced almost exclusively against males. Cainkar found that after 9/11 roughly twice as many Arab Muslim women than men reported experiences of hate crimes and harassment, whereas Arab Muslim men felt the brunt of anti-terrorism government measures (Cainkar, *Homeland Insecurity*, 5).

blow. United States Justice Department figures report that by 5 November 2001, 1,182 Muslims and Arabs were arrested under the act's auspices.

With Americans on tenterhooks about the presence of Muslims in their land, a culture of surveillance has endured on American soil years after 9/11. Muslims have continued to face religious and ethnic profiling at American airports, which prompted the coining of the phrase "Flying While Brown," a spinoff of the racial-profiling rallying cry "Driving While Black." On a Minneapolis runway in 2006, for example, six imams (religious leaders) were removed from their U.S. Airways flight and detained after passengers and crew members raised an alert of terrorism in the offing, having seen the imams pray before boarding and change seats and ask for seatbelt extensions on the aircraft. Demonstrating its extensive reach, post-9/11 surveillance has included mosque observation programs. The prevalence of such sacred space scrutiny swelled after 2008, when the United States Justice Department's Domestic Intelligence and Operations Guide expanded FBI power to use undercover sources. Alleged terrorists were subsequently arrested at mosques across the nation, based on finger-pointing by FBI agents and their Muslim informants. As Sally Howell elucidates, this utilization of insiders has devastated trust within mosque communities and has involved heavy reliance on questionable sources. Howell explains,

> The government's informers were frequently desperate men: the homeless, the terminally ill, the addicted, the siblings and kin of those with extensive medical bills, aliens about to be deported. Caught up in schemes to save themselves from jail time, deportation, or financial duress or offered quick and easy money (sometimes in the hundreds of thousands of dollars), they were willing not only to inform on their fellow Muslims, but also to entrap them.[46]

Building upon FBI endeavors or initiating efforts of their own, local police divisions such as the New York Police Department's "De-

---

[46] Sally Howell, "Muslims as Moving Targets: External Security and Internal Critique in Detroit's Mosques," in *Arab Detroit 9/11: Life in the Terror Decade*, ed. Nabeel Abraham, Sally Howell, and Andrew Shryock, 151–85 (Detroit: Wayne State University Press, 2011) 162.

mographics Unit"[47] also made mosque surveillance part of their operations. It emerged in 2013 that the Demographics Unit labeled twelve New York mosques as terrorist groups, thereby enabling "terrorism enterprise investigations" involving undercover informants making secret recordings in mosques.

In keeping tabs on Muslims in the Big Apple, the core of Demographics Unit surveillance included turning to the athletic field to pluck what it deemed rotten fruit. Spirits were high among members of the Arab American Association of New York in 2009, when the team it sponsored, the Brooklyn United, captured the championship of the NYPD's inaugural youth soccer league season. Two years later, AAANY spirits plummeted. It withdrew its sponsorship, outraged that the Demographics Unit monitored Muslim players and their families in order to inform its "Sports Venue Report," a thirty-eight-page memo documenting where members of twenty-nine ancestries of interest play and watch sports. According to Matt Apuzzo, whose *Enemies Within* documents NYPD surveillance activities,[48] the situation is shrouded in uncertainty. Apuzzo maintains it is unclear whether the NYPD established its youth and adult soccer and adult cricket leagues intentionally for surveillance purposes, or if measures such as encouraging detectives to join the adult leagues evolved as later developments after initially designing the leagues for the sake of community outreach.[49] For many New York Muslims, however, there is no uncertainty. They are convinced the NYPD set up the leagues from the start in order to watch their everyday moves. AAANY Executive Director Linda Sarsour bemoaned, "When the leagues started we thought they were trying to engage our community

---

[47] This unit was established in cooperation with the Central Intelligence Agency, which is prohibited from domestic spying. It has secretly infiltrated Muslim student groups, sent informants into mosques, and eavesdropped on conversations in a variety of settings.

[48] Matt Apuzzo and Adam Goldman, *Enemies Within: Inside the NYPD's Secret Spying Unit and bin Laden's Final Plot Against America* (New York: Touchstone, 2013).

[49] Dave Zirin, "Not a Game: How the NYPD Uses Sports for Surveillance," *The Nation,* http://www.thenation.com/blog/176082/not-game-how-nypd-uses-sports-surveillance (posted 10 September 2013; accessed 21 April 2014).

through sports. We were wrong."[50] Sarsour and others felt betrayed by local law enforcement, perhaps especially because the situation occurred in a sporting setting. Rinku Sen, president of the racial justice organization Race Forward, commented on the matter by stating that sports "are one area in which Hindus, Sikhs, Christians, Muslims, and others have been able to come together, especially in the diaspora. The NYPD spying brings a layer of suspicion into this world that has otherwise been an important place to build trust and camaraderie."[51] Resembling fissures that have emerged within mosque communities due to the possible presence of insider informants, significant cracks have formed between some New York Muslims and police officials, after what appeared to be opportunity for fun on the field ended up with these Muslims issuing a red card against the men in blue.

As detailed in later chapters, Muslims from the Atlantic to the Pacific share Sen's view that sports can bring individuals of different faiths together and "build trust and camaraderie." In a post-9/11 America where fear and negative caricatures of Muslims abound, the results of Muslims and non-Muslims coming together on the court or field transcend what is displayed on the scoreboard. Previously thinking in terms of a perspective that pits Islam versus America in an alleged clash of values, a non-Muslim who enjoys the balance between competitiveness and friendliness in a Muslim basketball league or celebrates a touchdown with Muslim teammates at the local mosque may experience a clash of his own, between his previously held mindset and what he sees around him. Witnessing a palpable passion for popular American sports from Muslim teammates who know the game's intricacies and lingo inside and out, his former sense that Muslims are out of step with, if not hostile toward, American societal norms may readily go down in defeat. Louise Cainkar argues that for many Muslims, life in twenty-first-century America is characterized by "de-Americanization," which "revolves around notions of perpetual foreignness and an implicit lack of national

[50] Ibid.
[51] Ibid.

loyalty."[52] Cainkar goes on to say that the message of de-Americanization "is one of exclusion: 'You Muslims, Middle Easterners, and South Asians are not true Americans'... When perceived as non-American, such communities can be easily placed outside the boundaries of constitutional rights and removed from national understandings of social justice."[53] De-Americanized, Muslim Americans stand within a regrettable trajectory of American history in which Catholics, Jews, and others have paid a steep price for being popularly pigeonholed as perpetually foreign and irreparably disloyal to their nation. Additionally, though, Muslim Americans have climbed aboard a parallel American track in which sports play an important role in diminishing de-Americanization's potency. Omar Abbassi of the Muslim Basketball league in New Jersey commented that non-Muslims who play in the league "see first-hand that we're just regular people."[54] Abbassi presented the message that is implicitly communicated to these non-Muslims in the following terms: "We're Muslims. We're cool people like you guys. We play basketball, we play sports."[55] Showcasing their common humanity with fellow Americans through their mutual athletic inclinations, Muslims' participation in popular American sports can help send de-Americanization of Muslims to the bench, never to re-enter the game.

[52] Cainkar, *Homeland Insecurity*, 232. Cainkar credits Bill Ong Hing for this notion of "de-Americanization" (Bill Ong Hing, "Vigilante Racism: The De-Americanization of Immigrant America," *Michigan Journal of Race and Law* 7 (2002): 441–56).

[53] Cainkar, *Homeland Insecurity*, 232.

[54] Omar Abbassi, personal interview, 1 May 2014, Parsippany NJ.

[55] Ibid.

4

Sports and Islamic Principles

I was hooked. I felt I had to read more. After hearing dozens of Muslim Americans detail their passion for athletic activities and expound upon sports' compatibility with Islamic principles, the words "Islam and Sport Do Not Mix" seized my attention, albeit mostly due to a heavy dose of skepticism regarding what I would read beneath this headline. Paul Wilkinson, former director of the University of St. Andrews Centre for the Study of Terrorism and Political Violence, compiled a bullet-point list with items such as the following to support his bold headline claim:

> Algeria's 1992 Olympic gold-winning female athlete, Hassiba Boulmerka, trained abroad due to Islamist death threats.
> Cricket nations cannot visit Pakistan because the risk factor is too high, especially after the attack on the Sri Lankan national cricket team's coach in Lahore during 2009. …The only possible way for visiting cricket teams to visit Pakistan now is if the Pakistan Cricket Board invest in bomb-proof buses.
> Somali football fans were told they will be publicly flogged—or worse—if they are caught watching the 2010 World Cup on TV. Playing football is also "banned" by Al Shaabab.[1]

Wilkinson's attempts to demonstrate that Islam and sports do not mix are stamped with the label of a thriving industry that churns out essentialist statements about Islam based on actions of its violent minority. This article's devil is not in the veracity of its details; its descriptions of various sports-related issues in the Islamic world tend to get the specifics

[1] Paul Wilkinson, "Islam, Sport, & Terrorism," Cherson and Molschky, http://chersonandmolschky.com/2014/01/23/islam-sport-terrorism/ (posted 23 January 2014; accessed 23 April 2014).

of the story right, though occasionally overstated for rhetorical effect. The misstep instead is the movement from these details to a generalization that places all Muslims in the same boat, captained by violent extremism, and occludes the reality that for countless Muslims the relationship between Islam and sports is filled with heavenly harmony, not cacophonous clashing.

Throughout this chapter, statements and stories from Muslim Americans I interviewed and from an array of writings about Islam and sports will form a stark contrast to Wilkinson's claim. In highlighting understandings of the compatibility of sports and Islamic principles, however, I need to warn myself not to counter Wilkinson's generalization with an essentialized picture of my own, namely one that depicts all Muslims likening the fit between every athletic activity and Islamic principles to that between hand and a snugly secure glove. Muslim conceptualizations of the relationship between sports and Islam are far too variegated and nuanced to be encapsulated by generalization, and so while ultimately spending more time exploring affirmations of sports' compatibility with Islamic principles, this chapter also journeys into territory of a different type. Occasionally this alternate terrain will include Muslim condemnation of sports so strident that, when looked at in isolation, would seem to support Wilkinson's headline. More frequently it will feature Muslims who embrace sports as largely in line with their faith but who also believe their religion sets unassailable limits that certain aspects of athletic experience tend to transgress.

Sports and Islamic Principles in Harmony

Considering its seminal role in informing all sorts of Islamic views, the argument can be made that the Qur'an shapes any understanding of the permissibility or impermissibility, and the benefits or detriments, of sports from an Islamic perspective. Yet the Qur'an's contributions to these understandings must rely heavily upon extrapolation and reasoning by analogy, since no Qur'anic statements save one possible exception specifically address sports or athletic endeavors. The possible lone sporting reference comes in Surah Yusuf (chapter 12) verse 17, in which, according to some translations, the brothers of Yusuf (Joseph) say to their father Yaqub (Jacob), "We went racing with one another." Expressing an idea appearing in other writings about sports and Islam, Islamic scholar Seraj Hendricks maintains that "nastabiq," the Arabic word translated as "racing" in this verse, "clearly refers to a type of competition the brothers claimed they participated in."[2] Whether or not they agree with Hendricks, Muslims need to search outside the Qur'an to find multiple references to sports in Islamic tradition. This search unearths its treasure in the Hadith, the vast compilation of sayings and actions attributed to Muhammad and his seventh-century companions. The Hadith exerts tremendous influence on Muslims as they seek to emulate their Prophet in various aspects of their lives. As Muslims pose the question "What would Muhammad do?" in regard to sports, the Hadith provides numerous answers.

Judging by how often I heard it, one statement is the clear frontrunner in references to the Hadith in order to argue for the compatibility of sports and Islam. In coffee shops, mosques, and myriad other settings, the likelihood of encountering the statement "Teach your children swimming, archery, and horseback riding" was almost as high as receiving the kindness I consistently enjoyed from those I interviewed. In most cases, this exhortation was drawn upon to assert that sports in general are highly encouraged based on the Prophet's personal counsel. A few individuals focused specifically on the three athletic activities mentioned in the statement and presented their understanding of Muhammad's rationale in endorsing these three pursuits in particular.[3] This rationale was discussed at great length by Reda Ahlouche, a first-generation immigrant from Algeria who teaches physical education and nutrition at a Massa-

---

[2] Shaykh Seraj Hendricks, "Sport and Islam," *Muslim Views,* http://mysite.mweb.co.za/residents/mfj1/sport.htm (published 24 November 1998; accessed 23 April 2014).

[3] Though no interviewees connected Muhammad's rationale in this statement with preparation for military success, Badi Aldousari makes this connection in regard to archery and horseback riding. Aldousari writes that the importance of archery in Islam is its "significance as a weapon that was crucial in wars and conquests" and that "the prophet linked horsemanship to the concept of holy war (preaching God's word peacefully or by conquest)" (Badi Aldousari, "The History and the Philosophy of Sport in Islam" (unpublished M.A. thesis, Ball State University, 2000) 22–24).

chusetts Islamic high school and whose extensive personal training client list has included Rodney Harrison, Richard Seymour, Kevin Faulk, and other New England Patriots. Displaying great gusto for both fitness and his faith, Ahlouche connected physical perks with each of the three athletic activities. He said about swimming, "It incorporates each and every muscle of your body. The healthiest athletes in the world are swimmers. Michael Phelps is an example. There is nothing that works your heart like swimming."[4] Ahlouche went on to argue that "there is nothing that has eye coordination like in archery,"[5] which he stated is especially helpful in developing proprioception[6] since "you measure a distance, you calculate it in your brain and you have a visual connection with it and release it. This demands a lot from your brain function and your motor skills."[7] Finally, Ahlouche arrived at horseback riding, proclaiming that when attempting to control a horse, "You're pumping your biceps, your triceps, your deltoids, your back. Your legs are also working."[8] While getting on and off a horse, he added, "You are using each and every muscle in your body."[9] Ahlouche's aim in his animated discourse was not to suggest that Muslims should value these three athletic activities above all others. Instead he asserted that Muhammad chose these three outstanding examples of physical fitness in order to emphasize the immense importance of physical activity in any form.

Coming in next, although a distant second place, in Hadith statements I heard most often in interviews is the declaration "A strong believer is better than a weak believer." Prominently displayed in promotional literature and on banners and medals for the Islamic Circle of North America New Jersey branch's 2013 Muslim Sports Day, this statement is cited in appeals for Muslims not only to adhere to their reli-

[4] Reda Ahlouche, personal interview, 10 March 2014, Mansfield MA.
[5] Ibid.
[6] This term refers to the "unconscious perception of movement and spatial orientation arising from stimuli within the body itself" ("Proprioception," http://medical-dictionary.thefreedictionary.com/proprioception (accessed 14 March 2015)).
[7] Reda Ahlouche, personal interview, 10 March 2014, Mansfield MA.
[8] Ibid.
[9] Ibid.

gion more avidly, but to head to the gym or athletic field more frequently. After quoting this statement, Qatari Islamic studies scholar Abdelhak Hamiche, for instance, insists that Muslims should play sports regularly since "Islam wants Muslims to be strong in their bodies, minds, morals, and souls, because it glorifies strength which is characteristic of Allah's perfection. A strong body is more capable of performing the obligations of life and religion."[10] From this perspective, engaging in athletic activity is an act of obedience to God,[11] making one's body stronger and taking care of it as a God-given trust. Muhammad Chowdhery of An-Noor Academy in New Jersey addressed this latter point, remarking that in Islam "one's body does not belong to that individual but rather it is a gift that God gives an individual... Therefore it's mandatory for boys and girls, men and women, to ensure that they take care of their bodies and they are active."[12] This viewpoint does not deny that sports are a great

[10] Abdelhak Hamiche, "Sports in Islamic Perspective," *The Peninsula*, http://thepeninsulaqatar.com/special-page/islam/225700/sports-in-islamic-perspective (posted 15 February 2013; accessed 23 April 2014).

[11] Playing sports, of course, is not the only option at a Muslim's disposal to strengthen his body or maintain her level of physical fitness. Proper diet or a regular commitment to take the stairs instead of the elevator can factor into the fitness equation, and some Muslims argue that, especially because of its act of prostration, the salat prayer is a physical fitness routine that Muslims can undertake five times daily. This idea is articulated by Hasina Zaman, who writes that "Islam has prescribed exercise as part of a daily routine for Muslims. This takes the form of five obligatory daily prayers" (Hasina Zaman, "Islam, Well-Being, and Physical Activity: Perceptions of Muslim Young Women," in *Researching Women and Sport*, ed. Gill Clarke and Barbara Humberstone, 50–67 (Houndsmill, England: Macmillan, 1997) 55). Zaman explains that the salat prayer includes seventeen circles of bodily movements that "are controlled and synchronised and exercise most of the large and small muscle groups in the body" (ibid.). According to Aldousari, physical fitness is enhanced in two additional ritual activities, fasting and pilgrimage. Aldousari writes, "Currently fitness consultants recommend dieting and exercising as the ideal formula for weight loss and fitness. Interestingly enough, Islam has preached dieting in the form of fasting and exercising in the form of praying and pilgrimage as a religious obligation of every Muslim for 14 centuries" (Aldousari, "The History and the Philosophy of Sport in Islam," 46).

[12] Muhammad Chowdhery, personal interview, 21 February 2014, Piscataway NJ.

deal of fun or that athletic activity can satiate a competitive appetite. Chowdhery happily mentioned that he enjoys his Muslim softball league immensely. This viewpoint does, however, up the significance of sports enormously, making athletic activity an opportunity for Muslims to express their obedience to God by taking care of what their Creator has bestowed to them.

Looking further into the Hadith, Islamic basis for playing sports is found not only in statements from Muhammad urging others to participate in athletic activities, but also in stories featuring the Prophet himself playing sports. One account features Muhammad running against his wife, Aisha, who declares, "I raced with the Prophet and beat him in the race. Later, when I had put on some weight, we raced again and he won." Hearing this story from multiple interviewees, I usually encountered emphasis placed on Muhammad himself engaging in an athletic contest and encouraging a woman to do the same, leading to the lesson that both men and women should participate in athletic activity. A few individuals extracted an ancillary nugget of wisdom from this story, digging into the detail that the previously victorious Aisha was outrun by Muhammad after she gained extra pounds. In these tellings of the story, a key takeaway was that negative consequences will result if individuals do not remain physically fit. Likewise, another Hadith narrative spotlighting an athletically active Muhammad lends itself to various explanations of its ultimate upshot. This story describes the Prophet grappling with Rukana, Arabia's leading wrestler of the day, and defeating him three times. This story may be referenced in order to maintain that Muslims should share Muhammad's predilection for sports, whereas significance may also be found in the Prophet's display of character traits that Muslims should put into practice. Badi Aldousari in "The History and the Philosophy of Sport in Islam" highlights Muhammad's demonstration of compassion in the story. Aldousari writes that Muhammad and Rukana originally agreed to wrestle one bout and give one sheep to the victor, but after going down in defeat Rukana requested a rematch with a sheep once again on the line. Following a second victory by the Prophet, the cycle was repeated again, leaving a thrice-beaten Rukana down three sheep. Aldousari asserts that because of his characteristic compassion, Muhammad chose to let Rukana keep his sheep, mercifully concluding that he "shouldn't lose the fight and the sheep at the same time."[13] Hendricks derives different didactic direction from this story, accentuating the pursuit of excellence as a Prophetic trait that Muslims should emulate. Hendricks proclaims, "The fascinating consequence of this duel was that Rukana, after being outclassed, embraced Islam. This is a striking example of the effect that excellence in performance can have on the minds and hearts of people. It is remarkable that here the example is clearly linked to the potential effect of excellence in sport."[14] Based on Hendricks's presentation of this story, two rewards await Muslims who reach athletic heights, the ability to follow in their Prophet's athletically adroit footsteps and the pleasure of seeing others become attracted to Islam.

Connections made by Aldousari and Hendricks between athletic activity and character development would stir up some doubters. Michael Novak in *The Joy of Sports*, for example, expresses skepticism that values learned in sports transfer to other spheres of life.[15] A large number of individuals I interviewed, however, would distance themselves from such doubt, believing instead that the athletic arena provides blue-ribbon instruction in character development. Remarking that "one of the things that defines our religion is character,"[16] Mujtaba Shahsamand of New

---

[13] Aldousari, "The History and the Philosophy of Sport in Islam," 26.

[14] Hendricks, "Sport and Islam."

[15] Novak writes that a "thought a clear mind should oppose is the notion that there is some simple transfer of values learned in sports to other areas of life. It is a mark of wisdom, Aristotle wrote, to see in every sphere of life its proper measure. Each sphere is unique. Each has its own proper conditions, laws, and contexts. ...The skills a quarterback learns in swiftly 'reading' the patterns set in motion by the defense are limited skills. ...In corporate bureaucratic life, the quarterback may be inclined to use the same schematic vision to grasp the obstacles arrayed against him. But the number of players in front of him is seldom so clearly arrayed, and the span of time during which obstacles may be set in motion is not nearly so instantaneous as the formations he faces on the gridiron. The rules in the real world are not so clear, nor so closely refereed. The scope for ambition and other motivations is infinitely vaster. And so forth" (Novak, *The Joy of Sports*, 226).

[16] Mujtaba Shahsamand, personal interview, 1 May 2014, Parsippany NJ. In terms of the importance of character in Islam, Craig Joseph and Barnaby Riedel assert the following amidst discussing their interviews with teachers and administra-

Jersey stated that basketball provides a clear mirror of character, enabling an individual to recognize which aspects of his personal makeup especially need to be refined. Shahsamand explained:

> It's easy to have a good character when your emotions are neutral, but I think your real character comes out during tough times, when you're angry, when you're upset—you're competitive. Basketball is a whole range of different emotions. It can bring the best out of you or it can bring the worst out of you. Islam, what it really teaches you is even during the tough times, to be patient, keep your composure. And basketball is competition, and competition is a test of your iman—your faith—so it's a way of practicing the religion. So I think competition is good. It's when your true character comes out. You can see what type of person you are and work on it.[17]

Shahsamand's description of sports as a test providing ample opportunity for character growth was reiterated by Adam Kareem, a former Division 1 college football player. The erstwhile Maryland Terrapin commented that playing a sport "really tests you in a lot of ways. It tests your patience, it tests things that we hold to as virtues as Muslims. And it's a really great way to practice those skills. I've become a lot more patient specifically through playing football."[18] Kareem underscored that patience and other Islamic virtues need to be cultivated, and sports can greatly facilitate this process as athletes are exposed to peaks and valleys of competition and must practice diligence if they want to taste the sweetness of sporting success. Northeastern University student Omar

---

tors at a Chicago area Islamic school: "Akhlaq [Character] is so important to Muslim moral thinking that many interviewees, in discussing it, made the point that the perfection of people's character, their akhlaq, is the fundamental purpose of Islam. Those who argued this pointed to a well-known hadith...: 'When the Prophet one time was asked about the purpose of his message, he said, I was sent for nothing but to perfect or complete the moral character or the high moral character of humanity or individuals or people'" (Craig M. Joseph and Barnaby Riedel, "Islamic Schools, Assimilation, and the Concept of Muslim American Character," in *Being and Belonging: Muslims in the United States Since 9/11*, ed. Katherine Pratt Ewing, 156–77 (New York: Russell Sage Foundation, 2008) 169).

[17] Mujtaba Shahsamand, personal interview, 1 May 2014, Parsippany NJ.

[18] Adam Kareem, personal interview, 20 February 2014, Alexandria VA.

Abdelkader also addressed diligence, saying that "Islam really preaches the idea of working hard to earn things rather than just have them given to you. We believe that God doesn't give us anything easy. We have to go earn it."[19] Abdelkader portrayed sports as a champion teacher of this principle because of the common correlation between hard work in training and victory on the court or field. Kareem echoed this point by mentioning having seen this correlation in his own athletic experiences, but he added he has also grown in character as a result of not having things go well in games despite working hard on the practice field and training room. Kareem stated that he prizes such experiences not only for their contribution to character development, but also because they illuminate events in the life of Muhammad, whose diligence was often followed by desirable results but sometimes by undesirable circumstances.[20]

Sports and Islamic Principles: Harmony and Dissonance

Interview comments galore essentially likened sports to an Islamic virtue Petri dish, creating optimum conditions for the cultivation of character. Yet standing alongside these cheers for sports were some words of warning, emphasizing a need to remain on guard for points of incompatibility between sports and Islamic principles so that this powerful promoter of positive character traits does not end up promoting immoral attitudes and actions instead. No interviewee took sports to task as vehemently as Hafez Ismail, who in his *Islam and Sport* casts aspersions especially on professional and major amateur sporting events.[21] Ismail fulminates against the Olympics, for instance, proclaiming they are "immoral and sinful because of the many harms and evils which are an essential com-

---

[19] Omar Abdelkader, personal interview, 10 March 2014, Boston MA.

[20] Adam Kareem, personal interview, 20 February 2014, Alexandria VA.

[21] Ismail acknowledges some benefits of sports on a recreational or smaller scale level, categorizing these benefits under the headings "physical" (health and fitness, preparation for Jihad, relaxation of the body and mind), "social" (development of social skills), and "economic" (employment). Nonetheless, he claims, "The harms and benefits of sport are many. In modern times, the harms exceed the benefits by far, in number and magnitude" (Hafez Afzal Ismail, *Islam and Sport*, https://archive.org/stream/IslamAndSportsByHafezAfzalIsmail#page/n0/mode/2up (accessed 31 January 2014).

ponent of the Games. These include the harms of commercialism, na-
tionalism, corruption, extravagance, and wastage, just to mention a few.
Hence, we as Muslims should call for the abolishment of the Olympic
Games."[22] Coming nowhere near Ismail's concluding statement in intensity, some interviewees nonetheless expressed significant concern with
particular behaviors commonly associated with certain sports cultures.
Drawing upon what he has witnessed in playing at the prep and college
levels, Kareem commented, "A lot of times the guys on sports teams talk
pretty foul, they're a little misogynistic in things they voice. There's a
heavy influence in pop culture, like music and drugs. These also make
their way to sports teams. And as Muslims these are things that are distinctly discouraged or removed from our culture."[23] Kareem included the
"strong encouragement from guys on the team to hang out with girls and
get girlfriends"[24] as an additional aspect of certain sports cultures that
Muslims should discourage, and mosque youth leader Omar Malik singled out another by speaking against tattoos. Malik lamented, "A tattooed sports athlete is like a norm now, and also they'll have obscene
stuff written on their bodies."[25] According to Malik, tattoos run afoul of
Islamic teaching since Muslims are "not supposed to change our body in
that manner. It's hurting your body."[26] Malik is dismayed by the mark
that tattooed athletes make on youthful minds, noting that many young
Muslims at his mosque model themselves after pro and college athletes
they see on television. Malik was not alone in turning to TV to identify
discord between sports and Islamic principles. A few individuals pinpointed televised coverage of sports as a potential stumbling block in regard to Islamic norms because of commercials that ballyhoo beer or depict sexually suggestive scenarios. This issue gave rise to an intriguing
dilemma during the 2014 Super Bowl, when members of the Muslim
Association of the Puget Sound (MAPS) near Seattle wanted to assemble at the mosque to watch their beloved Seahawks strive for the NFL

[22] Ibid.
[23] Adam Kareem, personal interview, 20 February 2014, Alexandria VA.
[24] Ibid.
[25] Omar Malik, personal interview, 21 March 2014, Warren MI.
[26] Ibid.

crown, but were troubled by the thought of Super Bowl commercials appearing within the mosque. As a result, the televised broadcast was shown in the mosque on a slight delay, providing a chance to substitute commercials with humorous YouTube videos and other entertaining, morally sound alternatives. These Seahawks fans needed to wait a little longer than others to watch Russell Wilson scramble for another first down or see the Legion of Boom defense force Peyton Manning off the field one more time, but from their perspective this was a small price to pay in order to fuse fanaticism for their team with faithfulness to their religion.

In addition to responding with boos to ads selling booze, many Muslims regard the mix between commercial sponsorship and sports to be a hazardous combination on fronts besides television advertisements. Though not a significant issue in America since most pro leagues in the United States keep sponsorship off players' attire, friction has sparked up elsewhere involving Muslims whose team jerseys display corporate logos. Due to Islamic interdictions on gambling, Frederic Kanoute objected to his Spanish soccer team's gambling website logo on uniforms. The star player from Mali agreed to wear the Sevilla FC jersey only without the logo, and to his delight the team provided him with a brand-free jersey for each of its matches in 2006.[27] A story with a similar beginning ended up with a dissimilar denouement in Lithuania, where corporate logos on uniforms formed a major motivational piece behind Muslim American Ibrahim Jaaber's decision to part ties with his pro basketball team. The 2007 Ivy League Player of the Year and conference career steals record holder enjoyed outstanding March Madness performances in which his Penn Quakers gave top-seeded teams all they could handle. Ibby followed his college career with five professional seasons in Europe, and in 2012 he began his sixth European campaign as a brand new member of Lithuania's top team, Zalgiris Kaunas. Six months into the season, Jaaber

---

[27] Kanoute responded by saying, "I am very pleased that Sevilla seem to understand my position, and are not obliging me to wear this shirt" (quoted in "Kanoute Refuses to Wear Gambling Logo," Deutsche Presse Agentur, http://www.ummah.com/forum/showthread.php?96249-Kanoute-refuses-to-wear-gambling-logo (accessed 14 March 2015)).

sent a letter to team administration announcing his decision to leave, citing religious opposition to alcohol and betting firm advertisements on team jerseys as well as to Zalgiris's use of cheerleaders in sexually provocative attire. Jaaber's missive acknowledged that his departure would result in forfeiting his salary, but he expressed willingness to make sacrifices for the sake of his beliefs. Jaaber extrapolated on this experience as we met at the Islamic Circle of North America's New Jersey branch headquarters. He professed that "because the professional arena is controlled by the secular aspect of the society, there are inevitable clashes that will always occur with Muslim professional athletes,"[28] especially because of the centrality of the concept of purity in Islam. Focusing on this concept, Jaaber stated that the "life of the Muslim is this: we are striving to regain and maintain purity, because purity in Islam is a prerequisite before you can enter paradise. And so all of our religious obligations surround this matter."[29] According to Jaaber, many pro Muslim athletes face an unavoidable obstacle in their quest for purity since they are required to "take money from impure sources"[30] at some point in their career. As Jaaber came to see it for himself, the response to this obstacle was clear; eternity in heaven could not be jeopardized by allying with impure sources, even if it meant foregoing a financially secure career playing the game he loves.

Running sports through the sieve of Islamic principles, the sediment found by one athletically oriented Muslim such as Jaaber might differ from that discovered by another. One source of varying judgment relates to whether a Muslim may participate in sports that involve a heavy dose of violent actions. Considering that a vast majority of Muslims view peacefulness as a core principle of their faith and believe their religion

---

[28] Ibrahim Jaaber, personal interview, 18 February 2014, Somerset NJ.

[29] Ibid. Jaaber expanded on this final statement by relating each of the five pillars of Islamic practice to the concept of purity. He declared, "The first pillar when you testify, all of your sins are wiped clean. You're deemed pure. The second pillar, the prayer, from prayer to prayer minor sins are being cleansed from us. Our third pillar, zakat, means purity pertaining to wealth. The fourth pillar which is fasting is a month of purification, you really refrain from some of the things you do during the year, on a higher level. And then the hajj is the pilgrimage, and when you come back it's as if you were born anew, pure" (ibid.).

[30] Ibid.

condones violent actions only for defensive purposes, the permissibility of playing football warrants inquiry. May a Muslim play a sport filled with tackling and other types of violent collisions? May a Muslim take part in an athletic activity in which the intensity of violence inflicted often increases the likelihood of victory, à la a bone-jarring tackle resulting in a game-changing fumble? For some Muslims, these questions produce black-and-white answers about football, but for others they call for a hue of situational gray. Shaykh Muhammad al-Kawthari asserts that a shariah-based ruling on the permissibility of football "will depend on how one plays the sport."[31] The cleric seeks to clarify this vague claim by continuing to say, "If the sport is played in a very aggressive way whereby there is a high risk of the players getting injured, then it would be disapproved if not permissible. ...However, if the sport is not played in an aggressive and hostile way, there seems to be no reason for its impermissibility, especially when the sport provides a very good opportunity to exercise the body."[32] Al-Kawthari apparently would not cheer for chop blocks or helmet-first tackles, and some may doubt that football can even be played without aggression and with low risk of injury. Al-Kawthari might quell some of this doubt, however, by advocating flag football or two-hand touch, or he might point to an exhibition game like the NFL Pro Bowl, where players who normally lower the boom on opponents will put on the brakes. Similarly for boxing, participating without aggression and with low risk of injury may be difficult to fathom, yet sparring without intent to injure would provide one nonviolent alternative. A fatwa (legal ruling) by the European Council for Fatwa and Research takes an interesting twist on the permissibility of boxing, roping its acceptability solely within the limits of striking a punching bag for the sake of physical training. The fatwa identifies striking a human target and boxing professionally as impermissible acts "due to the great harm and untold risk it involves, especially to the body and life of the victim. Islam

---

[31] Shaykh Muhammad ibn Adam al-Kawthari, "The Fiqh of Sports and Games," http://sunnahmuakada.com/2013/02/14/the-fiqh-of-sports-and-games/ (posted 14 February 2013; accessed 23 April 2014).
[32] Ibid.

never allows inflicting harm on any person; Muslim or non-Muslim."[33] Explaining its rationale further, the fatwa alludes to a Hadith statement in which Muhammad forbids directing blows to the head and face,[34] which also appears in a body blow against competitive boxing by Masud Khan. The British Muslim states that he "used to pour scorn" on those who wanted to ban "such an exciting and exhilarating sport,"[35] but he took a 180-degree turn after watching Chris Eubank pummel Michael Watson in a 1991 super-middleweight title bout that left Watson with severe brain damage and confined to a wheelchair. Khan came to the conclusion that boxing "must be a sport that the *Shari'ah* cannot justify,"[36] largely because it violates the principle that one's body is a trust given by God. Khan contends that our bodies are "given to us for safe keeping, they do not belong to us to do as we choose, so we have no right to participate in a sport or any other activity that violates the *amanah* [trust] and whose objective is intense physical damage."[37] Khan goes on to encourage parents to have their children learn semi-contact karate or kung-fu instead of boxing, since in these martial arts children learn "vital self-defence techniques that are needed in an increasingly violent society"[38] without seeking to dish out physical harm upon others.

As Muslims participate in martial arts, football, or any other athletic activity, their emphasis, of course, might not be placed upon competition. Playing simply for fun or exercise in a pick-up game or a league in which scores are not recorded, a focus on winning and losing or competitiveness in any other guise might be far removed from Muslims' sporting experiences. Yet, speaking at least for those I interviewed, the slaking of competitive thirst is a major motivator for athletic activity among many Muslim Americans, who consider competitive desire to be compatible

[33] "Boxing as a Sports [sic] in Islam," http://en.allexperts.com/q/Islam-947/2009/2/boxing-sports-islam.htm (posted 22 February 2009; accessed 23 April 2014).

[34] "If anyone of you fights a person, he should not hit him in the face."

[35] Masud Ahmed Khan, "Islam and Boxing," http://www.masud.co.uk/ISLAM/misc/boxing.htm (accessed 23 April 2014).

[36] Ibid.

[37] Ibid.

[38] Ibid.

with Islamic teachings provided no Islamic principles or virtues are toppled in its wake. Humility was often identified as one virtue that is especially flammable amidst competitive fire. Rizwan Butt, president of a Pennsylvania mosque, described an ever-present tension between competitiveness and arrogance, stating that in the heat of competition Muslims must maintain vigilance against arrogance, a paramount sin in Islamic tradition.[39] Butt commented that Muslims "can never put down somebody else, or pump ourselves up to the point where we think we're superior, because this goes back to arrogance."[40] According to Butt, the competitive pursuit of athletic excellence is fully in line with Islamic precepts, but only if accompanied by an attitude of humility. Komail Lakha of Minnesota made a similar point while talking about nationwide East African-style volleyball tournaments involving Khoja Shia congregations.[41] Remarking that some tournament teams have "rock star players," Lakha declared that "the key thing for them to realize and keep doing is being humble."[42] In keeping their hubris in check, Lakha believes, these volleyball aces serve not only themselves by spiking the sin of arrogance; they also benefit youth who view them as role models. Elsewhere in America's heartland, Lakha's desire for young Muslims to learn to keep their feet on the ground while reaching for athletic heights reverberated in comments from Habeeb Quadri. The Chicago-area Islamic school principal noted that a motto of his school's athletic teams is "Dominate Humbly." Calling arrogance "the first sin in our faith,"[43] going back to the devil in the Garden of Eden, Quadri stressed that humility need not squelch athletic excellence and competitive zeal. One more variation on this theme came from Kareem Shahin, a twenty-something member of Southern California's competitive Muslim Basketball League. Shahin proclaimed that he wants to be "a menace to people when I'm on the

---

[39] One Hadith statement, for example, proclaims, "No one will enter Paradise in whose heart is an atom's weight of arrogance."[40] Rizwan Butt, personal interview, 4 May 2014, Easton PA.

[40] Rizwan Butt, personal interview, 4 May 2014, Easton PA.

[41] Khoja Americans' athletic activities, including East African-style volleyball tournaments, will be discussed in chapter 9.

[42] Komail Lakha, personal interview, 26 April 2014, Brooklyn Park MN.

[43] Habeeb Quadri, personal interview, 17 March 2014, Morton Grove IL.

court."[44] He added, "I don't want people to say, 'Oh, you can leave him open,' or 'If you're guarding him, you can help out.' I want to be a guy where you might have to get one or two extra players on this guy, because he's a menace."[45] Shahin attributed this ambition to his naturally competitive bent, which he considers to be consonant with Islamic principles as long as it does not include arrogance or produce rifts in brotherhood. In reference to his competitiveness, Shahin said, "I don't want it to break ties with anybody. I want to be competitive but I don't want to belittle your activities or your competition or not be appreciative of whatever you're doing."[46] Shahin takes pleasure in being a thorn in opponents' sides in order to lead his team to victory, but he is ready to bench his competitive ardor immediately if it might cause a defeat for Muslim unity.

Expressing concern that competitiveness can cleave camaraderie, Shahin finds himself in the same arena as Alfie Kohn and other humanist critics of competition.[47] Importantly, though, because Kohn argues for an *inevitable* break in camaraderie due to competition, Shahin would separate himself from Kohn and take a seat in a completely different section of the arena. Kohn propounds that competition involves "mutually exclusive goal attainment," or MEGA, in which one person or team's success requires another's failure, thereby turning opponents into dehumanized obstacles to success rather than shareholders of common humanity. Kohn claims that MEGA is an inherent component of competition, [48] which inescapably "acts not only to strain our existing relationships to the breaking point, but also to prevent them from devel-

[44] Kareem Shahin, personal interview, 11 April 2014, Fontana CA.

[45] Ibid.

[46] Ibid.

[47] A humanist criticism of competition suggests that it "encourages purely instrumental social relations rather than encouraging relationships in which people are valued as ends in themselves" (Michael L. Schwalbe, "A Humanist Conception of Competition in Sport," *Humanity & Society* 13 (1989): 47).

[48] Kohn argues that MEGA is not a matter of "the *way* we compete or the *extent* of our competitiveness," but an inherent quality of competition in any form (Alfie Kohn, *No Contest: The Case Against Competition*, rev. ed. (Boston: Houghton Mifflin, 1992) 10).

oping in the first place. Camaraderie and companionship—to say nothing of genuine friendship and love—scarcely have a chance to take root when we are defined as competitors."[49] From the standpoint of Shahin and other interviewees who spoke highly of competition provided it is kept in check, Kohn's antithesis between competition and companionship should be heeded as warning of potential pitfall, but by no means taken as documentation of unavoidable peril. Along the lines of scholars who express their disagreement with Kohn by stating that competition presupposes cooperation not only between teammates, but opponents as well,[50] many Muslim Americans believe that if handled with care, competition can build bonds and lay bridges among athletic foes in addition to athletic allies.

Sports and Fasting

As stated by a few interviewees, Islam calls each of its followers to compete with oneself in a continual striving for excellence. The Belief Statement of the Islamic Society of Central Jersey contains the following exhortation:

---

[49] Ibid., 134. John Gerdy similarly declares, "The very nature of sport serves to divide rather than to bring people together. Inherent in any sporting event is the dichotomy of 'winner' and 'loser,' 'us' versus 'them,' 'home team' versus 'visitors.' The fundamental premise upon which sports is based is to pit competitors against each other in a battle for domination" (John R. Gerdy, *Sports: The All-American Addiction* (Jackson: University Press of Mississippi, 2002) 58).

[50] Portraying competition "as a special form of cooperation," David Shields and Brenda Bredemeier argue, "In a contest, two or more competitors cooperate, each providing the other with a worthy challenge that enables each participant to exhibit her or his best performance. Determination of a 'winner' requires that all cooperate in upholding the conditions of fairness" (David Lyle Light Shields and Brenda Jo Light Bredemeier, *Character Development and Physical Activity* (Champaign IL: Human Kinetics, 1995) 22). Randy Martin and Toby Miller approach this idea from a different angle. They argue that the body's "ability to anticipate what the other may do—which lies at the heart of the effect called competition—already presupposes a deep dependence on those others in the contest, to make one's own participation possible" (Randy Martin and Toby Miller, "Fielding Sport: A Preface to Politics?" in *SportCult*, ed. Randy Martin and Toby Miller, 1–13 (Minneapolis: University of Minnesota Press, 1999) 5).

Excellence cannot be compromised. We impose upon ourselves an obligation to reach beyond the minimal. Though we may be better today than we were yesterday, we are not as good as we could become tomorrow. None of us can settle for less than our best, and we can never stop trying to surpass what has already been achieved. We must continuously challenge and compete with ourselves.[51]

Such competition is not solely a solipsistic endeavor. It may also entail competing against others[52] who push individuals to recognize and transcend their personal limitations.[53] As a result, athletic competition has plenty to offer Muslims in helping them strive for excellence. Additionally, a link between sports and the recognizing and transcending of personal limitations resides in the intermingling of athletic activity and fasting during Ramadan. From a pro playing under bright NFL lights to a high-schooler pushing herself in the shadows to run one more mile, scores of Muslim Americans take themselves beyond their apparent physical and psychological limits as they play sports while abstaining from food and drink from sunup to sundown during Ramadan's thirty days. Physiological studies attest to this commitment's toll,[54] and anecdo-

---

[51] "Islamic Society of Central Jersey Belief Statement," Islamic Society of Central Jersey, http://www.iscj.org/AboutBeliefStatement.aspx (accessed 28 April 2014).

[52] The Qur'an upholds competing against others in personal righteousness as a desirable pursuit: "Each of you chooses the direction to follow; you shall race towards righteousness. Wherever you may be, God will summon you all. God is Omnipotent" (Q2:148); and "They are eager to do righteous works; they compete in doing them" (Q23:61).

[53] Randolph Feezell writes, "Sport, as the quest for a certain kind of physical excellence within a complicated web of rules and strategic know-hows, challenges persons to come to grips with their limitations, to understand themselves in order to succeed or to become better. Sport requires self-expansion and self-knowledge, insofar as sport participants must acknowledge their limits in order to overcome them and become better or succeed in various ways" (Randolph Feezell, *Sport, Philosophy, and Good Lives* (Lincoln: University of Nebraska Press, 2013) 227).

[54] David Kahan notes "the slowing of diurnal metabolism for energy conservation, the psychological stress from the attenuation of training intensity and duration, and the modification of training schedules to keep with the fasting obligations" (David Kahan, "Islam and Physical Activity: Implications for American Sport and Physical Educators," *Journal of Physical Education, Recreation, & Dance* 74/3 (2003): 50).

tal evidence I encountered supports these findings. Kareem Shahin described playing high school basketball during Ramadan as "some of the hardest times of my life,"[55] especially when his team ran to and back from its rival high school in the morning before school started, leaving Shahin thirsty but unable to drink until sundown. Nonetheless, Shahin expressed deep appreciation for this experience, saying "it built a lot of discipline"[56] and made him a stronger person and follower of his faith.

Shahin's story combining being pushed to the limits with experiencing personal growth matches Hamza and Husain Abdullah's accounts of fasting in the NFL. The defensive back brothers and their ten siblings were raised in a devout Southern California Muslim family in which they began fasting at an early age. Both brothers fasted throughout their college careers at Washington State and in the NFL, where Hamza played for seven seasons with the Denver Broncos, Cleveland Browns, and Arizona Cardinals, and Husain's 2014 campaign with the Kansas City Chiefs was his sixth in the league, following a stint with the Minnesota Vikings. Astoundingly, when Ramadan happened to fall in September of Husain's rookie 2008 season, none of his Vikings teammates or coaches knew that the newbie was fasting while sweating it out in practices and games. Seeking to avoid the media spotlight and special treatment from coaches, Husain chose not to tell anyone in his new organization. In 2009 the Islamic calendar had Ramadan beginning during the pre-season in August,[57] and this time Husain decided to inform one team member, assistant defensive backs coach Derek Mason. Soon, though, the cat was completely out of the bag. Husain's fasting became common knowledge following a meeting with head coach Brad Childress, who had noticed his player seeming to lack energy and struggling to keep up his weight. Due to this meeting, a Vikings nutrition consultant devised a special Ramadan diet for Abdullah. The defensive back executed the game plan, waking briefly at 2 A.M. for a protein and carbohydrate shake and again at 5 A.M., when he and his wife would pray and eat their predawn suhoor

[55] Kareem Shahin, personal interview, 11 April 2014, Fontana CA.
[56] Ibid.
[57] Ramadan advances approximately ten days each year relative to the Gregorian calendar.

meal, which Husain capped off with another shake. The diet helped him maintain his target playing weight, but by no means did it knock down every hurdle associated with fasting in the NFL. According to both Husain and his brother, these obstacles are especially daunting during the rigors of training camp, and Hamza identified two particular points of the typical training camp day, namely lunchtime when teammates are chowing down in the cafeteria and the lull between afternoon practices and his after sundown meal, as the most challenging of them all.[58] Hamza was able to pass these tests of fasting willpower thanks to strategies such as sitting in a cool tub in a team therapy room and going home during lunchtime to play with his daughter. Finding further fortification for fasting during the dog days of training camp, the brothers have turned to the Qur'an. Husain has often reminded himself of the verse "On no soul does God place a burden greater than it can bear" (Q2:286) in order to help himself push ahead when feeling like breaking his fast during daylight hours. Husain has also noted non-Muslim teammates serving as sources of inspiration, recalling a sweltering practice in which five teammates ended up in a medical tent dehydrated. Husain recollected that he "was struggling internally to keep going"[59] without liquid replenishment, but he was invigorated to continue after teammates expressed their respect for his fasting commitment.

For devout Muslim athletes such as the Abdullahs, the eternal reward accompanying obedience to God is fasting's primary perk. As a significant secondary benefit, Hamza has pointed out that he grabbed his first and only NFL interception while fasting.[60] Like Latter Day Saint stories that associate adhering to the Word of Wisdom with gaining an athletic edge, Hamza's claim of correlation between fasting and increased

[58] Neil MacFarquhar, "Muslim Player Thrives with Nourished Spirit," *New York Times,* http://www.nytimes.com/2007/10/13/sports/football/13fasting.html?_r=1/ (published 13 October 2007; accessed 21 April 2014).

[59] Quoted in Aliyah Mohammed, "Muslim NFL Players Fast During Ramadan," NBC Bay Area, http://www.nbcbayarea.com/news/local/Muslim-NFL-Players-Come-to-Bay-163640676.html (published 7 August 2012; accessed 21 April 2014).

[60] MacFarquhar, "Muslim Player Thrives."

sporting success has been asserted by other Muslim jocks. Former NBA All-Star Shareef Abdur-Rahim has mentioned that his best game as a pro took place while fasting during Ramadan, when in 2001 he piled up fifty points to help his Atlanta Hawks soar over the Detroit Pistons. No one has claimed this correlation as vociferously as NBA Hall of Famer Hakeem Olajuwon, who averaged nearly eight extra points per game while fasting. According to Olajuwon, "When your stomach is full, you get tired and lazy and too relaxed. You get tremendous energy from fasting. Everything is crisp. When your stomach is empty, you get a lot of oxygen and you can breathe."[61] Ramadan was the crowning month of this powerful post player's year, not only for delivering spiritual highs, but also for raising his game to its highest level.

NFL defensive lineman Ryan Harris resonates with Olajuwon in connecting Ramadan with enhanced athletic performance, having declared that the month "is about reflection, reordering your priorities and focusing on what's important. That's why it helps me be a better player."[62] A huge difference, however, marks Harris's Ramadan experience with that of Olajuwon. Harris has made the choice not to fast when Ramadan coincides with NFL seasons or training camps. Harris entered his rookie year in Denver poised and ready to fast, but he had a change of heart between a demanding morning workout and an afternoon practice on the sixth day of training camp. As Harris describes it, "After the lift I was just out of gas and I needed something that would get me ready for practice."[63] Prompted further by concern that refraining from food and drink would inhibit his recovery from off-season back surgery, Harris stuck with his decision not to fast, which in accordance with Islamic tradition, he has compensated for by donating to the poor. Harris has subsidized meals at homeless shelters in Denver and in Houston, where he

---

[61] Quoted in ibid.

[62] Quoted in Dale Robertson, "Ryan Harris Is Making the Most of His Opportunity," *Houston Chronicle,* http://blog.chron.com/ultimatetexans/2013/07/ryan-harris-is-making-the-most-of-his-opportunity/ (posted 29 July 2013; accessed 23 April 2014).

[63] Quoted in MacFarquhar, "Muslim Player Thrives."

has gone on to play with the Texans, and he has served at a soup kitchen in his hometown of St. Paul, Minnesota.

By comparing Harris's Ramadan experience to that of Olajuwon, the Abdullah brothers, and others who have fasted while playing, I intend to illustrate that the mix of Ramadan and sports elicits a range of response. A gold medal example of such variety took place at the 2012 Summer Olympics in London, where hundreds of devout Muslims fasted and hundreds did not. Those who fasted were following in the fleet footsteps of Suleiman Nyambul of Tanzania, who won the 5,000-meter silver medal while fasting at the 1980 Moscow Games, the last time the Olympics coincided with Ramadan. After gaining second place, Nyambul proclaimed, "Once you decide to do something, Allah is behind you."[64] The London Games were well equipped to meet the needs of fasting Olympians, who faced more than seventeen hours of daylight and peak British summer temperatures. London officials made arrangements to offer special pre-dawn suhoor meals that met Islamic dietary regulations, and they prepared fast-breaking packs containing water, fruit, and energy bars. For many Muslim Olympians in London, though, such arrangements were unnecessary, since these athletes chose not to fast either during the entire Games or on days when they competed. In many cases, this decision came with explicit backing from Islamic legal scholars in the athletes' home countries. The High Egyptian Islamic Council issued a fatwa (legal ruling) that excused its Olympians from fasting while competing or coaching, a position taken by legal scholars in numerous other Islamic lands. Citing a tradition that Muslims do not need to fast while traveling during Ramadan but must compensate for missed days by fasting for an equivalent amount of time later, Bahrain Olympic Committee executive Sheik Khalid bin Abdulla Al Khalifa explained, "Our athletes will not be fasting during the Olympics. It's simple in Islam. Since they are traveling, they can take these days at the Olympics on loan and then

---

[64] Quoted in "Many Muslim Athletes to Fast After London Olympics," CNN/SI, http://sportsillustrated.cnn.com/2012/olympics/wires/07/20/2090.sp.oly.ramadan.ol ympics/index.html (posted 20 July 2012; accessed 22 April 2014).

make up for them until next Ramadan."[65] Demonstrating further variety in response to Ramadan, some London Olympians made amends for not fasting during the Games by following the tradition of donating food to the poor, like Ryan Harris of the NFL. British rower Mohammed Sbihi, for example, found himself in smooth Islamic tradition waters by providing sixty meals for every day he missed to impoverished individuals in his father's homeland of Morocco.

Returning my fasting focus to American soil, a highly unusual scenario at a Michigan public high school provides greater insight into the multifarious ways in which Muslims have negotiated the demands of sports with religious dictates regarding Ramadan. With its ninety-eight percent Arab American student body, fasting is the norm among athletes at Dearborn's Fordson High School, America's first million-dollar high school, built in 1922 under the direction of Henry Ford. Fordson football coaches faced a quandary in 2010, when Ramadan coincided with the intense pre-season practice period at the conclusion of summer vacation. Concerned about the safety of players practicing for hours in intense heat without water or any other replenishment, coaches came up with a creative solution. Practices were held in the middle of the night, enabling players to arrive well-nourished and to guzzle as many fluids as they pleased without violating their commitment to fast from sunup to sundown. The plan's chief architect was Fouad Zaban, long-time head coach of his beloved alma mater. Zaban spoke fondly about the middle-of-the-night practices since they averted putting his players at excessive physical risk, but he also noted difficulties. Zaban said it was "hectic staying up all night and sleeping during the day and then trying to adjust again"[66] to a normal schedule, especially because the season began directly after the two weeks of midnight practices. To Zaban's surprise, one challenge he thought he might encounter but did not was resistance from parents of the few non-Muslim players on the team. The coach received only one parental complaint, from a Muslim concerned with having a son out well after midnight, as practices typically wound down around 4 A.M. Other parents may not have been thrilled, but considering the threat

[65] Ibid.
[66] Fouad Zaban, personal interview, 20 March 2014, Dearborn MI.

of dehydration and other medical mishaps that may have arisen if practices were held during daytime hours, health and safety concerns ultimately tackled any negative response they may have had. Moreover, with the vast majority of the squad made up of Muslim players, many parents were delighted to see the school accommodate its young athletes' faith. Fordson assistant football coach and head basketball coach Osama Abulhassan commented that if Fordson coaches would say, "'Hey guys, you're fasting, that's great, but we're going to practice when it's 100 degrees and you can't drink water'—we're not really respecting the faith"[67] of these players. According to some Americans, this may be a matter of overstepping bounds in the tenuous relationship between religion and public schools. For other Americans like Abulhassan, Fordson's Ramadan decision was not only completely consonant with the First Amendment, but also an apt acknowledgement of the devotion of particular Americans to core aspects of their religion.

[67] Osama Abulhassan, personal interview, 20 March 2014, Dearborn MI.

5

Challenges to Muslim American Athletic Activity

America was caught unawares, taken by surprise by events in New York. This, though, was no cataclysmic act of terror that turned the world upside down. This was a feel-good story that made waves throughout the sporting world. Eleven years after 9/11, Linsanity spread from its New York epicenter to NBA arenas and media devices across America. Chinese American point guard Jeremy Lin rose from obscurity to stardom almost as quickly as his swift crossover dribble. With each point, assist, and steal he tallied and with each dazzling move he contributed to ESPN highlight reels, Lin was doing more than taking down New York Knicks opponents. He was uprooting assumptions implanted deep within American minds about Asian Americans and their athletic abilities. Like Hank Greenberg hammering away at the image of the weak, athletically incompetent Jew, Lin made fans across America reconsider stereotypes that cast Asian Americans as all-stars in the classroom but benchwarmers in the arena.

Muslim Americans of South Asian and Arab descent are still waiting for their version of Linsanity to arrive. Countless South Asian and Arab Muslim Americans are passionate about playing and watching sports, but so far only African Americans and Nigerian Hakeem Olajuwon have entered the ranks of Muslim athletic stardom in America. As Stanley Thangaraj claims in his study of South Asian basketball leagues, Americans tend to "overemphasize the South Asian 'brain'" and depict South Asians as lacking "a body to claim normative sporting masculinity."[1] Arabs, too, are rarely associated by Americans with proficiency in popular American sports. Former college basketball player Maher

---

[1] Stanley Thangaraj, "Playing through Differences: Black-White Racial Logic and Interrogating South Asian American Identity," *Ethnic and Racial Studies* 35/6 (2012): 990.

Abuawad recalled his experience growing up in a Brooklyn neighborhood where he was one of only a few Arabs who played basketball. Abuawad commented that until he proved himself on the court, opponents and teammates alike "would make fun of me, that I couldn't dunk, I couldn't do this and that"[2] because of his Arab descent. One day a Jeremy Lin or Hank Greenberg of South Asian or Arab ancestry may hold the shovel that starts to bury these stereotypes, but up to this point a particular barrier has played a significant role in preventing this burial from beginning. Diluting the pool of potential South Asian and Arab American sporting stars, immigrant parents have frequently discouraged and sometimes prohibited their children from making sports a significant part of their lives. The first part of this chapter considers a common cause of this sports sidelining,[3] parental prioritization of academics over athletics.

[2] Maher Abuawad, personal interview, 21 February 2014, Lawrenceville NJ.

[3] Another cause that might be considered is the argument that South Asian and Arab immigrant parents devalue sports due to being shaped by cultures that lag behind American esteem for competitiveness and athletic activity. Michael Mandelbaum writes, "Contemporary Americans are perhaps the most competitive people since the ancient Greeks. Virtually any activity in the United States sooner or later becomes the subject of a competition, from animal husbandry to architecture and even including eating" (Michael Mandelbaum, *The Meaning of Sports: Why Americans Watch Baseball, Football, and Basketball, and What They See When They Do* (New York: Public Affairs, 2004) 30). Examining the cultural, moral, religious, and political values of inhabitants of over ninety nations, the World Values Survey has indicated that Americans approve of competition more highly than any other country ("World Values Survey," World Values Survey, http://www.worldvaluessurvey.org/wvs.jsp (accessed 15 March 2015)). When supplemented by analyses that connect the forging of American competitiveness with nineteenth-century national characteristics like an expansionist spirit and a Protestant ethic (see Miracle and Rees, *Lessons of the Locker Room*, 43; and Overman, *The Protestant Ethic and the Spirit of Sport*, 235), these suggestions of extraordinary American competitiveness warrant serious scrutiny. Problematically, though, they may be easily accompanied by generalized pictures of hypercompetitive Americans juxtaposed with images of members of other cultures, including Arabs and South Asians, with no competitive bone in their body. Furthermore, an argument that involves casting the United States as a sports-crazed country whereas Arab and South Asian nations kick sports to the curb would occlude a passion for soccer, cricket, and other sports as well as huge athletic success from individuals residing in Arab and South Asian lands. As I learned from

Parental Prioritization of Academics Over Athletics

Not all Arab and South Asian Muslim immigrant parents have shared this prioritization, and as I will eventually address, the tables have started to turn. Struck by how often this issue was raised by those I interviewed, however, I am presenting it as one significant challenge related to Muslim American athletic activity. I build upon the observations of David Kahan, who explored athletic activity and inactivity in Muslim American communities near the end of the twentieth century. Kahan concluded, "The strongest explanation for relative physical inactivity in the Muslim populations that were investigated appears to be parental influence. Muslims who immigrated 30 to 40 years ago and prospered in the educational system and workforce instruct their children to follow in this path, thus frowning upon sport as an impediment to achieving educational and career goals."[4] Multiple individuals I interviewed would nod their heads at Kahan's claim, maintaining that Muslim immigrant parents have frequently regarded the relationship between academics and athletics in either-or terms, with athletics getting trounced in this binary battle.

Particularly strong commentary on this matter came from Odsen Piton, director of the Muslim Athletic League in Boston. Piton proclaimed that Muslim immigrant parents want their children "to focus on school only, and they tend to forget that the kids want sports and they're growing up in an environment that values sports."[5] New Jersey Islamic school athletic director Abir Catovic reminisced about seeing this mindset firsthand after arriving in the United States from Egypt as a young child. Catovic commented, "When I came here, the most important thing was your education—that's what Muslim families value."[6] These

Southern California mosque sports director Hashim Zaman, for example, players from Pakistan and Egypt have been dominant in squash; the longest winning streak ever in any sport is held by Pakistan's Jahangir Khan, who tasted victory in 555 squash matches in a row (Hashim Zaman, personal interview, 10 April 2014, Irvine CA). Arab and South Asian Muslim athletic ardor is also conspicuously displayed at the Islamic Solidarity Games, which was inaugurated in Saudi Arabia in 2005 when 7,000 athletes from fifty-four Islamic countries competed in thirteen sports.

[4] Kahan, "Islam and Physical Activity," 51.

[5] Odsen Piton, personal interview, 9 March 2014, Cambridge MA.

[6] Abir Catovic, personal interview, 1 May 2014, Monmouth Junction NJ.

values of her parents came to clash with her own, as she discovered through her public school physical education class that she loved sports and was excited by the prospect of joining an afterschool athletic team. Fortunately for Catovic, this family dissonance resolved in a harmonious key. Her parents decided to permit her to play on school sports teams as long as she maintained straight A's on report cards. Hitting the books hard, she was able to hit jump shots and fastballs for her high school, where she played on the basketball, softball, and soccer squads. For other Muslim youth from immigrant families, on the other hand, athletic aspirations may not see such a happy ending. Parents' emphasis on education may ground these young Muslims' yearnings to watch their athletic talents soar. IBall Academy basketball training director Maher Abuawad recalled honing the hoops skills of an exceptionally adept Muslim highschooler with strong potential to play at the Division II, if not Division I, college level. Abuawad lamented that this potential was zapped; the budding star's immigrant parents insisted that he put basketball aside and focus on his studies to become a doctor or lawyer. Pushed to the library instead of the locker room, he lost his chance to play college basketball and do what Abuawad called "the thing that he loved."[7] Abuawad's wife, Amnah Elbarrad, added to the discussion, providing her perspective on why Muslim immigrant parents often prevent their children from stepping on the court or field so they can concentrate on academics instead. Basing her comments on what she has seen in her ancestral Egyptian homeland, Elbarrad stated that in Islamic nations rarely does success in sports translate into a lucrative career. Instead, education to become a doctor or lawyer is a well-worn path to a well-paid walk of life, a path that, according to Elbarrad, many immigrant parents urge their children to follow in order to lead prosperous lives in America.[8] As illustrated by Abuawad's tale of his tremendously talented trainee, in some cases this educational emphasis might not lead parents to ban their children from recreational leagues or afterschool sports at younger ages, but it might mean adamant opposition to sports at the college level, thereby blocking shots to play professionally. Southern Californian Mujahid Chandoo cast

[7] Maher Abuawad, personal interview, 21 February 2014, Lawrenceville NJ.
[8] Amnah Elbarrad, personal interview, 21 February 2014, Lawrenceville NJ.

this obstacle as rubbing against the tenet of Islam as a complete way of life." After expressing a wish that Muslim immigrant parents would "give the same opportunity to their kids to excel in professional sports" as they do in the medical and legal fields, Chandoo professed, "Islam is a balanced life, so if it's possible to earn your living by playing sports then you should be allowed to do that."[9] Chandoo hopes for a major mindset shift in Muslim American immigrant culture, saying he awaits the day when parents will encourage their sons to "be the next Kobe"[10] just as readily as they prod their progeny to walk the hallowed halls of hospitals or courthouses.

American immigrant youth have been down a similar road before. First-generation Eastern European Jewish parents commonly curtailed their children's clamoring to play popular American sports,[11] regarding them as a foolish way to fritter away the day and as morally dubious pursuits. Steven Riess writes that many of these parents considered baseball to be "a ridiculous amusement in which adults wearing short pants tried to hit a ball with a stick and ran around in circles,"[12] and many judged football and boxing to be morally inadmissible because of their violence. Riess continues to construct a vivid vignette of Eastern European Jewish parents putting the kibosh on their kids' athletic activity, asserting that they "exerted pressure on sons against playing sports that were dangerous, distracted them from study or work or both, or encouraged behavior that drew them away from a traditionally strict Orthodox upbringing."[13] Perhaps just a stone's throw away from the Jewish neighborhood, many Italian immigrant parents also viewed their children's daydreams to play sports as a nightmare. These parents tended to see sports as a waste of time that kept children from fulfilling their primary obligation of con-

---

[9] Mujahid Chandoo, personal interview, 12 April 2014, Fullerton CA.

[10] Ibid.

[11] For most of these immigrants, their familiarity in their native homelands "with physical culture was at best limited to ice-skating, sledding, and ball playing" (Steven A. Riess, "Sports and the American Jew: An Introduction," in *Sports and the American Jew*, ed. Steven A. Riess, 1–59 (Syracuse NY: Syracuse University Press, 1998) 15).

[12] Ibid.

[13] Ibid.

tributing to the family's welfare. Carmelo Bazzano comments that Italian parents in America "were astonished that schools would provide recreation even at the high school level. Among other reasons, they felt that play could cause injury, hence loss of income and burden to the family."[14] The father of Joe DiMaggio exemplifies a common mindset of Italian American parents. A San Francisco fisherman, Giuseppe DiMaggio looked to clip the future Yankee Clipper's athletic wings, especially as Joe would sneak away from his duties on his father's boat to play baseball with friends. The eventual legend who would one day be showered with cheers from adoring fans was pelted as a youth with appellations of *lagnusu* (lazy) and *meschinu* (good-for-nothing) from his exasperated father.[15]

In the twenty-first century, Eastern European Jewish and Italian immigrant parental pushback against sports is now a distant memory, and signs suggest that the same might be said of Muslim American immigrant communities in the next century. New Jersey Islamic school principal Amanny Khattab asserted that Muslim immigrant parents used to believe there were "so many other things that are important to accomplish other than sports,"[16] since they had "other priorities because they were still establishing themselves as immigrants, as people who wanted to be financially stable."[17] Khattab claimed that this mindset "is completely shifting," as many second- and third-generation immigrant parents' experience of economic stability leads them to tell their children that sports are "just as important"[18] as academic endeavors. IBall Academy director Abuawad agrees that the parental pendulum is swinging. Comparing his younger generation of Muslim Americans to an older

---

[14] Carmelo Bazzano, "The Italian American Sporting Experience," in *Ethnicity and Sport in North American History and Culture*, ed. George Eisen and David K. Wiggins, 103–16 (Westport CT: Greenwood Press, 1994) 109.

[15] Ibid., 111.

[16] Quoted in Matthew Stanmyre, "New Jersey Islamic Students See Basketball League Taking Shape," NJ.com, http://www.nj.com/hssports/blog/boysbasketball/index.ssf/2013/04/new_jersey_islamic_students_see_basketball_league_taking_shape.html (published 14 April 2013; accessed 21 April 2014).

[17] Quoted in ibid.

[18] Quoted in ibid.

generation that has placed academics above athletics, Abuawad remarked, "You have these upcoming parents interested in fantasy football and all that stuff, so we're going to see that change."[19] As this change takes its course, what would have seemed like a far-fetched fantasy might become reality; an Arab or South Asian American child of one of these fantasy football-loving parents might grow up and become the top pick in fantasy leagues across America.

Muslim Females and Athletic Activity

"Intisar continued to play in secret from her family. While other teenagers hid condoms and pot from their parents, Intisar guarded *her* big secret—sports."[20] Shabana Mir tells this tale of a pseudonymous Somali American whose mother forbade her from playing basketball, considering it an unacceptable activity for a young Muslim woman. On one level, Intisar's plight simply continues the story already started in this chapter, since she was prevented by her immigrant parents from participating in sports. For Intisar, however, parental benching was not primarily about academics superseding athletics. It was her gender that made Intisar's parents cry foul to her hoop dreams. Continuing my exploration of barriers to Muslim American sports participation, I now turn to athletic obstacles faced specifically by Muslim women and girls.

Discouragement of female athletic activity was typically tucked securely within Muslim immigrant baggage, an accepted way of life in the old country carried into the new American homeland. New Jersey Islamic school athletic director Abir Catovic described her limited athletic experiences in her birthplace of Egypt, stating that in elementary school boys would play soccer while female students were told they had to jump rope instead. Catovic recalled, "I would just stand there, looking at the soccer—I still remember it. I wanted to go play soccer."[21] Catovic and

---

[19] Maher Abuawad, personal interview, 21 February 2014, Lawrenceville NJ.

[20] Mir, *Muslim American Women on Campus*, 2.

[21] Abir Catovic, personal interview, 1 May 2014, Monmouth Junction NJ. For a discussion of a similar mindset in a South Asian rather than Arab nation, see Hasina Zaman's analysis of athletic activity among young Bangladeshi women (Zaman, "Islam, Well-Being, and Physical Activity," 61).

her New Jersey Islamic school seek to write a different script for Muslim girls by offering them afterschool basketball and volleyball, but she suggested that a significant percentage of girls at her school still bear the mark of a culture that has discouraged females from playing sports. Many within Coach Catovic's crew are basketball neophytes, having no knowledge of the difference between offense and defense or other basics of the game. Speaking with laughter but also with obvious respect for her greenhorn players, Catovic remarked that she needs to take small steps such as saying, "Your homework tonight is to watch a basketball game to see how they're standing and that I'm not crazy in telling you to stand like this... Where are their hands? Did you notice that?"[22] As noted by Michigan mosque sports director Haaris Ahmad, because of the historical paucity of Muslim female athletic participation, qualified Muslim American female coaches are hard to find. The result has often been a self-perpetuating cycle of little female athletic involvement, as Muslim girls are discouraged or barred from playing sports if coached by a man, but very few Muslim women are competent and confident to take the man's place as coach since they themselves did not grow up playing sports.[23]

Importantly, however, this cycle has started to slow down. Athletic opportunities specifically designed for girls and women have curtailed its momentum at Catovic's school, Ahmad's mosque, and dozens of other Muslim American settings. Like the changing tide of immigrant parental attitudes regarding the relationship between athletics and academics, a new chapter of female athletic opportunity is being written by a slew of Muslim Americans. One of its earliest authors was Semeen Issa, who in 1997 founded the Muslim Girls' Sports Camp in Pasadena, California. Girls aged seven to sixteen enjoyed basketball, soccer, volleyball, and martial arts, interspersed with camp songs, water fights, daily prayers, and talks relating Islamic principles to everyday life and athletic experiences.[24] Issa's vision for the two-week camp was sparked by seeing her

---

[22] Abir Catovic, personal interview, 1 May 2014, Monmouth Junction NJ.

[23] Haaris Ahmad, personal interview, 21 March 2014, Canton MI.

[24] A development such as the Muslim Girls' Sports Camp stands within the stream of immigrant female experience in American religious history, as the early

two daughters enjoy their recreational soccer league and wanting other Muslim girls to be able to have a ball through sports as well. Issa disclosed a further piece of her vision by declaring, "Learning to play sports helps give Muslim girls self-confidence, develops their leadership skills. They get a different message here than they might get at home or at school: 'Get out there. Don't be afraid to try something new.'"[25] Moving ahead into the twenty-first century, another contributor to Muslim American female athletic activity's new chapter is the Ahmadiyya Muslim Community.[26] Beginning in 2011, Ahmadi women and girls from the Mid-Atlantic have assembled for the Regional Sports Tournament. The 2013 version brought 500 participants to a Maryland mosque, where they strengthened sisterhood through soccer, volleyball, badminton, table tennis, and running competitions.[27]

stages of at least one other religious immigrant group involved a gradual development of athletic opportunities for its female members despite opposition from some individuals. Linda Borish focuses on early twentieth-century Jewish associations and settlements that "provided a forum for preserving religiosity for Jewish women and autonomy to create a Jewish environment whilst incorporating physical activities and sport for their physical well-being and to gain access to American practices" (Linda J. Borish, "Women, Sport, and American Jewish Identity in the Late Nineteenth and Early Twentieth Centuries," in *With God on Their Side: Sport in the Service of Religion*, ed. Tara Magdalinski and Timothy J. L. Chandler, 71–98 (New York: Routledge, 2002) 72). Giving access for immigrant Jewish women and girls to calisthenics, basketball, swimming, tennis, track and field events, and bicycling, Jewish associations like the Young Women's Hebrew Association or the Chicago Hebrew Institute generated controversy among some members of the Jewish immigrant community for making this access possible.

[25] Quoted in Sandy Banks, "Mixing Girls' Sports and Muslim Tradition," *Los Angeles Times*, http://articles.latimes.com/2001/aug/14/news/cl-33980 (published 14 August 2001; accessed 21 April 2014).

[26] Ahmadi Muslims have viewed their Indian founder Ghulam Ahmad (1835–1908) as the Christian Messiah and the Islamic Mahdi, the bringer of peace and justice to the world. The Ahmadi belief that Ghulam Ahmad was a prophet has drawn disapproval from many Muslims considering the central mainstream Islamic belief that Muhammad is the final prophet (Curtis, *Muslims in America*, 31).

[27] Shahina Bashir, "Muslim Women Develop Sisterhood Through Sports," http://www.examiner.com/article/muslim-women-develop-sisterhood-through-sports (posted 18 April 2013; accessed 21 April 2014).

Though in some Islamic nations, individuals continue to strongly oppose female athletic participation, a female-only event in America such as the Regional Sports Tournament has its share of counterparts in the twenty-first-century Muslim world. The mother of them all is the Islamic Countries Women Sport Games, held every four years[28] in order to provide Muslim women with a chance to compete internationally without compromising Islamic principles. Organized by the Iranian-based Islamic Countries Women Sport Federation, precautions are taken to ensure the Games are devoid of male presence, whether athletes, officials, referees, coaches, or spectators, and no portion of the event is broadcast as a further step to keep the male gaze completely at bay. The Games grew from eleven participating Islamic nations in its first installment in 1993 to twenty-three in 1997. Non-Muslims began participating in the Games in 2005, constituting a small but symbolically large portion of the 1,587 athletes from forty-two countries taking part in eighteen different sports, some of which included special competitions for disabled athletes. A smaller-scale female-only multi-sport event took its inaugural flight in 2011 in Abu Dhabi, where 350 athletes engaged in seven sports at the Gulf Cooperation Council (GCC) Women's Games.[29] These sportswomen came from every GCC nation besides Saudi Arabia, an absence reflecting the Kingdom's historically tight leash on female sports participation. This Saudi leash has been among the Islamic world's tautest; however, loosening is underway. Perhaps not as intensely as a sandstorm but more stiffly than a zephyr, changing winds blew through Saudi air in 2012 when two women, a judo athlete and an 800-meter runner from California with dual Saudi and American citizenship, became the first females to represent the Kingdom at an Olympic Games.

[28] The Games were not held in 2001. Scheduled to take place in Pakistan, the first time outside of Iran, organizers were forced to cancel the Games due to lack of sponsorship and other financial difficulties.

[29] Mohammed al-Mahmood, general secretary of the Abu Dhabi Sports Council, proclaimed that the long-term objective of the GCC Women's Games is to "encourage all the ladies in the [Gulf] to participate in sports... We have the talent and this talent needs to be well trained so they can achieve their targets, win medals, and raise the flag of the country in international competition" (quoted in Amara, *Sport, Politics and Society in the Arab World*, 118).

Saudi winds were again stirred in 2014 when, in response to high obesity rates among Saudi women, the government advisory Shura Council called on the Saudi education ministry to lift a ban on sports for girls at state-run schools, provided that strict rules for dress and gender segregation are followed. Cleric Abdullah Al Dawood left no doubt about his opinion, tweeting that "these steps will end in infidelity and prostitution."[30] Dawood's cries were not those of a lone voice in the desert; other Saudi Islamic scholars sounded similar alarms. Yet in line with a number of twenty-first-century Saudi developments granting more rights to its female citizens,[31] a chorus calling for Saudi female athletic change ultimately drowned out these alarms.

This Saudi snapshot of strident opposition to female athletic participation juxtaposed with increasing sporting opportunities for women and girls captures the climate of some Muslim American communities. Often this contrast finds older Muslims on one side of the fence and a younger generation on the other. Northeastern University student Omar Abdelkader provided invaluable insight into such intergenerational difference by discussing an example of second- and third-generation Muslim American immigrants seeking to adapt the Islam of their parents in light of their American surroundings, while doing so in a way these younger Muslims consider to reside squarely within the framework of overarching Islamic principles. Abdelkader described a highlight of his week, when he and his Boston-area Muslim male and female friends get together on Sunday mornings to play flag football. Abdelkader declared,

> Many may view Islam as an ultraconservative, male-dominant religion in which women and men are always completely separated. This may have been the case for older-generation Muslims and may unfortunately still be the case in certain cultures. But this is not an accurate repre-

[30] Quoted in "Physical Education for Saudi Girls Stirs Debate," *Muslim Women in Sports*, http://muslimwomeninsports.blogspot.com (posted 15 April 2014; accessed 8 May 2014).

[31] In 2009, for example, Norah al-Faiz was appointed deputy minister for education, and in 2014 thirty women joined the Shura Council, a consultative body of 150 members.

sentation of what Islam is. We as the new generation of Muslims are looking to dispel these false notions about our way of life.[32]

Abdelkader stated that he and his friends negotiate a space between conservative and liberal extremes by having men and women play together, but taking measures to keep opposite-gender touching to an absolute minimum. Girls are split up on opposing squads and only guard one another, and Abdelkader emphasized that even if this protocol were not in place, by pulling a flag instead of tackling, significant contact never occurs. Abdelkader acknowledged that many Muslim Americans would state that mixed-gender flag football steps out of Islamic bounds since males and females past puberty should never play sports together under any circumstances. He presented his perspective on the matter, though, by pronouncing,

> There are no Islamic rulings via the example of the Prophet Muhammad (peace be upon him), or in other Islamic teachings that forbid male and female non-sexual interactions. That includes playing sports with one another. The Prophet Muhammad (peace be upon him) was known to race with his wife, Aisha (God's blessings upon her), for fun. Although not every male and female is related or married on the playing field, it is well understood between all males and females participating that they are playing in a respectful manner that does not violate any Islamic decrees.[33]

For a group of young Boston Muslims, co-ed flag football brings a new color to the Muslim sporting palette, providing an athletic opportunity for females that, according to these young Muslims, matches nicely with Islamic principles.

As more Muslim women play sports in Saudi Arabia, Boston, or any other location, questions regarding appropriate athletic attire inevitably arise. Some types of traditional Islamic dress are extremely restrictive in terms of athletic activity. In their study of sports among Muslim women in Norway, Kristin Walseth and Kari Fasting quote women who find it nearly impossible to play sports while wearing a krimar, a garment that

---

[32] Omar Abdelkader, personal e-mail to author, 19 February 2015.
[33] Ibid.

covers the hair and chest.[34] For some female Muslim athletes, however, the restrictiveness of traditional dress is a non-issue, since they choose to dress just like their non-Muslim competitors. Persuaded that the Qur'an does not prohibit women from competing in front of a mixed-gender audience while wearing Western-style sportswear, Algerian 1992 1,500-meter Olympic gold medalist Hassiba Boulmerka ran before the world's watching eyes in a tank top and shorts, much to the dismay of a cohort of compatriots who labeled Boulmerka an immoral and corrupt woman and issued death threats that compelled her to move to Europe.[35] For many Muslim women, on the other hand, Boulmerka's option is not an option. Based on their personal understanding of Islamic teachings, or required by the laws of an Islamic land or the dictates of a family member, a significant proportion of Muslim women would not join Boulmerka in competing uncovered.[36] Fortunately for these women, the twenty-first-century Muslim sportswoman can reap the rewards of a new industry that develops garb that maintains modesty codes while maximizing comfort and mobility. Sprinter Ruqaya Al Ghasara served as a virtual billboard for this industry in 2004 and 2008, decked out in a full-body covering designed to minimize air resistance at the Athens and Beijing Olympic Games. As a covered woman going for the gold, Al Ghasara recognized she was representing more than just her home country of Bahrain. She proclaimed, "I have a great desire to show that there are no problems with wearing these clothes. Wearing a veil proves that Muslim

---

[34] Kristin Walseth and Kari Fasting, "Islam's View on Physical Activity and Sport: Egyptian Women Interpreting Islam," *International Review for the Sociology of Sport* 38/1 (2003): 54.

[35] A similar situation was faced by eighteen-year-old Sania Mirza from India, who was provided with heavy police protection at a tournament in Kolkata after receiving threats due to playing in sleeveless shirts and shorts. Mirza considered ending her tennis career in 2008 because of these threats but chose to stay away from tournaments in her home country instead (Coakley, *Sports in Society*, 527–28).

[36] An expression of this variety is documented by Wirdati Radzi, whose book represents a diversity of opinions about hijab and sports based on research she conducted during the 22nd Southeast Asian Games in Hanoi in 2003 (Wirdati Mohammad Radzi, *Muslim Women and Sports in the Malay World: The Crossroads of Modernity and Faith* (Chiang Mai, Thailand: Silkworm, 2006)).

women face no obstacles and encourages them to compete in sport."[37] Inspired by such an example and supplied by sartorial innovations, athletic doors are open for Muslim women to play comfortably and competitively while conforming to Islamic dress codes.

Yet, in some cases, Muslim women have passed through a recently opened door only to find another locked by an international sports governing body. Arguing that a player could incur serious injury if her headscarf was pulled in the course of play, the international soccer federation FIFA announced in 2007 what came to be known as its "hijab ban" in international games. The prohibition slide tackled a large number of players and teams, perhaps none more injuriously than the Iranian women's national team, which forfeited qualifying matches for the 2012 Olympics due to the ban. Effects also trickled down to the local level in countries where youth soccer organizations chose to follow FIFA's lead. In separate instances, nine-year-old and eleven-year-old Canadian girls were forced to watch their teammates from the sidelines after resolving not to remove their headscarves, and a fifteen-year-old from Quebec was told she could no longer referee if she continued to sport her hijab during games.[38] Whistles were blown against the ban with increasing intensity, and FIFA overturned it in 2012. FIFA vice-president Prince Ali bin Al-Hussein of Jordan had a heavy hand in this reversal, yet no amount of persuasion on his part may have convinced fellow FIFA leaders to overturn the ban if not for the development of a headscarf specially designed to alleviate safety concerns. After testing several prototype possibilities, FIFA favored a headscarf created by a Montreal fashion designer that, thanks to a magnetic system, can be opened and released instantly if pulled from anywhere around the neck.

Though the FIFA prohibition has grabbed the most headlines, other international sporting agencies have followed suit in sidelining Muslim

---

[37] Quoted in Coakley, *Sports in Society*, 528.

[38] Andy Radia, "Rayane Benatti, 9-Year-Old Quebec Girl Banned from Soccer Game for Wearing Hijab," Yahoo! News, https://ca.news.yahoo.com/blogs/canada-politics/9-old-quebec-girl-banned-soccer-game-wearing-182157253.html (posted 10 July 2012; accessed 8 May 2014).

female athletes because of their attire. The International Boxing Association prevented competitors from entering the ring in hijab until changing course for the 2012 Olympics, and for a while it seemed that one of the two aspiring Saudi female Olympians would not be competing in London, having overcome objections within her home country but about to be brought down by the International Judo Federation. Stating concern for Wojdan Ali Seraj Abdulrahim Shaherkani's safety, the IJF announced she would not be allowed to compete in the Olympics while wearing hijab. Fortunately for Shaherkani, a compromise was hammered out just days before the Games. The IJF permitted her to compete wearing a black swimming cap, a condition she and Saudi officials found acceptable. Shaherkani's story resembles a weightlifting saga starring a Muslim American athlete. Born in the United States to Pakistani parents, Kulsoom Abdullah became the first weightlifter to compete at the international level while wearing hijab when she represented Pakistan at the 2011 World Weightlifting Championships. The Ph.D.-holding computer engineer subsequently qualified for the American Open, but was told she could not participate unless she wore the standard singlet donned by other competitors. The bearers of bad news were U.S.A. Weightlifting officials, who identified the problem not to be Abdullah's headscarf but an International Weightlifting Federation requirement that competitive attire must not cover the elbows or knees. This regulation was in place to keep lifters from gaining an unfair advantage by hiding a support mechanism on a body joint and to help judges correctly determine whether a lifter's elbows and knees are locked. Because of this rule, U.S.A. Weightlifting officials rejected Abdullah's request to take part in the American Open clad in loose pants, a long-sleeve Under Armour shirt with a short-sleeve loose t-shirt on top, and a headscarf. Dismayed by this rejection, Abdullah insisted, "I want to be able to compete and follow my faith at the same time. My faith and desire to compete in Olympic lifting are not mutually exclusive. I should not be excluded from participating based on dress restrictions of my faith."[39] The lifter got a lift from the Council on

[39] "Lifting Covered FAQ," http://www.liftingcovered.com (accessed 24 April 2014). Abdullah points out that "Olympic Lifting" is the name of her sport, consist-

American-Islamic Relations, who took up her cause. U.S.A. Weightlifting responded to CAIR's calls for change and allowed Abdullah to compete in the American Open, and her initial frustration turned even further to joy when the IWF modified its dress regulations because of her protest. The IWF now allows lifters to wear body-length unitards, albeit tight-fitting ones, which Abdullah considers to be an acceptable compromise to balance weightlifting's technical rules with Islamic dress standards.

While not the subject of international governing body restrictions, swimming has provided a pool of challenges for Muslim women and girls. One option for swimmers is a full-body suit complete with head covering such as the Bodykini,[40] but as University of Delaware student Madinah Wilson pointed out, this option has its difficulties. Wilson stated that she was deterred from swimming for her high school team by the exorbitant price of a full-body suit and also by the adverse effect this kind of suit has on a swimmer's speed.[41] Standing as arguably an even greater challenge, for a large number of Muslim women Islamic modesty requires refraining from swimming in the presence of men, even if wearing a full-body suit.[42] Efforts to ensure that Muslim females can swim in

ing of the snatch as well as clean-and-jerk lifts, not a reference to her competing at the Olympic level (ibid.).

[40] According to its website, the Bodykini Muslim swimsuit "has been designed to respect Islamic values and aims to enhance the lifestyle of active Muslim women. Islamic women can now enjoy wearing our modest swimming suits and participate in water sports, swim in the pool or at the beach, or simply relax in the jacuzzi. Our Muslim swimwear is especially designed to enhance athletic performance while upholding the Koranic principle of modesty by only exposing face, hands, and feet. The Bodykini provides protection for women who prefer to limit their exposure to the sun's harmful rays. The Bodykini performs well during active swimming and is generously proportioned to provide comfort, allowing maximum movement whilst in or out of the water" ("Bodykini Modest Sportswear," http://www.bodykini.com/ (accessed 11 March 2015)).

[41] Madinah Wilson, personal interview, 19 February 2014, Newark DE.

[42] Monika Stodolska and Jennifer Livengood note that according to interviews with Muslim American women, "Participation in activities such as volleyball, softball, soccer, and karate did not require any particular adaptations on the part of Muslim women, other than wearing sweatpants and scarves. Swimming, however,

isolation from men have stirred the waters in a few nations where Muslims are in the minority. In Finland, for example, the setting aside of specified female-only hours at a public Helsinki pool was temporarily canceled due to objection from non-Muslim Finns who wanted to finish the practice completely.[43] In the United States, some Americans were troubled by a St. Paul, Minnesota YMCA partnership with a local police department to hold a swim group exclusively for Somali American girls. Offering instruction in basic swimming skills for girls aged five through seventeen, organizers left no stone unturned to make sure the hour-long weekly sessions would have absolutely no male onlookers. With female lifeguards and locked men's locker room doors, the pool's location on the YMCA's windowless third floor provided swimmers and their parents with extra assurance that male eyes would not be fixed upon the pool. Given this opportunity to swim apart from men, participants and their parents expressed deep appreciation for the program, noting it supplied these girls with a rare chance to learn swimming skills and boost their self-confidence while upholding Islamic modesty norms. A mother named Ubah Ali sang the program's praises, mentioning that the alternative for her twelve-year-old daughter to learn to swim in a female-only setting would have been lessons at 5 in the morning.[44] Fox News, on the other hand, intoned a very different tune. During a December 2013 episode of "Fox and Friends," anchor Heather Nauert followed a report about the swim group by warning, "Sharia law is changing everything... The classes are now starting across the Midwest."[45] Promising that Fox

appeared to pose significant problems for informants" (Monika Stodolska and Jennifer S. Livengood, "The Influence of Religion on the Leisure Behavior of Immigrant Muslims in the United States," *Journal of Leisure Research* 38/3 (2006): 308–309). These problems, though, could be greatly alleviated by setting up female-only times at pools, which interviewees said "would significantly reduce their constraints on participation" (ibid.).

[43] Nussbaum, *The New Religious Intolerance*, 5–6.

[44] Nicole Norfleet, "St. Paul YMCA and Police Start Somali Girls Swim Group," *Star Tribune*, http://m.startribune.com/?id=232082231 (published 18 November 2013; accessed 22 April 2014).

[45] Quoted in Travis Waldron, "Fox News on Swim Class for Muslim Girls: 'Sharia Law Is Changing Everything,'"

News would "keep watching this story for you,"[46] Nauert intimated that Americans must remain vigilant against the possible overflow of Islamic dictates beyond the St. Paul pool, spilling throughout an unsuspecting American society.

Nauert's warning sounded similar to the clamoring against a different incident involving the setting aside of public space for Muslim American females to engage in athletic activity apart from the presence of men. Harvard University officials granted the 2008 request of a group of Muslim female students to prohibit men from using a university gym for six hours each week. From 3–5 P.M. on Mondays and 8–10 A.M. on Tuesdays and Thursdays, male patrons and staff were barred from the Quadrangle Recreational Athletic Center. In support of the measure, Harvard College Women's Center director Susan Marine contended the university would fail its Muslim female population in its "moral and ethical responsibility to make sure our students can stay healthy"[47] if arrangements for female-only exercise space were not made. Marine added that the measure would cause merely minimal inconvenience for Harvard men, since it entailed only six of the seventy hours when Harvard's least-used gym was open and because other university gyms were available to men during these six hours. Some members of the Harvard community were unpersuaded by these arguments and sought to sink Marine's position. Student Lucy Caldwell opined in a *Harvard Crimson* editorial, "I think that it's incorrect in a college setting to institute a policy in which half of the campus gets wronged or denied a resource that's supposed to be for everyone."[48] This story, too, found its way onto Fox News, where Caldwell debated her position with a Council on American-Islamic Relations representative.

http://thinkprogress.org/sports/2013/12/02/3009111/fox-news-fond-muslims-participating-sports/ (posted 2 December 2013; accessed 22 April 2014).

[46] Ibid.

[47] Quoted in "Harvard Gym Accommodates Muslim Women," *USA Today*, http://usatoday30.usatoday.com/news/health/2008-03-04-muslim-gym_N.htm (posted 4 March 2008; accessed 8 May 2014).

[48] Ibid.

In a Harvard gym, on a flag football field, or within any other athletic setting, Muslim American women and girls have a great deal to gain from sports staking a significant claim in the configuration of their lives. As Christa Kleindienst-Cachay avows about athletic participation among Turkish Muslim girls and young women in Germany, sports for Muslim American females can provide "an enormous enrichment to their lives" for a host of reasons, including "developing friendly relationships through sport" and empowering them to "re-define the relationship of gender, bodies, and faith."[49] Such perks make Muslim women and girls themselves the chief beneficiaries of sporting opportunities for Muslim females in the United States, yet a significant subsidiary bridging benefit also blooms. As a greater number of Muslim American women and girls play sports, non-Muslims are likely to increasingly regard Muslim females in their country not as exotic milquetoasts, but as strong fellow human beings sharing common American interests. Continuing her aforementioned depiction of the young Somali American woman whose mother banned her from basketball, Shabana Mir writes, "The woman who blocked and dribbled the ball also labored to shatter stereotypes about weak, timid, secluded, and immobile Muslim women."[50] With tongue planted firmly in cheek, Mir goes on to say, "Surely Muslim femaleness and basketball were opposed to each other. Surely the very *American* qualities we see in the sportswoman—mobility, flexibility, and freedom—are not qualities the immigrant and Muslim woman can or should share."[51] Like the damage done by Jewish athletes to the stereotype of the weak, anti-American Jew, when non-Muslims learn about a

[49] Christa Kleindienst-Cachay, "'Balancing Between the Cultures...' Sports and Physical Activities of Muslim Girls and Women in Germany," in *Muslim Women and Sport*, ed. Tansin Benn, Gertrud Pfister, and Haifaa Jawad, 92–108 (Abingdon, UK: Routledge, 2011) 101–102. Kleindienst-Cachay declares, "With the women's decision to go on doing sport at the onset of puberty, often in spite of their parents' initial opposition, and to tie themselves to the German system of sport and education, the girls made a conscious decision in favour of working towards excellence in sport, and becoming totally different types of role models than their families could have anticipated" (ibid., 102).

[50] Mir, *Muslim American Women on Campus*, 2.

[51] Ibid.

superlative Muslim sportswoman such as Ibtihaj Muhammad, this African-American fencer from New Jersey can poke lasting holes in the caricature of the fainthearted Muslim woman clashing with American values. Poised to earn a spot on the 2016 United States Olympic team, the hijab-wearing Muhammad is one of the world's greatest at her sport. Admittedly, most Americans who hear the word "fencing" may think of a barrier marking boundaries rather than a sport. Yet, if she does indeed become the first-ever Muslim American female Olympian, stories about Muhammad are bound to grab national attention, perhaps especially because of the intriguing connection between her Islamic dress and her initial attraction to her sport. Muhammad recalls, "If I played tennis, if I played soccer or if I ran track, and my teammates wore shorts or short sleeves, I would always have to wear long sleeves or long pants, and it was hard for me as a kid, because I didn't feel like I fit in."[52] When she discovered fencing, Muhammad finally found a sport in which, as a covered Muslim woman, she felt like she belongs, since competitors wear full-body and head coverings. According to Muhammad, "Once I put my mask on—that's the beauty, I feel, of my sport—it almost becomes an equal playing field. People look at me as an athlete, and solely as an athlete, as opposed to being a woman or a Muslim or being black. And I love it."[53]

[52] Quoted in Jennifer Lazuta, "American Female Muslim Athlete Inspires Girls in Dakar," *Voice of America,*
http://www.voanews.com/content/first-american-female-muslim-athlete-inspires-girls-in-dakar/1846731.html (posted 7 February 2014; accessed 22 April 2014).
[53] Ibid.

6

Professional Muslim Athletes

Young Muslims around the world look up to you as heroes. You inspire them to dream big and work hard. And when all Americans take pride in your achievements, it underlines what is best in our nation.[1]

The setting was the White House, the speaker was Secretary of State Hillary Clinton. In honor of the Ramadan-ending holiday Eid al-Fitr, the White House guest list included football players from Fordson High School, Muslim college sportsmen and sportswomen,[2] and two stars of the previous chapter, Kulsoom Abdullah and Ibtihaj Muhammad. Also among the guests of honor were pro basketball player Kenneth Faried and football pro Ephraim Salaam. In exploring bonding and bridging through Muslim American sports, the warp and woof of this book's investigation will entail local-level amateur athletic activities. First, though, the present chapter spotlights pro athletes such as Faried and Salaam.

As stated by the Secretary of State, Muslim youth may view fellow followers of Islam who have reached the pinnacle of their sport's mountain as heroes worthy of emulation. Hearing about the Abdullah brothers fasting during a rigorous NFL training camp day might ramp up the resolve of a Muslim high school player to push on without fluids at his afterschool football practice. Reading about NBA All-Star Shareef Abdur-

---

[1] Quoted in Farah Pandith, "Eid Reception Recognizes American Muslims' Achievements in Athletics," U.S. Department of State. http://blogs.state.gov/ stories/2011/09/09/eid-reception-recognizes-american-muslims-achievements-athletics (posted 9 September 2011; accessed 21 April 2014).

[2] These college athletes were Oday Aboushi (football player at the University of Virginia), Noor Amr (basketball player at Coe College), Omar Kaddurah (long-distance runner at Georgetown University), Sarah Kureshi (middle-distance runner who was the sole American competitor in the 4th Islamic World Games in Tehran), Dahir Nasser (basketball player at California Polytechnic University, Pomona), and Natalie Zeenni (soccer player at the University of New Mexico).

Rahim never missing a salat prayer might trigger a young Muslim hoopster to try to be like Shareef and prostrate five times a day. Moreover, pro Muslim athletes are in prime position to make a difference in the psychological well-being of Muslim American youth. According to former European league pro Ibrahim Jaaber, "Especially in this time we're in, the youth are in dire need of good Muslim examples, because there is an identity crisis that we suffer from, not knowing where we fit in in the social dynamics of the greater society."[3] From Jaaber's perspective, pro Muslim athletes can alleviate some of this angst and help bolster young Muslims' commitment to their faith by modeling the maintenance of Islamic devotion while playing on American sports' biggest stages.

These boons for bonding form a fundamental fragment of the important impact of Muslim professional athletic activity, an impact that features bridging as well. As Muslims excel at sports that reside deep within American society, the proposition that Islam and America fundamentally clash might become increasingly mulled over in non-Muslim minds and lose much of its lifeblood. As non-Muslims celebrate their home team's triumph sealed by a Muslim rookie's buzzer-beating three-pointer, their curiosity might be piqued to learn more about this phenom and the religion he follows. University of Minnesota student Amer Sassila gave his take on what may transpire when a non-Muslim fan wants to learn more about a Muslim athlete he admires, referring to basketball legend Hakeem Olajuwon and the community service and generosity that have defined his life due to his Islamic faith. Likening the process to the gradual "piece by piece" dismantling of the Berlin Wall rather than "an immediate window-shattering break,"[4] Sassila asserted that negative stereotypes of Islam can fall as Muslim athletes such as Olajuwon demonstrate athletic excellence combined with laudable character traits that are worlds apart from images of Islamic extremism.

In connecting pro Muslim athletes with bonding and bridging, I make no claim of absolute association. I enter a speculative realm, not one of guarantee. I present bonding and bridging as potential consequences, not certain results, of Muslims playing sports at a professional

---

[3] Ibrahim Jaaber, personal interview, 18 February 2014, Somerset NJ.
[4] Amer Sassila, personal interview, 26 April 2014, Minneapolis MN.

level, just as I claim of any Muslim American athletic activity. Neither do I propose that these connections are always intentional. At times, Muslim sportsmen have made conscious choices to conduct themselves in a manner that might inspire Muslim fans to devote themselves more strongly to Islamic piety and fellowship or might lead non-Muslim fans to take a step towards seeing Islam in a more favorable light. At other times, such bonding and bridging may result from an athlete's actions without any intention on his or her part to foster these results. According to Council on American-Islamic Relations spokesman Ibrahim Hooper, "As with other people of faith, Muslim athletes don't have to wear their religion on their sleeve. These athletes will tell you their first objective is to win games, not hearts and minds."[5] As Hooper suggests, dawah may be far removed from a pro Muslim athlete's mind. Executing a pick and roll or running out of bounds to preserve precious fourth-quarter seconds may be more pressing concerns. Reflecting this reality, this chapter makes bonding and bridging only one aspect of the tales it tells about pro Muslim athletes. In some of these tales, connections with bonding and bridging are brought to the fore, while in others these connections remain in the shadows.

The national pastime receives negligible notice amidst these tales, since Major League Baseball has seen only one Muslim player,[6] a shortstop with a short stay of three years in the league. Sam Khalifa found himself in the Pittsburgh Pirates' starting lineup for part of his brief big league career, but he found his name nowhere near the top of lists of All-

[5] Quoted in Omar Sacirbey, "A Source of Pride and Hope," Religion News Service, http://m.spokesman.com/stories/2007/feb/03/a-source-of-pride-and-hope/ (published 3 February 2007; accessed 22 April 2014). On the other side of the coin are Muslim Americans who "want to see more Muslim athletes playing public roles," such as Muzammil Mohamed Stevens, president of Muslim Athletes International Inc., an organization that supports and recognizes Muslim athletes. Stevens declares, "If we can use sports as a vehicle to be an example, then that's what we should do" (quoted in ibid.).

[6] As of 2015, there are two Muslim executives in Major League Baseball. Farhan Zaidi became the first Muslim general manager of any American pro sports franchise when he was named Los Angeles Dodgers GM in November 2014. Shiraz Rehman is Assistant General Manager of the Chicago Cubs.

Star Game vote recipients. Khalifa retired from his rather inconspicuous baseball career in 1990 after the murder of his father, the controversial founder of an Arizona mosque.[7] Like Major League Baseball, the National Hockey League has had sparse Islamic representation, with just four Muslims having laced up skates for NHL teams. Notably, though, one of these four may be destined for stardom,[8] taking his game far beyond what Khalifa accomplished in big league ballparks. A Canadian Muslim of Lebanese descent, Nazem Kadri was selected by the Toronto Maple Leafs as the seventh overall pick in the 2009 draft. Kadri noted the significance of his unique position as a Muslim first-round draft pick, telling reporters, "A lot of Muslim kids are going to start playing hockey because they see someone like them be successful in that area."[9] Kadri also acknowledged that these youth might encounter bumpy ice as hockey-playing Muslims, akin to what he faced en route to the NHL. Unlike Khalifa, who claimed that teammates good-naturedly called him "the Shaikh" but never exhibited prejudice because of his religion,[10] Kadri reports having anti-Islamic comments hurled his way from opposing players and fans at different stages of his hockey development. Nonetheless, Kadri finds a silver lining in these Islamophobic clouds. He points to these acerbic comments as sources of inspiration to push himself harder to "prove he belongs"[11] in the sport that he loves.

[7] Khalifa's father Rashad founded the Masjid of Tucson in response to what he believed was a midlife revelation that he was a messenger of God. His teachings about the Qur'an were often steeped in numerology.

[8] The other three Muslim NHL players are Canadian Ramzi Abid (member of the Phoenix Coyotes, Pittsburgh Penguins, Atlanta Thrashers, and Nashville Predators from 2000–2007), Canadian Alain Nasreddine (member of the Chicago Blackhawks, Montreal Canadiens, New York Islanders, and Pittsburgh Penguins from 1998–2008), and Russian Nail Yakupov (with the Edmonton Oilers since 2012).

[9] Quoted in Michael Traikos, "Muslim Nazem Kadri Is Emerging from the Background as One of the Best," *The National*, http://www.thenational.ae/sport/north-american-sport/nhl-muslim-nazem-kadri-is-emerging-from-the-background-as-one-of-the-best (published 5 April 2013; accessed 23 April 2014).

[10] Alex Remington, "Why Aren't There More Muslims in Baseball?" www.fangraphs.com/blogs/why-arent-there-more-muslims-in-baseball/ (posted 8 August 2013; accessed 22 April 2014).

[11] Traikos, "Muslim Nazem Kadri Is Emerging."

Muslim Boxers

Compared to baseball or hockey, Muslim presence has been much more strongly established in three other professional sports in America. The remainder of this chapter looks at Muslim pros in boxing, basketball, and football, focusing on Muslims born in the United States, with one foreign-born Muslim NBA star thrown into the mix. I begin in the ring, noting the oldest boxer ever to win and defend a world title and to be recognized by all three major boxing federations as champion of a weight division. Taking the World Boxing Association light heavyweight crown in 2014 at the venerable age of forty-nine, Bernard Hopkins boasts the additional distinction of possessing at least one boxing federation middleweight belt from 1994 to 2005. Hopkins has never been one to draw attention to his faith, yet Muslim sports websites refer to his commitment to Islamic piety. One declares that Hopkins's "nickname may be The Executioner, but he remains humbled by his duties as a devout Muslim."[12] Hopkins converted to Islam while in prison, thus mirroring a major crossroads in the life journey of another boxing behemoth, Mike Tyson. Among the most recognizable individuals on the planet during his seemingly invincible late 1980s boxing prime, the first heavyweight to simultaneously hold World Boxing Association, World Boxing Council, and International Boxing Federation titles pummeled opponents into submission. Tyson then submitted to God in prison, where he was doing time for a rape charge. Iron Mike's 1995 release was met by a media onslaught covering his newfound Islamic faith. Images of Tyson wearing a white kufi (prayer cap) were beamed across the globe. Tyson further brought his adopted faith to the fore upon defeating World Boxing Council titleholder Frank Bruno the next year. After the referee determined Bruno had taken enough punishment and called off the fight in the third round, Tyson dropped to his knees in the center of the ring and bowed three times to God. Despite such public display of devotion,

---

[12] "Bernard Hopkins: An American Muslim Boxing Success Story," *The Muslim Observer*, http://muslimmedianetwork.com/mmn/?p=6362 (posted 17 June 2010; accessed 22 April 2014).

Tyson told an *Esquire* reporter in 1996, "I'm a very private Muslim,"[13] stating he prays daily and fasts during Ramadan not to draw attention to himself but to strengthen his awareness of God and submit to his Creator. Akbar Ahmed speaks to Tyson's religious devotion by writing that he donated $250,000 to help a Las Vegas Muslim community construct a new mosque building, where on occasion he vacuums the prayer carpet.[14] Statements of Tyson's fidelity to Islamic piety may raise some eyebrows, especially considering a series of highly publicized events both inside and outside the ring following his conversion. Tyson repeatedly punched Orlin Norris after the end of the first-round bell in their 1996 fight, rendering Norris unable to continue the bout. A year later, fans witnessed one of the most bizarre events in boxing history, when Tyson bit off a chunk of Evander Holyfield's ear in the heat of battle in the ring. Tyson then found himself behind bars once again, this time for nine months, for assaulting two motorists after a traffic accident in 1998.

Taking the boxing world by storm, Tyson may have defined the sport for nearly a decade, but another Muslim fighter has been the face of boxing for at least a generation. A Muhammad Ali biographer pronounces, "There have been more words written about, and photographs taken of, and more attention lavished upon Ali than any athlete ever."[15] Some of these words address Ali's promotion of both bonding and bridging, describing ways in which he has inspired fellow Muslims in their faith and has given innumerable non-Muslims a more positive picture of Islam. Reflecting on Ali's influence, Deborah Caldwell declares, "As the first bona fide American celebrity to embrace the faith, Ali was a hero to millions of Muslims here and around the world. Many African-American Muslims were inspired to convert to Islam because of Ali.

---

[13] Quoted in Baker, *Playing with God*, 236.

[14] Akbar Ahmed, *Journey into America: The Challenge of Islam* (Washington DC: Brookings Institution Press, 2010) 188.

[15] Thomas Hauser, *Muhammad Ali: His Life and Times* (New York: Simon & Schuster, 2006) 9.

Now, post-September 11, he remains the most visible American Muslim celebrity."[16]

Early in his career, however, Ali was neither a hero to a large proportion of Muslim Americans nor lionized by most non-Muslims, because of his affiliation with the Nation of Islam. This exclusively African-American organization was captained by Elijah Muhammad, who steered the Nation of Islam away from mainstream Islamic belief by teaching that Black Muslims were enslaved, converted to Christianity, and brought to the New World by Whites, who were genetically bred as a devilish race. According to this teaching, God was on the verge of bringing Blacks back to Islam and restoring their rightful rule over the evil White race. From a mainstream Islamic perspective, Elijah Muhammad took his Nation of Islam ship into even deadlier waters by professing that God appeared on earth in human form, namely a man he met in Detroit named Wallace Fard. Though placed outside the pale of orthodoxy by many Muslims in America, the Nation of Islam became the lens through which a multitude of African Americans viewed and practiced Islam, attracted by Nation of Islam principles such as Black financial independence and political self-determination as well as its emphases on clean living, dignity, and discipline.[17] The Nation of Islam provided African Americans with racial pride, but to innumerable Americans the group was a cauldron of trouble rather than a fount of blessing. Considering Elijah Muhammad's call for Black separation from White society and his insistence that members put allegiance to the Nation of Islam

[16] Deborah Caldwell, "Muhammad Ali: The Reassuring Face of American Islam," in *Taking Back Islam: American Muslims Reclaim Their Faith*, ed. Michael Wolfe, 146–49 (Emmaus PA: Rodale, 2002) 147.

[17] Muhammad encouraged his followers to start and to patronize their own businesses, and he emphasized that Nation of Islam members should be "pure, hardworking, punctual, disciplined, and modestly dressed. Children were taught these values in the Nation of Islam's primary and secondary schools. Women in the organization joined the Muslim Girls Training-General Civilization Class to learn home economics, etiquette, and later, self-defense. Men joined the Fruit of Islam and practiced military drills and various religious catechisms. Men wore bow ties and dark suits; women wore robes and often a head scarf" (Curtis, *Muslims in America*, 38–39).

above allegiance to the United States,[18] Ali's conversion was no attempt to get most boxing fans in his corner. Stepping into a firestorm of criticism, Ali tried to extinguish some of these flames by encouraging Americans to see his newly adopted religious organization in a new light. After defeating Sonny Liston for the heavyweight crown in 1964, the freshly minted champ made his conversion public and proclaimed, "People brand us a hate group. They say we want to take over the country. They say we're Communists. That is not true. Followers of Allah are the sweetest people in the world. ...All they want to do is live in peace. They don't want to stir up any kind of trouble."[19] Americans were generally unpersuaded by Ali's positive portrayal. Caldwell writes that "[m]ost people were simply appalled"[20] when Ali joined the Nation of Islam, and at least for a while a number of media mavens refused to use his new name, opting for his pre-conversion name, Cassius Clay, instead. Public outrage over Ali's affiliation with the Nation of Islam flared up again three years after his conversion, as principles inspired by the organization significantly shaped his refusal to register for the Vietnam War draft,[21] which resulted in the revoking of his heavyweight title and boxing license and a sentence of five years in prison and a $10,000 fine.[22]

At the same time Americans threw him under the bus for following the Nation of Islam, Ali experienced a bumpy ride with his organization's leader. Elijah Muhammad was tickled pink by the exposure Ali gave the Nation of Islam to potential African-American converts, but he

---

[18] Muhammad instructed his followers not to vote in national elections or serve in the American military.

[19] Quoted in Hauser, *Muhammad Ali*, 82–83.

[20] Caldwell, "Muhammad Ali," 146.

[21] Ali proclaimed his opposition to serving in the Vietnam War at a Houston military induction center in April 1967. He declared to the press, "I am a member of the Black Muslims and we don't go to war unless they're declared by Allah himself" (quoted in Jay, *More Than Just a Game*, 121).

[22] Ali's title was revoked by the New York State Athletic Commission and his boxing license withdrawn because his stance was said to violate the "best interests of boxing" (quoted in ibid., 122). After three and a half years away from boxing, Ali won a lawsuit against the Boxing Commission to overturn its previous ruling.

was also green with envy due to being overshadowed by the world champion. Nation of Islam minister Jeremiah Shabazz proposed,

> When Elijah Muhammad spoke, his words were confined to whatever city he had spoken in. But Ali was a sports hero, and people wanted to know what he had to say, so his visibility and prominence were of great benefit to the Nation. His voice carried throughout the world, and that was a true blessing for us. There's no doubt, our following increased enormously, maybe a hundred percent, after he joined the Nation.[23]

Elijah Muhammad occasionally applauded Ali for acting as an ambassador of the Nation of Islam,[24] but at other times he condemned Ali and his exploits in the ring. Uncovering the ambiguity of this relationship, Maureen Smith demonstrates that although the Nation of Islam leader temporarily relaxed his strictures against professional sports[25] in order to take advantage of Ali's ability to draw droves of devotees into Nation of

[23] Quoted in Maureen Smith, "*Muhammad Speaks* and Muhammad Ali: Intersections of the Nation of Islam and Sport in the 1960s," in *With God on Their Side: Sport in the Service of Religion*, ed. Tara Magdalinski and Timothy J. L. Chandler, 177–96 (New York: Routledge, 2002) 189.

[24] Elijah Muhammad's first public reference to Ali as champion came in a March 1964 issue of *Muhammad Speaks*, in which he proclaimed, "I'm so glad that Cassius Clay admits he is a Muslim. He was able, by confessing that Allah was the God and by following Muhammad, to whip a much tougher man. ...Clay had confidence in Allah, and in me as his only Messenger. This assured his victory and left him unscarred" (ibid., 181).

[25] Muhammad wrote the following condemnation of sports in an October 1962 edition of *Muhammad Speaks*: "America, more than any other country, offers our people opportunities to engage in sports and play, which cause delinquency, murder, theft, and other forms of wicked and immoral crimes. This is due to this country's display of filthy temptations in this world of sport and play... Hundreds of millions of dollars change hands for the benefit of a few to the hurt of millions, and suffering from the lack of good education, with their last few pennies they help the already helped to try winning with these gambling 'scientists' who have prepared a game of chance that the poor suckers have only one chance out of nine hundred to win. Therefore, the world of sports is causing tremendous evils... [S]port and play (games of chance) take away the remembrance of Allah (God) and the doing of good" (quoted in ibid., 179–80). Muhammad spoke against sports alongside "secular entertainment, sexual promiscuity, obesity, tobacco, and other vices" (quoted in ibid., 180).

Islam doors, Muhammad pulled no punches against Ali in his publication *Muhammad Speaks*. Following Ali's fight against George Chuvalo, for example, in which the champ responded to his opponent fighting below the belt by dealing Chuvalo a flurry of blows deemed excessively violent by some observers, Muhammad urged his followers to see this act as an exhibition of Ali depending on his own "natural ability" instead of on "his previous open acknowledgement and dependence upon Allah and His messenger."[26] Muhammad went on to vent, "We cannot back one who will not acknowledge the Divine Guidance of Allah and His messenger from which all strength derives which has made such success possible."[27] The Nation of Islam head ended up removing his backing of Ali completely. Muhammad suspended the champ from the Nation of Islam and revoked his bestowal of the name "Muhammad Ali" after the boxer told sportscaster Howard Cosell that his return to the ring after his Vietnam War draft saga was motivated by a need for money. According to Muhammad, Ali's statement revealed that he had irremediably placed his trust in the enemy of God for his survival. Knocked out by his leader, Ali would need to search for a different religious ring.

This search ended up with Ali remaining within the vast arena of Islam, this time in its mainstream Sunni version. Ali's second Islamic conversion, eleven years after his first, was strongly influenced by Elijah Muhammad's son Wallace, who repudiated his father's tenets that Whites are a devilish race and that God appeared on earth. Wallace distinguished himself further from his father by calling for the American flag to be displayed in mosques and by instructing his followers to base their understanding of Islam on the Qur'an and Hadith instead of an alleged modern-day prophet such as his father. Looking back on his second conversion, Ali declared, "Wallace taught us the true meaning of the Qur'an. He showed us that color don't [sic] matter. He taught that we're responsible for our own lives and it's no good to blame our problems on other people."[28] Incorporating this understanding of Islam into his own worldview, Ali came to regard the relationship between his faith

[26] Quoted in ibid., 187.
[27] Ibid.
[28] Quoted in Hauser, *Muhammad Ali*, 294.

and his country no longer as antithetical but in much more harmonious terms. William Baker writes that following his second conversion, Ali "evolved from an angry rebel to a patriotic, conservative American."[29] Thanks to this metamorphosis, as Zareena Grewal affirms, for Americans of all faiths Ali has become "a national icon, the quintessential American,"[30] light years away from what most Americans thought of Ali amidst his years with the Nation of Islam. Illustrative of this national icon status, Ali was granted the honor of representing his country by lighting the cauldron flame at the 1996 Summer Olympics in Atlanta, and the United States Congress eulogized Ali with a glowing resolution on his sixty-fifth birthday. Among a long list of statements feting his athletic and humanitarian achievements, the resolution announced that "Ali is a devout Sunni Muslim and travels the world over, working for hunger and poverty relief, supporting education efforts of all kinds, promoting adoption, and encouraging people to respect and better understand one another."[31] According to the math of Talib Abdur-Rashid, imam of Harlem's Mosque of the Islamic Brotherhood, such altruism outside the ring plus Ali's accomplishments inside it equals immeasurable bridging influence. Addressing this equation in the climate of post-9/11 America, Abdur-Rashid stated, "A lot of Americans turn on their TV sets these days and see this about 'Islam,' and that about 'Muslims'—and they don't have a human face to relate what they see and hear about Islam. But over the past thirty-five years, Muhammad Ali was that human face the average person in America came to know and associate with being a Muslim."[32] In an era when the face of Islam is commonly conceptualized as covered with rancor and violent intent, Ali's visage has symbolized love for humankind in many Americans' mind's eye. Ali has embraced this role as an ambassador of Islam, striving to translate his high profile into opportunities to put Islamophobia out for the count and

[29] Baker, *Playing with God*, 223.

[30] Zareena Grewal, "Lights, Camera, Suspension: Freezing the Frame on the Mahmoud Abdul-Rauf-Anthem Controversy," *Souls: A Critical Journal of Black Politics, Culture, and Society* 9/2 (2007): 118.

[31] Quoted in Sacirbey, "A Source of Pride and Hope."

[32] Quoted in Caldwell, "Muhammad Ali," 149.

to encourage non-Muslims to consider turning to Islam in their own journeys of faith. For many years during his retirement, Ali faithfully followed a routine of autographing Islamic tracts for two hours every morning.[33] Describing this ritual to biographer Thomas Hauser, Ali remarked, "I'm not trying to convert anybody. Only God can do that. I just want to open people's minds, so they'll think about God and Islam."[34] The former world champ who in his glory days flamboyantly dubbed himself "the Greatest" completely changed his tack. Dialing down the volume, though with a similar degree of inner conviction, Ali came to name God as "the Greatest" instead.

Muslim Basketball Players

Two decades after Ali's Vietnam War draft decision led many Americans to stick him with an unpatriotic traitor tag, this label was pinned on another pro Muslim athlete, this time a member of the NBA. Known as Chris Jackson during his ascent to college basketball stardom at Louisiana State, Denver Nuggets point guard Mahmoud Abdul-Rauf took on his new name meaning "praiseworthy, merciful, and kind" after converting to Islam in 1991. Though, like any religious conversion, Abdul-Rauf's was not completely attributable to one sole cause, his Tourette's syndrome was a prime factor.[35] Prior to his conversion, Tourette's sent Abdul-Rauf searching for more structure in a life racked by disorder due to his neurological disease. Finding this structure in Islam, Abdul-Rauf told a reporter, "God has given me, through His blessing, Tourette's, and

---

[33] According to Thomas Hauser, Ali "has spent two hundred thousand dollars on books and pamphlets, which he carries in a large briefcase where he goes. 'If I just handed out pamphlets,' he explains, 'most people would throw them away. But if I sign each one and put on the person's name, people will keep them and read what the pamphlets say.' For two hours, Ali autographs religious tracts. On each one, he writes the word 'to' followed by a space and the legend 'from Muhammad Ali.' The pamphlets will go in his briefcase. Then, whoever he meets, if they want his autograph he'll ask their name, insert it in the space, and date the pamphlet beneath his signature" (Hauser, *Muhammad Ali*, 464).

[34] Quoted in ibid.

[35] Tourette's syndrome is a neurological disorder involving involuntary movements and vocalizations known as tics.

he has given me basketball and Islam to cope with Tourette's. Through basketball, I get a little peace. And through Islam I get total peace."[36] Conversion also sparked within Abdul-Rauf a rising sense of social awareness and global responsibility. Unnoticed by most fans for a while, this emerging consciousness became conspicuous in the 1995–1996 season, when Abdul-Rauf remained in the locker room or arena hallway during the pre-game National Anthem. Abdul-Rauf's protest went on without objection for over sixty games, but in March a Denver radio station caller voiced complaints. These gripes led to a morning practice television interview in which Abdul-Rauf made the blood of some of his countrymen boil. After identifying the American flag as "a symbol of oppression, of tyranny," he went on to announce, "I think this country has a long history of that. If you look at history, I don't think you can argue the facts. You can't be for God and for oppression. It's clear in the Qur'an."[37] The NBA responded to Abdul-Rauf's utterance by suspending him indefinitely without pay,[38] and allegations of disloyalty to his country and disrespect to its flag filled airwaves across the nation.[39] Scores of Americans shared the opinion of Colorado branch American Legion veterans organization commander Ed Wearing, who judged Abdul-Rauf guilty of treason and demanded that he renounce his American citizenship. Former Boston Celtics all-star and coach Tommy Heinsohn

---

[36] Quoted in Grewal, "Lights, Camera, Suspension," 112.

[37] Quoted in ibid., 113.

[38] The NBA justified its suspension based on the following league rule: "Players, coaches, and trainers are to stand and line up in a dignified posture along the sidelines or the foul line during the playing of the national anthem" (quoted in ibid., 113).

[39] In a statement released after the controversy broke, Abdul-Rauf said his decision not to participate in the national anthem was not meant to be "disrespectful to those who regard the national anthem as a sacred ceremony. It is my understanding that 100 percent honesty and sincerity is the requirement for participation in the national anthem. As such, I chose not to disrespect anyone and remain in the locker room or hallway area while the anthem was being played" (quoted in Don Lattin, "Standoff Over the National Anthem/NBA Suspension of Muslim Stirs Free-Speech Debate," http://www.sfgate.com/news/article/PAGE-ONE-Standoff-Over-the-National-Anthem-2990682.php (published 14 March 1996; accessed 22 April 2014)).

joined in the castigating chorus, asking about Abdul-Rauf, "Is he an American? Is he taking all those greenbacks with George Washington's face on them?"[40] Abdul-Rauf replied by calling his Islamic beliefs "more important than anything"[41] and expressing willingness to completely give up his sport in order not to compromise his religious convictions. As it turned out, the suspension lasted only one game. The NBA agreed to reinstate Abdul-Rauf under the condition that he stand with his teammates while praying silently during the National Anthem. Abdul-Rauf returned to the court but not to life as he had known it. Abdul-Rauf fell out of favor with Nuggets brass, who traded him in the offseason to the Sacramento Kings. Unable to find his groove in Sacramento, after two seasons with the Kings, Abdul-Rauf left the NBA to play in Turkey.

Just as damage was done to Abdul-Rauf's NBA career, perceptions of Muslim Americans took hits as well. Suspicion of Muslim American sedition was stirred up by Abdul-Rauf's saga, which led two Denver radio station disc jockeys to blare music outside a Mile High City mosque in an attempt to disrupt prayers inside. While one Muslim American author put a positive spin on the controversy by proposing that it prompted non-Muslims to interact with Muslims to inquire about Islamic beliefs,[42] Muslim Americans who spoke publicly tended to portray it as a public relations disaster for Muslims in the United States. A statement issued by the American Muslim Council, for instance, insisted that Abdul-Rauf was motivated by "very personal reasons that do not have to do

[40] Quoted in Baker, *Playing with God*, 231.
[41] Quoted in Grewal, "Lights, Camera, Suspension," 113.
[42] Asma Gull Hasan argues, "In truth, though, I think American Muslims actually came out on top in the end. For about two days, our friends, neighbors, and colleagues asked us questions about Islam. They wanted to know if it really was against our religion to stand for the flag. We had an opportunity to talk to our fellow Americans about what Islam is and what being a Muslim means" (Asma Gull Hasan, *American Muslims: The New Generation*, 2nd ed. (New York: Bloomsbury, 2002) 163). Hasan comments further, "Much good came out of the event in the end, with the radio station agreeing to apologize publicly for a period of time, to conduct seminars on Islam for their employees, and to set up an internship program for Muslim college students interested in going into broadcasting" (ibid., 165).

with Islamic beliefs."[43] Notably, as Grewal points out, nearly every spokesman who dissociated Abdul-Rauf's protest from Islamic principles was an immigrant Muslim. Grewal writes, "Abdul-Rauf's stance, although consistent with the political orientation of many African-American Muslims...perplexed many immigrant Muslims consumed by a different set of political issues, an international rather than domestic focus, and who, in large part, do not possess the cultural reference to understand Abdul-Rauf's decision in the context of a long history of American dissent."[44] Whereas immigrant and African-American Muslims have typically shared rousing acclamation for Muhammad Ali since his conversion to mainstream Islam, rifts between the two were exposed through their conflicting reactions to Abdul-Rauf's National Anthem boycott. African-American Muslims have often claimed that many immigrant Muslims do not respect them as equals in Islamic faith.[45] African-American Muslim scholar Sherman Jackson argues that the post-1965 rise in Muslim immigration "laid the foundations for an effective 'immigrant supremacy,'" in which Black converts to Islam were forced to move "from the back of the bus to the back of the camel."[46] Jackson and

---

[43] Quoted in Baker, *Playing with God*, 231.

[44] Grewal, "Lights, Camera, Suspension," 110.

[45] Aminah Beverly McCloud writes, "In an effort to prevent African Americans from defining Islam, immigrants have declared much of African-American culture inappropriate for inclusion in any definition of Islam. Using both Salafism and Wahhabism as models, transnational Muslims from South Asia and the Arabic-speaking world declared music prohibited, American clothing inappropriate, contact with Christian relatives abhorrent, and dismissed African Americans' knowledge of America as irrelevant. They then cast Islam as unknowable for those who had been Muslim for decades. Arabic was cast as an extremely difficult language and thus, indigenous Muslims could have only limited access to Islam and thus, only limited authority" (Aminah Beverly McCloud, *Transnational Muslims in American Society* (Gainesville: University Press of Florida, 2006) 132).

[46] Sherman A. Jackson, *Islam and the Blackamerican: Looking toward the Third Resurrection* (New York: Oxford University Press, 2005) 60. Jackson says that "the priorities, insights, perspectives, historical experience, and understandings of the Arabs, followed by those of other immigrant groups, were established as both normal and normative, the 'Islamicity' of the Blackamerican (and other American) Muslims being measured in terms of how intimately they identified with these" (ibid.).

other African-American Muslims have also maintained that some immigrant Muslim Americans demonstrate little concern for African-American Muslims' needs and struggles.[47] Future chapters will highlight some steps towards mending interracial rifts by way of immigrant and African-American Muslims joining together on the court or athletic field, but in the case of the Abdul-Rauf ordeal, sports served not as a mending needle but as a microscope displaying split Muslim American interracial seams.

Albeit on a much smaller scale, controversy surrounding the Islamic faith of an NBA player again reared its head about a decade after Abdul-Rauf's protest. At the center of this affair stood Shareef Abdur-Rahim, a 2002 NBA All-Star who played twelve seasons with the Vancouver Grizzlies, Atlanta Hawks, Portland Trail Blazers, and Sacramento Kings. The son of an Atlanta imam, Abdur-Rahim fasted during Ramadan and prayed the salat steadfastly throughout his career, telling a reporter during his NBA tenure that he had not missed a salat prayer since childhood. Speaking to the salat's significance in his life, Abdur-Rahim commented, "It's hard for me to get away from what I believe in if I'm praying five times a day. Regardless of everything else going on, it's what God is telling me to do. I don't want to miss them, and I stay cognizant of that. It's part of me staying in tune to who I am."[48] Such fidelity to religious practice might elicit cheers of admiration and respect from an assortment of Americans, but one of Abdur-Rahim's compatriots led a campaign to shower his Islamic devotion with catcalls. Blogger Debbie Schlussel alleged that Abdur-Rahim "has been using his status in the NBA (and accompanying wealth) as a platform for and tool in the Islam-

---

[47] Jackson asserts that for immigrant Muslim Americans, issues such as "police brutality, exploitation of blacks in the media and entertainment industry, the drug-prison complex, joblessness, education, urban violence and single parentage, Affirmative Action, or the wholescale criminalization of aspects of Blackamerican culture, were all suppressed by a single-minded focus on the problems of the Muslim world—Palestine, Kashmir, Egypt, Saudi Arabia, Afghanistan" (ibid., 73).

[48] Jason Quick, "During Ramadan, Forward Fasts in the Daylight Hours, Reads the Quran, and Doesn't Complain," *The Coli*, http://www.thecoli.com/threads/shareef-abdur-rahim-being-a-muslim-i-think-thankfullness-thread.70004/ (posted 9 November 2004; accessed 22 April 2014).

ic propaganda and proselytizing machine. He's been actively spreading the false 'Islam is peaceful and likes all peoples of all colors' baloney."[49] As so-called substantiation of Abdur-Rahim's link to Islamic violence, Schlussel noted his appearance on "The Deen Show,"[50] which, according to Schlussel, "won't condemn Hezbollah and Hamas and their terrorist attacks."[51] Schlussel continued her full-court press against Abdur-Rahim by singling out the Future Foundation, his charity organization that since 2001 has helped youth in Abdur-Rahim's hometown of Atlanta. The foundation website proclaims the following:

> Our mission is to level the playing field for youth in metro Atlanta by providing quality education, health, and life skills programs. We call ourselves the Future Foundation because we encourage kids to dream about, invest in, and prepare for their futures. We prepare students and parents to have the self-confidence to envision a better life, and stand out from the cycle of negativity and hopelessness, and affect change in their lives and communities.[52]

For Schlussel, however, this positive presentation is a ruse; nefarious intent lurks hidden beneath these stated niceties. Noting that Abdur-Rahim's organization donates to the Boys and Girls Clubs of America, Schlussel remarked, "Let's hope he only gives them money and doesn't use this as a window to spread his Islamic ideology to inner city boys and girls across America. It's no loss to see Shareef Abdul-Rahim [*sic*] leave

---

[49] Debbie Schlussel, "Buh-Bye: NBA Gravy Train Ends for Muslim Proselytizer Who Supports Cop Killers,"
http://www.debbieschlussel.com/4261/buh-bye-nba-gravy-train-ends-for-muslim-proselytizer-who-supports-cop-killers/comment-page-1/ (posted 23 September 2008; accessed 22 April 2014).

[50] According to its website, since 2006 "['The Deen Show'] has been working on clearing up misconceptions about Islam, condemning terrorism and at the same time delivering the simple Message of the 'Purpose of life' in a fun and exciting way... 'The Deen Show' is viewed internationally, reaching millions of viewers on several satellite and cable stations all over the world" ("'The Deen Show': About," http://thedeenshow.com/page/about (accessed 11 March 2015)).

[51] Schlussel, "Buh-Bye."

[52] "Future Foundation: About," Future Foundation, http://future-foundation.com/about/ (accessed 22 April 2014).

the NBA. It's just one less giant paycheck for the jihad."[53] As a point of irony in Schlussel's derisive intent behind her use of the term, Abdur-Rahim might gladly label his charity work as "jihad," considering that this word's primary connotation among Muslim Americans has to do with striving peacefully to follow God's path through various actions including charity. Demonstrating tunnel vision shaped by extremist versions of Islam, however, in Schlussel's lexicon "jihad" has one meaning alone: aggressive proselytization with violence typically in tow.

As a former All-Star and career 15,028-pointscorer, Abdur-Rahim would be a likely pick for a starting five of all-time greatest Muslim NBA players. Whether or not Shaquille O'Neal should crack this starting line-up creates an intriguing debate. Talent is not the issue. The fifteen-time All-Star and four-time NBA champion on many a night dominated the paint and seemed to score against overmatched defensive foes at will. The sticking point pertains to whether O'Neal should indeed be selected to a team of *Muslim* players. Born to a Muslim father, Shaq has suggested that he follows in his father's religious path. While playing for the Los Angeles Lakers in the 2002 Western Conference Finals, O'Neal explained that his pre-game practice of hugging and touching cheeks with Hedo Turkoglu of the Kings was an expression of the opponents' shared Muslim faith. At times, though, O'Neal has given many Muslims pause to consider him a fellow follower of Islam, especially on occasions in which he has resisted tying his religious identity to Islam alone. On one such occasion, O'Neal proclaimed to a reporter, "Fact is I'm Muslim, I'm Jewish, I'm Buddhist, I'm everybody 'cause I'm a people person."[54]

Perusing NBA stat sheets, it is also debatable whether a Muslim on a 2014–2015 roster would make the all-time greatest Muslim NBA player starting five. The likeliest candidate would be Denver Nuggets power forward Kenneth Faried. Recognized for his relentless drive on the court and by his nickname "the Manimal," Faried followed his third NBA sea-

---

[53] Schlussel, "Buh-Bye."

[54] Quoted in Allison Kugel, "Shaquille O'Neal Talks Kobe Bryant, Pat Riley, & NBA Politics: 'I Did It My Way,'"

http://www.pr.com/article/1191 (posted 11 November 2011; accessed 22 April 2014).

son by playing for the United States national team at the 2014 FIBA Basketball World Cup. Faried's experience of choosing to embrace his religion is no run-of-the-mill story about coming to Islamic faith. Faried was raised by his mother and her female life partner, both Muslims. As a young child, Faried attended a Baptist church with his father, but he ultimately devoted himself to his mother's religion. Describing his dedication to Islam, Faried has stated, "I try to follow my faith to a T... Sometimes it's hard, but I'm just happy that Allah gave me a chance to be in the position I'm in—and gave me this talent, this hustle, this heart. And the parents I have and the great people around me to push me."[55]

Further push to greatness for Faried or any other Muslim hoopster can come from recognizing that the foundation has already been laid for a Muslim to achieve tremendous success in the NBA. Thanks in large part to his unstoppable skyhook, Kareem Abdul-Jabbar rose straight to the top of the NBA career scoring register, netting 38,387 points during his twenty years in the league. Known by his pre-conversion name, Lew Alcindor, Abdul-Jabbar was twice named national Player of the Year and played on three national title teams during his college days at UCLA. Abdul-Jabbar kept the outstanding accomplishments coming as a pro, capturing six NBA titles and six MVP awards and making nineteen All-Star Game appearances as a member of the Milwaukee Bucks and Los Angeles Lakers. Unlike his college exploits, Abdul-Jabbar achieved most of these titles and honors as a Muslim, having converted after his second season in the NBA. Disenchanted with the Catholicism of his youth, Abdul-Jabbar gave serious consideration to joining the Nation of Islam but decided against it, concluding that Elijah Muhammad's group perpetuated "negative power that feeds on itself"[56] similar to White racism. Abdul-Jabbar's quest led him to choose mainstream Sunni Islam instead after an intensive month-long study of the Qur'an.

Enjoying one of the greatest careers in NBA history while playing on only two teams, Abdul-Jabbar was by no means a basketball journey-

---

[55] Quoted in Benjamin Hochman, "Nuggets' Power Forward Pick Faried Creates Buzz," *The Denver Post*, http://www.denverpost.com/ci_18400591 (posted 3 July 2011; accessed 22 April 2014).

[56] Quoted in Baker, *Playing with God*, 224.

man. Spiritually, though, Abdul-Jabbar has possessed a journeying disposition that led him to visit a number of Muslim communities in the
Middle East and Southeast Asia in order to gain greater insight into
what following Islam might mean in his own life. During this whirlwind
summer 1974 tour, Abdul-Jabbar met Muslims who practiced their religion less strictly than those who influenced the formation of his faith in
America, and as a result, he gravitated toward a more casual approach to
Islam. Baker states that Abdul-Jabbar continued to pray and read the
Qur'an but "less rigorously than he did as a new convert,"[57] and he chose
not to fast when NBA seasons coincided with Ramadan. Despite this
decision, the holy month remained highly significant for Abdul-Jabbar,
as he adhered to the traditional practice of reading one thirtieth of the
Qur'an during each of Ramadan's thirty days. As Ramadan happened to
fall amidst the thick of the playoffs during the final two years of his career, Abdul-Jabbar regarded this practice as mental nourishment to fortify himself for each intense post-season battle. Additionally, Abdul-
Jabbar has given Islam props by saying its dietary principles propped up
his career. Abdul-Jabbar maintains that his body could not have paid the
toll demanded by twenty NBA seasons without refraining from pork and
alcohol.

Interestingly, alcohol brewed at the center of discord between Abdul-Jabbar and fellow Muslim Americans who took exception to his appearance in a Coors beer television commercial after his retirement.
Although producers honored Abdul-Jabbar's insistence that he not hold
a beer bottle in the commercial, an Islamic Society of North America
spokesman criticized him for his appearance and called the ad "devastating."[58] ISNA secretary general Sayyid M. Sayeed enjoined Abdul-Jabbar
either to request that Coors no longer air the commercial or to donate his
earnings for the ad to institutions that combat excessive use of alcohol.
Some Muslim American leaders, on the other hand, judged it inappropriate to whistle Abdul-Jabbar for a religious foul. Islamic Center of

[57] Ibid., 225.
[58] Julie Cart and Larry B. Stammer, "Kareem Rebuked Over Beer Ad," *Los Angeles Times,* http://articles.latimes.com/1997-01-18/sports/sp-19764_1_kareem-
abdul-jabbar (published 18 January 1997; accessed 23 April 2014).

Southern California's Maher Hathout remarked that Abdul-Jabbar "should be approached in a more private and dignified way,"[59] and Salam Al-Marayati of the Muslim Public Affairs Council stated, "Kareem Abdul-Jabbar never claimed to represent Islam or Muslims and therefore his decision to accept a role in the commercial was personal. We disagree [with the commercial], but it has no bearing on Islam and Muslims in America."[60]

Unlike the flak he took on this occasion from fellow Muslims, Abdul-Jabbar has received extremely little faith-related public criticism from non-Muslims, besides a smattering when he originally announced his conversion and change of name. Quite possibly, though, Abdul-Jabbar has been the subject of a discreet Islamophobia on the part of NBA fans and executives, as suggested by an online posting from an individual identified as "Buckus Toothnail." The posting proposes that Lakers fans would choose Magic Johnson or Kobe Bryant, not Abdul-Jabbar, as the greatest Laker of all time and also mentions Abdul-Jabbar's inability to land a head coaching gig in the NBA. Toothnail writes, "[W]hy hasn't Abdul-Jabbar's legacy lived up to his accomplishments? Very few people will dare to say it, but it's likely Abdul-Jabbar being Muslim has altered the public's perception of him for the worse since the tragic events of 9/11."[61] Toothnail acknowledges that, especially due to his introverted nature, "it's doubtful that Abdul-Jabbar's religion is the *only* factor" in hindering him from getting the acclaim he deserves, yet Toothnail contends that this factor nonetheless calls for consideration.[62]

Over the course of my interviews, Abdul-Jabbar's name popped up periodically as a Muslim sports hero, but reference was made far more frequently to another ex-NBA center. Judging from these conversations,

[59] Ibid.

[60] Quoted in ibid.

[61] Buckus Toothnail, "Has Kareem Abdul-Jabbar's Religion Affected His Legacy?" *Bleacher Report,* http://bleacherreport.com/articles/437893-has-kareem-abdul-jabbars-religion-affected-his-legacy (posted 17 August 2010; accessed 23 April 2014). Toothnail adds an intriguing query: "[S]ince 9/11 would Abdul-Jabbar still be able to land a role as an airplane pilot in a major Hollywood film like *Airplane?*" (ibid.).

[62] Ibid.

Hakeem Olajuwon is the quintessential Muslim sports hero, packaging ardent piety with athletic prowess. Born and raised in Nigeria, Olajuwon brought his skills to the University of Houston, where he and fellow members of the creatively monikered Phi Slama Jama reached the Final Four three years in a row. Hakeem the Dream built upon his illustrious college stint by continuing to excel on the NBA floor. During a career comprising seventeen years with the Houston Rockets followed by one with the Toronto Raptors, the Hall of Famer and twelve-time All-Star scored 26,946 points, stood atop the NBA all-time blocks list, led the Rockets to back-to-back NBA titles, and captured the 1994 league MVP and Defensive Player of the Year awards. Even more importantly from Olajuwon's perspective, his NBA career also included a dramatic spiritual transformation right at its start. Born to devout Muslim parents, Olajuwon did not emulate their piety while starring at the University of Houston, but shortly after being drafted by the Rockets he decided to visit a mosque near his new team's home arena. He describes leaving as a changed man. Olajuwon recalls, "I felt goose bumps all over my body. Everything I had known growing up came back to me in that instant: the feeling of my knees on the floor of the mosque, the sound of the words of Allah as they washed over me. I remembered walking to school on Friday mornings and having the Call on every radio, as if I was being shepherded. It was the most beautiful sound I had ever heard."[63] Countless visits to this mosque ensued, and Olajuwon developed the habits of praying at mosques near opponents' arenas and reading the Qur'an voraciously in airplanes and hotel rooms during away-game travels. Olajuwon asserts that his piety acquired an added ardency when he performed the hajj pilgrimage in 1991. He notes returning from Saudi Arabia to the mecca of the basketball world even more determined to use his hoops skills "to do good and to encourage others, for the pleasure of Allah."[64]

Comments from a number of Muslim Americans suggest that Hakeem's dream was fulfilled. His stardom illuminated both a commitment to piety that inspired fellow Muslims toward deeper devotion and a representation of his religion that led non-Muslims to view Islam more fa-

---

[63] Quoted in Baker, *Playing with God*, 207–208.
[64] Ibid., 229.

vorably. According to basketball buff Mohamed El-Housiny of Houston, "Hakeem represented the best of what Islam was and made us all proud."[65] Muslim Americans far away from Olajuwon's Houston backyard agree with these accolades, and many feel personally connected to Olajuwon because of his visits to mosques in NBA cities across the nation. Referring to adult Detroit-area Muslims, Chris Blauvelt commented that it seems as if "everyone has their Hakeem Olajuwon story"[66] in which they have talked with him or at least seen him pray. Northeastern University student Omar Abdelkader identified Olajuwon's example as fortification for his fasting resolve. Abdelkader stated that Olajuwon's ability to fast while playing grueling NBA games almost every other day is "really inspirational for any Muslim: 'If he can do that, after going through all that, why can't I fast?'"[67] Olajuwon has further inspired fellow Muslims' faith through his stated aspiration for every second of his life to be guided by taqwa, or God-consciousness. Olajuwon has described taqwa as an "internal voice" that presides over his every action, saying that when coached by taqwa, "You play competitively, but you don't do things that are cheating or unfair or foul play. You report to a higher authority."[68] University of Minnesota student Amer Sassila believes that Olajuwon's consistent demonstration of virtue in the heat of competition, along with his kindness and generosity off the court, has had significant effects in altering non-Muslims' thoughts about Islam. Citing Olajuwon's interactions with fans during his playing days and in retirement, Sassila stated that he is "friendly to them, kind to them, always smiling at them. He's out there giving back to the community rather than the NBA asking him to go give back to the community just for publicity. He's doing this out of his own will."[69]

[65] Quoted in "U.S. Muslims [*sic*] Love Story with Basketball," http://www.onislam.net/english/news/americas/457590-us-muslims-love-story-with-basketball.html (posted 16 June 2012; accessed 22 April 2014).

[66] Chris Blauvelt, personal interview, 19 March 2014, Detroit MI.

[67] Omar Abdelkader, personal interview, 10 March 2014, Boston MA.

[68] Quoted in Deborah Caldwell, "A Basketball Player Finds Peace," *Taking Back Islam: American Muslims Reclaim Their Faith*, ed. Michael Wolfe, 228–32 (Emmaus PA: Rodale, 2002) 232.

[69] Amer Sassila, personal interview, 26 April 2014, Minneapolis MN.

Muslim Football Players

In terms of number of Muslims having played in its ranks, the NFL is neck and neck with the NBA. Shifting the comparison to number of star Muslim players, however, the NFL is outscored by the NBA, unable to get a safety and reach a scoreboard display of two. It seems safe to say that the NFL Muslim standout total stands at one, wide receiver Ahmad Rashad. Leaving Pentecostal Holiness roots behind in the nascent stage of his NFL career, the erstwhile Bobby Moore converted to Islam, much to the chagrin of fans in his new St. Louis home. Thankfully for Rashad, Cardinals backers' jeers soon became cheers, as his on-field adroitness trumped anti-Islamic sentiment. Rashad moved on to hear more hometown applause in Buffalo and then Minnesota, where he spent seven of his ten years in the NFL with the Vikings. Over the course of this career, Rashad snatched forty-four touchdown receptions, appeared in four Pro Bowls, and earned a reputation for resilience by starting in all but one game with the Vikings from 1976 to 1982. Rashad continued to make a splash after retirement as a sports broadcaster and as host of an array of television shows.

A comprehensive exploration of Muslims in the NFL might spend some quality time in the office of Shahid Khan, owner of the Jacksonville Jaguars. Khan became the league's first Muslim owner in 2012, when the first-generation Pakistani American tapped into his auto parts company fortune to purchase the team.[70] Rather than aiming for a comprehensive picture of Muslims in the NFL, though, I progress in my selective sampling to Oday Aboushi, the league's first Palestinian American player. The offensive lineman has embraced this distinction, commenting after being drafted by the New York Jets in 2013 that he considers it "an honor"[71] to represent Palestinian Americans on the NFL stage. He added

---

[70] Khan is owner of Flex-N-Gate Corporation, which holds the distinction of making at least one part on two-thirds of all cars and trucks sold in the United States ("Jaguars' Owner Bought Team Undeterred by Racism," CBS News, http://www.cbsnews.com/news/jaguars-owner-bought-team-undeterred-by-racism/ (posted 25 October 2012; accessed 15 March 2015)).

[71] Quoted in Dennis Waszak, Jr., "Oday Aboushi, Jets' Palestinian-American Rookie, Defends Against 'Muslim Extremist' Claim," Associated Press,

that to "open the door" for other Palestinian Americans and "show them that it is possible" to make it to football's highest level is "a great feeling."[72] According to Aboushi, teammates each stage of the way have consistently accepted him, undeterred by his Islamic faith. Expressing a popular theme throughout this book, Aboushi has proclaimed, "Once we're on the field, we're all one. That's the great thing about us being in a sport, on a team. No matter where you come from—your background, your practice, your religion—when you get on a field, you're all brothers, you're all there to help each other, and you're all working toward one goal."[73] Much different than what he has experienced on the field, Aboushi's religious background was singled out when a 2013 *FrontPage Magazine* article, re-posted by Yahoo Sports, linked Aboushi to Islamic extremism. The article alleged that Aboushi showed his true Muslim stripes by giving a speech at a gathering of the Al Bireh Society,[74] portrayed by the piece as a "radical Muslim conference sponsored by a group denying Israel's right to exist and associated with blatantly anti-Semitic and terrorist propaganda."[75] In a statement issued by the Jets organization, Aboushi sharply distinguished his personal views from the anti-

http://www.huffingtonpost.com/2013/07/12/oday-aboushi-jets-palestinian_n_3588928.html (posted 12 July 2013; accessed 21 April 2014).

[72] Quoted in ibid.

[73] Renee Ghert-Zand, "First Palestinian-American in NFL," *The Times of Israel*, http://www.timesofisrael.com/first-palestinian-american-in-nfl/ (published 28 April 2013; accessed 21 April 2014).

[74] According to its website, the Al Bireh Society is a "non-profit charitable educational American Palestinian organization whose proud members derive their ancestry from the orginal [sic] family from the city of Al bireh, Palestine. Our objective is to serve our membership and the Palestinian, Arab, non-Arab, and charitable communities in the United States and abroad. Our mission is to perpetuate the Al Bireh family by means of providing educational, humanitarian, financial, charitable, and cultural programs as well as social interaction, and to enhance and promote the interaction of its members to the Arabic culture and to promote our culture and heritage to those outside our community, to the American public at large, and to the descendants of Al Bireh living throughout the world" ("Al Bireh Society: About Us," Al Bireh Society, http://albirehsociety.org (accessed 11 March 2015)).

[75] Quoted in Waszak, "Oday Aboushi."

Semitic brush with which he was painted, declaring, "As for the Israeli-Palestinian conflict, I hope that both sides make peace and live in prosperity."[76] Turning his attention to the author of the article's scurrilous claims, Aboushi went on to say, "It is upsetting to see people try and tarnish my reputation without even knowing me."[77] He then thanked those who supported him in the affair, which included backing from a Jewish organization. Anti-Defamation League director Abraham Foxman announced, "Absolutely nothing in the public record suggests Aboushi is anything other than a young American athlete who takes pride in his Palestinian heritage. His participation in a conference organized by the El-Bireh Society, a Palestinian community organization that was until recently defunct, should not be used to tar him as an extremist."[78] Aboushi made it to the pinnacle of his sport by dutifully blocking defensive foes and supporting his quarterback. Now it was his turn to receive support from a Jewish spokesman blocking Aboushi from defamatory accusations of anti-Semitism and violent extremism.

Time will tell if Aboushi becomes a popular role model among athletically inclined Muslim Americans. If so, he will join Hamza and Husain Abdullah, the brothers whose steadfast commitment to fasting was discussed in an earlier chapter. Having heard their names brought up fondly in interview after interview, I suggest that Hamza and Husain are pro football's closest equivalents to Hakeem Olajuwon as Muslim American sports heroes. Neither brother inhabits Olajuwon's Hall of Fame stratosphere in regard to athletic accomplishment, but as professional athletes who place Islamic piety at the center of their lives, the Abdullahs stand right alongside the NBA legend. Admired by many Muslims for fasting while playing in the NFL, the Abdullahs endeared themselves further to fellow Muslims when they chose to put their NFL careers on hold in order to perform the hajj pilgrimage during the 2012 season. The brothers recognized this decision would mean forfeiting million-dollar salaries and could place their NFL careers in jeopardy. After three years of mostly back-up and special teams roles in the league, Husain earned a

[76] Quoted in ibid.
[77] Quoted in ibid.
[78] Quoted in ibid.

starting spot as free safety for the Vikings in 2011, and Hamza enjoyed respect as a seven-year veteran of the league. Hamza was unable to land an NFL roster spot after his hiatus for the hajj, but despite this disappointment and the financial loss incurred, he expressed no regrets in what to him was a huge spiritual gain. Commenting on the decision to perform the hajj, Hamza declared, "It has been a blessing to play in the NFL for both Husain and I, but we would be remiss if we didn't give thanks to the One who made it all possible."[79] A few months before traveling to Mecca, the Abdullahs traversed America in their "30 Mosques in 30 Days" tour during Ramadan. Hamza, Husain, and older brother Abbas shared the fast-breaking iftar meal at thirty different mosques after each setting of the holy month sun, and Hamza and Husain capped off each meal with a talk about playing in the NFL as practicing Muslims. Packed mostly with young Muslims, audiences were dotted with non-Muslim youth as well. The Abdullahs' bridging intentions were demonstrated in the tour's promotional material, which stated that the brothers "will travel across America to promote interfaith dialogue and to deconstruct the negative connotations often associated with Islam."[80] An additional feature of many of the tour's thirty audiences was racial diversity, which, according to one individual I interviewed, carried interesting implications in light of Muslim American division along racial lines. Referring to immigrant parents who tend not to view African-American Muslims as Islamic equals, Chris Blauvelt proposed that some placed these views aside, at least temporarily, as they were delighted to see their children go to the mosque to hear the Abdullahs testify to their strong commitment to Islamic piety.[81]

Such testimony took unique non-verbal form during the 2014 NFL season, on the prominent stage of Monday Night Football. After inter-

[79] Quoted in Dan Hanzus, "Abdullah Brothers Put NFL on Hold to Pursue Faith," NFL.com, http://www.nfl.com/news/story/09000d5d82a06d69/article/ abdullah-brothers-put-nfl-on-hold-to-pursue-faith (published 21 June 2012; accessed 15 March 2015).

[80] Quoted in "Muslim NFL Players Hamza and Husain Abdullah '30 for 30' Ramadan Tour," Salatomatic, http://www.salatomatic.com/cbe.php?id=127 (posted 29 June 2012; accessed 15 March 2015).

[81] Chris Blauvelt, personal interview, 19 March 2014, Detroit MI.

cepting a Tom Brady pass and returning it for a touchdown, Husain marked the first pick six of his pro career by falling to both knees in the end zone and performing a prostration of thanksgiving.[82] Social media was atwitter due to the Kansas City Chiefs defensive back's action, especially because of what ensued. An official flagged Abdullah, interpreting his genuflection as a violation of the NFL's excessive celebration penalty. Religious acts are not supposed to be included under this penalty, and so NFL overseers subsequently threw a flag of their own at the official who made this call. However, for some Muslim Americans, upon further review the penalty's damage could not be overturned. A few online commentators construed the penalty as anti-Islamic targeting of a Muslim in prayer, pointing out that officials keep their flags in their pockets after demonstrative on-field praying from Tim Tebow and other Christian players.

Albeit only for a day or two, Abdullah's pick-six prostration raised an unusually high level of awareness of Muslim presence in the NFL. Few football followers have knowledge of an important part of some Muslim NFL players' lives, their personal charity organizations. This knowledge would likely have significant bridging effects, since it reveals Muslims at the highest stage of a popular American sport working to improve American communities and lives. Admittedly, non-Muslims may arrive at strikingly different conclusions in evaluating Muslim American athlete charity work, ranging from the Congressional resolution honoring the humanitarianism of Muhammad Ali to Debbie Schlussel's association between Shareef Abdur-Rahim's Future Foundation and Islamic violence. Islamophobic voices such as Schlussel's might always be heard, but stereotypes of Muslims as threats to American society can nonetheless be tackled by Muslim pro football players investing their time and money in greatly enhancing this society.

One investor is New York Jets defensive end Muhammad Wilkerson, who has displayed his heart for bridging in a variety of ways. Commenting before his very first regular-season NFL game, which happened

---

[82] The Hadith reports Muhammad falling to his knees in gratitude after receiving good news, and a number of Muslim athletes outside the United States have adopted this practice in response to moments of sporting success.

to take place on the tenth anniversary of 9/11 just miles away from the site of the World Trade Center, Wilkerson proclaimed, "I'm going to go out there and play as if I was part of those families that were hurt that day."[83] Wilkerson also builds bridges by giving back to the area where he grew up, Northern New Jersey's Union County. Wilkerson's charity organization is called T.E.A.M. 96, a reference to his jersey number following an acronym standing for "Togetherness, Education, Achievement, Motivation." T.E.A.M. 96 provides "a variety of assistance to both male and female college-bound 12th-grade high school student-athletes" from Union County high schools and aims to enable these students to "become our next generation of leaders, scholars, and positive role models for the world."[84] Like Wilkerson's focus on high school seniors hailing from one particular county, retired NFL wide receiver and kick returner Az Hakim aspires to make a powerful impact upon a specific subsection of American youth, those with incarcerated parents. Amidst a ten-year career with the Detroit Lions, New Orleans Saints, San Diego Chargers, Miami Dolphins, and St. Louis Rams, including an important role in propelling the 1999–2000 Rams "Greatest Show on Turf" to a Super Bowl ring, Hakim developed the Az Hakim Foundation in response to his own childhood struggles with a parent in prison. The foundation has grown since Hakim hung up his cleats to retire, reaching many with its mission to "provide academic, personal, professional, and athletic resources to children with incarcerated parents through direct contact or by assisting other organizations."[85] The foundation coordinates an assortment of enrichment programs and outings in an attempt to help youth of incarcerated parents "grow into confident, caring, and courageous individuals" and to "allow them to see that there is a brighter tomorrow through making better decisions."[86] Adding one more truss to

[83] Quoted in Bob Glauber, "Debut of Jets' Wilkerson Falls on Sept. 11," *Newsday,* http://www.newsday.com/sports/columnists/bob-glauber/debut-of-jets-wilkerson-falls-on-sept-11-1.3152791 (published 7 September 2011; accessed 23 April 2014).

[84] "T.E.A.M. 96," http://www.mwteam96.com (accessed 23 April 2014).

[85] "Az Hakim Foundation: About Us," http://www.hakim4kids.com/about (accessed 23 April 2014).

[86] Ibid.

Muslim NFL player bridging via charity organizations, retired offensive tackle Ephraim Salaam started the EMS (Ephraim Mateen Salaam) Foundation to provide mentorship and financial assistance to youth in need and their families. During his playing days with the Atlanta Falcons, Denver Broncos, Jacksonville Jaguars, Houston Texans, and Detroit Lions, and after retirement as an analyst with the cable network Fox Sports 1, Salaam has awarded numerous scholarships to inner-city students, and according to a *Muslim Journal* profile, he has "fed the needy at Thanksgiving, provided toys, clothing, and food for thousands of foster children throughout America at Christmas time, and mentored hundreds of youth."[87] Salaam was honored by the Los Angeles City Council in 2012, when it proclaimed March 17 to be Ephraim Salaam Day in recognition of his contributions to youth in Los Angeles and elsewhere in the United States and Africa.

[87] "Ephraim Salaam Represents Muslim Athletes at U.S. State Department," http://muslimjournal.net/?p=455 (posted 10 February 2012; accessed 23 April 2014).

7

Muslim Basketball Leagues

> Some of these guys that play in MBL…just love it. It's all they want to
> talk about, it's all they want to do. They can't wait. During the week
> they're always talking about what's going to come this coming Sunday
> or what just happened this past Sunday.[1]

Enjoying a beautiful April afternoon outside a Starbucks in Southern
California, I saw a familiar look on Sulaiman Dadabhoy's face. Lighting
up with excitement, Dadabhoy's countenance accentuated the words
above, reflecting his love for his Muslim basketball league. Dadabhoy
exhibited a passion I had seen many times before in conversations with
players and directors of Muslim leagues from Southern California to
New England. Hearkening back to sociologist Charles Page's coining of
the phrase "basketballization of American religion"[2] to describe a mid-
twentieth-century boom of Christian basketball leagues and organizations, this chapter looks at what might be called a basketballization of
American Islam. In the twenty-first century, more and more Muslim
Americans have embraced basketball not only as a fount of fun or wellspring of wellness, but as a deep source of dawah, in both its bonding and
bridging forms. I recognize that not all athletically active Muslim Americans head to the hardwood or asphalt; University of Minnesota MSA
president Amer Sassila stated that within his MSA chapter it is soccer,
not basketball, that reigns supreme.[3] Sassila's group, however, is in the
minority among twenty-first-century Muslim Americans. Based on interviews and on Internet searches, I concur with a *Houston Chronicle*
claim that while "soccer and cricket remain important for immigrant

---

[1] Sulaiman Dadabhoy, personal interview, 12 April 2014, Norco CA.
[2] Quoted in Nicholas J. Demerath and Philip Hammond, *Religion in Social Context: Tradition and Transition* (New York: Random House, 1969) 182.
[3] Amer Sassila, personal interview, 26 April 2014, Minneapolis MN.

Muslims, basketball has soared past them for the generation of Muslims raised in the U.S."[4] This chapter testifies to the preeminence of basketball as the sport of choice among Muslim Americans, especially second- and third-generation immigrants and African Americans.

Omar Sacirbey's article "Why Basketball Is Muslims' Favorite Sport" offers invaluable insight into answering the question embedded within its title. Laying down cards with faces such as Hakeem Olajuwon, Kareem Abdul-Jabbar, and Shareef Abdur-Rahim, Sacirbey places one answer on the table by arguing that basketball "has provided Muslim Americans with more heroes than any other major sport in America."[5] Sacirbey offers another response by discussing the close affiliation between basketball and African Americans.[6] Stating that African Americans comprise about thirty percent of the Muslim American community,[7] he also asserts that many immigrant Muslim Americans "identify with blacks as a fellow minority in a country still marked by prejudice, so they

---

[4] "Basketball a Slam-Dunk for Area Muslims," *Houston Chronicle,* http://uhdnews.uhd.edu/news/

stories.aspx?articleid=302&zoneid=1 (published 4 June 2012; accessed 22 April 2014).

[5] Omar Sacirbey, "Why Basketball Is Muslims' Favorite Sport," *Religion News Service,* http://www.huffingtonpost.com/2012/05/

21/basketball-muslim-favorite-sport_n_1528495.html (posted 21 May 2012; accessed 21 April 2014).

[6] Todd Boyd traces basketball's evolution to a game heavily influenced by African Americans. He writes, "For many years basketball was performed in the manner of classical music. A player was supposed to follow what was called textbook style, and not deviate in the process. Showmanship was discouraged" (Todd Boyd, *Young, Black, Rich, and Famous: The Rise of the NBA, the Hip Hop Invasion, and the Transformation of American Culture* (New York: Doubleday, 2003) 29). Boyd goes on to say that "as many Black players from the inner city came to dominate the game...[t]he style of the playground reigned, and a more athletic style of play— which assisted in the improvisation – was what made you significant. Your ability to create and do so with flair was what made the crowds gasp, not some adherence to an elusive and outdated textbook. This was similar to a jazz musician playing his instrument with a style all his own. Imitation would get you derisively dismissed, while originality would separate you from the pack" (ibid., 29–30).

[7] Estimates of the African-American proportion of Muslim Americans tend to fall somewhere between twenty-five and forty percent.

embrace popular culture associated with black culture, especially basketball and hip-hop music."[8] Each of these observations has much to contribute towards theorizing why basketball wins the Muslim American sporting trophy, but ultimately Sacirbey's pragmatic considerations of accessibility and cost may be most salient. Noting that basketball teams require roughly half the number of players as football, soccer, and baseball and that basketball demands little space, no protective gear, and no equipment besides baskets and balls, Sacirbey writes that basketball is "the easiest and most affordable sport for Muslims to organize. Those are important considerations for a faith whose numbers and communal finances are still small."[9] Sacirbey's concluding statement might belie the numerical and financial strength of more than a few Muslim American communities, but he nonetheless puts his finger on a practical reality driving droves of Muslim Americans to head for the hoops.

Building upon Sacirbey's suggestions, an additional proposal for basketball's Muslim American popularity resides in its role in enabling immigrants to make connections with other Americans, thereby helping them integrate into American society. Sunaina Maira compares a group of Bangladeshi immigrant high school boys who became heavily involved in basketball in relation to a separate cohort of Bangladeshi highschoolers in the same Massachusetts town who were devoted to cricket, demonstrating that selection of sport significantly shaped the entry of the former but not the latter group into the social world of non-Muslim peers.[10] Maira's observations about the basketball-playing cohort match the experience of Maher Abuawad, a second-generation Palestinian American. Growing up in Brooklyn, Abuawad found basketball to be "the easiest way to connect"[11] with non-Muslims in his neighborhood, fulfilling a yearning to relate to American peers shared by Mohamed El-Housiny, a Kansas City architect appearing in the article "U.S. Muslims [sic] Love Story with Basketball." El-Housiny, who came to the United

---

[8] Omar Sacirbey, "Why Basketball Is Muslims' Favorite Sport."
[9] Ibid.
[10] Maira, *Missing*, 159–60.
[11] Maher Abuawad, personal interview, 21 February 2014, Lawrenceville NJ.

States from Gaza at age five, said he "longed to fit in"[12] with non-Muslims around him but found language barriers and cultural differences blocking his way. Through basketball, though, he claims he "could communicate in a language Americans understand very well," and as his English skills grew, he enjoyed the realization that "after a good game of basketball you can talk to anyone."[13]

Such links between basketball and integration have been a big deal for a number of Muslim American youth, as stepping onto the court with non-Muslim peers has helped them step past sidelines drawn by religious and ethnic difference. Having pointed to these sidelines, I, too, now want to leave them behind, moving on to a different arena in analyzing the basketballization of American Islam. Due in large part to a concern that journeying farther down the integration framework road would entail entering hazardous essentialized Islam vs. America conditions, I take up the themes of bonding and bridging instead as I look at Muslim American basketball leagues. Akin to Lee, Dunlap, and Scott's findings in their examination of Korean basketball clubs,[14] Muslim basketball leagues help Muslim players reconceptualize who they are and reorient their everyday lives by means of strengthening Islamic fellowship and piety. At the same time, these leagues foster relationship building between Muslims and non-Muslims, prompting non-Muslims to view Islam in a more positive light. I recognize that concentrating on organized leagues provides only a half-court view of Muslim American basketball dawah, since bonding and bridging also occur in pick-up games throughout the nation. Kareem Shahin described how his commitment to honesty on a Southern California fitness center court dishes out an assist to his aspiration to represent Islam to teammates and opponents. Contrasting this pick-up environment to the refereed Muslim Basketball League, Shahin stated that sometimes a game is "point up, fourteen-fourteen, and nobody knows who it went off of. But if it went off of me...even if it's

[12] Quoted in "U.S. Muslims [*sic*] Love Story with Basketball."
[13] Ibid.
[14] Kangjae Jerry Lee, Rudy Dunlap, and David Scott, "Korean American Males' Serious Leisure Experiences and Their Perceptions of Different Play Styles," *Leisure Sciences* 33 (2011): 290–308.

going to cost us the game, I'm going to say, 'You know what guys, I hit it out.'"[15] Even something as seemingly inconsequential as calling out a teammate's name in pick-up play could be a bridging game changer, as suggested by Chris Blauvelt of Detroit. In light of likely associations made between the name "Osama" and this name's most infamous holder, Blauvelt commented, "If your friend's name is Osama and you're playing basketball, you're going to keep yelling, 'Osama, Osama, pass me the ball!' If he's on another team for the next pick-up game, those non-Muslims are going to have to yell out, 'Osama!' And all of a sudden that kind of means a lot."[16] Acknowledging that more of these pick-up scenarios would help to create a full-court presentation of dribbling for dawah, I nonetheless narrow the discussion to organized leagues.

New Jersey's Muslim Basketball

Competing against the din of shouts, whistles, and a jarring scoreboard buzzer, Muslim Basketball (MB) co-founder Essad Malik recalled the summer of 2005. Malik and his Muslim college student pals played pick-up games, progressing at first from a struggle to gather together ten people to ending up with three full courts of action. Excitement spilled over into the following year, leading Malik and friends to pull off something they had never heard of before, the formation of an organized Muslim basketball league. Though getting off the ground with humble beginnings, on a sloping outdoor court with rims more than ten-feet high, Malik discovered "there was a passion in the community for something like this."[17] Eight teams registered for the league's initial launch, and quickly the league skyrocketed to a total of twenty-eight teams. With two seasons per year, MB's spring 2015 season was its seventeenth, and as of March 2015 the league had seen 891 players, 1,301 games, and 135,732 points scored.[18] The league moved indoors into its current Police Athletic League facility in its sophomore season, when teams were

[15] Kareem Shahin, personal interview, 11 April 2014, Fontana CA.
[16] Chris Blauvelt, personal interview, 19 March 2014, Detroit MI.
[17] Essad Malik, personal interview, 1 May 2014, Parsippany NJ.
[18] "Muslim Basketball: About Us," http://muslimbasketball.org/about.asp (accessed 12 March 2015).

split into two separate competitive tiers. League director Sami Shaban remembers it taking three seasons for many players to accept this change, initially saying something to the following effect: "I'm not going to go to Division 2. Are you saying that I'm not as good? I'd rather not play."[19] Fast-forwarding to 2015, Division 2 is MB's largest level, with extremely competitive games and highly skilled players, albeit not quite of the caliber of many in Division 1, some of whom have honed their craft at the college or semi-pro levels. The league has also adopted a third tier, which commissioner Omar Abbassi identified as great for expanding competitive options, but occasionally a challenge for league administrators due to the pre-season approval process for second- and third-division teams. In order to ensure competitive balance, tentative team rosters are distributed to captains for their seal of approval, and Abbassi recounted a situation when multiple Division 2 captains turned their thumbs down in response to one team proposing to include a Division 1-caliber player on its roster. The story continued with the team folding and league administrators scrambling to find a replacement squad two weeks before the season's opening tip.[20]

Commitment to competitive balance is a common draw to MB for those who choose to join the league, a decision that in some cases is initially loaded with reluctance. This hesitancy comes not only from non-Muslims with negative impressions of Islam. Abbassi reminisced about his low expectations upon first hearing about the league, assuming it would basically be a glorified version of pick-up games he played, but hardly enjoyed, with unskilled Muslim players at New Jersey colleges and universities. Abbassi remembers thinking, "It's a Muslim basketball league. How good can it be?"[21] Willing to give the league a shot, Abbassi was pleasantly surprised by MB's high level of play and organizational structure. According to Malik, players keep coming back to MB largely because of its emphasis on quality, which includes tacking one new element onto the league's offerings every season, such as hiring referees very early in its history, paying statistics keepers later on, and introducing a

[19] Sami Shaban, personal interview, 1 May 2014, Parsippany NJ.
[20] Omar Abbassi, personal interview, 1 May 2014, Parsippany NJ.
[21] Ibid.

custom-made tablet-based statistics program for the spring 2014 season.[22] As reflected by these latter two additions, stats are an important part of the MB package. At first, Malik had reservations about keeping individual statistics, concerned it might promote self-centered play and deflate the league's focus on brotherhood.[23] Eventually, though, he came to believe that tracking individual as well as team statistics would pump air into MB's attractiveness, especially with a league website making these figures easily accessible.[24] The website has grown to contain a statistical smorgasbord, including team and individual records for most points, rebounds, assists, blocks, and steals, sortable by individual season, postseason, or division, as well as best career marks in each of these categories. Players can feast further on personal stats in every season and each division in which they have participated, along with message boards, game action photographs, contests to predict league game winners, and many other website features. Abbassi declared that the website "really sets this league apart," making MB "not just another basketball league where you come and play and you're not affiliated with the league until the next time you play. It gives you a way to interact and be a part of the league throughout the entire week, and not just on game day."[25]

Given the privilege of talking with six MB directors or players over the course of a basketball-packed Thursday evening at the Police Athletic League, I heard other voices echo Abbassi in dubbing the website one of MB's most appealing attributes. Similarly, another league distinctive received a chorus of cheers. I was told multiple times about MB's "no cursing and no fighting" policy, in which cursing results in a technical foul and fighting during a game may eventuate in expulsion from the league. Administrators remarked that for a few league participants these rules may seem unduly harsh, but administrators find them necessary in

[22] Essad Malik, personal interview, 1 May 2014, Parsippany NJ.

[23] Michigan mosque youth director Omar Malik spoke negatively of young players' request for statistics, believing that an individualistic mentality "takes over. They start worrying about their stats more than playing together as a team," thereby counteracting the central goal of building fellowship (Omar Malik, personal interview, 21 March 2014, Warren MI).

[24] Essad Malik, personal interview, 1 May 2014, Parsippany NJ.

[25] Omar Abbassi, personal interview, 1 May 2014, Parsippany NJ.

order to maintain an atmosphere consistent with Islamic values and to promote bonding and bridging through the league. Malik said, "We want to try and promote brotherhood as much as possible. We structure our rules around that... We don't allow any cursing, any taunting, any trash talk, any fighting, flashy jewelry, no dunking—anything that can really instigate negative feelings."[26] MB directors esteem these rules' contribution toward creating a climate that strengthens Muslim piety and fellowship, a climate from which commissioner Edriss Froogh claims to have highly benefited. Froogh stated he fell away from Islamic practice as a teen but then experienced a personal revival, crediting MB relationships for triggering this transformation. Froogh was especially affected by interacting with MB players whose devotion he wanted to emulate, and by the generosity of league members who helped him find jobs while unemployed. Froogh characterized this charitableness as par for the league course and noted that it is facilitated by the MB website message board on which players request and offer assistance in all sorts of areas.[27] Both on and off the MB court, Muslims connect with fellow followers of Islam, many of whom they likely would not meet otherwise. Malik explained one way in which the league brings erstwhile strangers together, saying that whereas players in MB's early years "had their set crew that they ran with every season,"[28] most league veterans have subsequently paired up with players from other teams or with league newbies. Froogh suggested that this tendency to shake things up encourages a level of Muslim fellowship across ethnic and racial lines that is rarely found outside the league. As opposed to the almost exclusively Afghan mosque he attends, Froogh mentioned playing on an MB championship winning squad with seven other Muslims, only one of whom was of Afghan descent.[29]

MB directors treasure brotherhood in the league not only for the sake of bonding, but also because they view exposure to Muslim camaraderie as a pot of bridging gold, demonstrating to non-Muslim players a

[26] Essad Malik, personal interview, 1 May 2014, Parsippany NJ.
[27] Edriss Froogh, personal interview, 1 May 2014, Parsippany NJ.
[28] Essad Malik, personal interview, 1 May 2014, Parsippany NJ.
[29] Edriss Froogh, personal interview, 1 May 2014, Parsippany NJ.

palpable pouring forth of Muslim love and respect. While Muslim players form a slight majority in its three divisions overall, MB includes a large number of non-Muslims especially in its most competitive division, which has grown to be approximately eighty percent non-Muslim. Supplying these non-Muslim players with a positive picture of Islam is a prominent MB priority for directors such as Malik, who told a local journalist that the "fact that non-Muslims are willing to wear the name Muslim Basketball on their jerseys, and that we can show them that they don't need to be afraid of the word Muslim is a key thing for us."[30] Unlike leagues that implement a Muslim to non-Muslim player ratio, MB places no restriction on the number of non-Muslims per team. According to Malik, the league started out with unwritten rules that kept the number of non-Muslims per team at one and then at two or three, but he and other administrators came to believe that it was contradictory to "the interest of inclusion and brotherhood to exclude people"[31] based on their religious affiliation. Malik proclaimed that Muslims who play in MB want in their everyday lives "to be included, to say, 'We're just like everyone else. We enjoy basketball just like everyone else.' So why should we exclude other people?"[32] Amidst this spirit of inclusion, non-Muslims come face to face with expressions of Islam that are primed to pull the plug on negative generalizations about Islam, as they learn about the religion not from the nightly news but from Muslim teammates and opponents.

Southern California's Muslim Basketball League

Nearly 3,000 miles westward from New Jersey, dribbling for dawah also resonates within the Anaheim Sports Center in Southern California. On the scene since 2004, the Muslim Basketball League (MBL) started with eight teams and, as of 2015, has reached a total of forty. Similar to MB, MBL offers winter and summer seasons and is split into three competi-

[30] Eric Angevine, "U.S. Muslims Find 'Love and Camaraderie' on Court," NBC Sports, http://www.nbcsports.com/other-sports/us-muslims-find-love-and-camaraderie-court#page=1 (posted 23 August 2012; accessed 21 April 2014).
[31] Essad Malik, personal interview, 1 May 2014, Parsippany NJ.
[32] Ibid.

tive levels. During the winter 2015 campaign, its third division was the largest, teeming with eighteen teams as opposed to six in Division 1 and sixteen in Division 2. The third division is filled with high school hoopsters but also includes players in their twenties and thirties. As I learned from league administrator Sulaiman Dadabhoy, many of these high-schoolers intend to eventually take their game to a higher MBL level, whereas most older third-division players plan to stay put, playing in MBL primarily for fun and fellowship instead of for fine-tuning their fundamentals. At the opposite end of the spectrum lie Division 1 players, highly competitive and supremely skilled. Most first- and second-division players are in their twenties, although one Division 2 squad had an average age of thirty-three, including a forty-two-year-old player. Also like MB, MBL's website maintains a mélange of individual and team records and statistics, sorted by season and by career. Website visitors are greeted by an abundance of items such as team power rankings, message boards, playoff analysis, and poll questions, in addition to previous season award winners in categories including MVP, Defensive Player of the Year, Rookie of the Year, Most Improved, 6th Man, Sportsmanship, and All-Star Game MVP.[33]

Enjoying his ride with MBL since it set out into uncharted territory as America's first Muslim basketball league, Dadabhoy is a Pakistani American league board member and former commissioner who loaded me up with insight into the league. Dadabhoy devotes numerous hours to the league each week, alongside family life, a full-time job, and his volunteer work with Uplift Charity, an organization he co-founded to assist poor Southern Californians. Dadabhoy noted the time-intensive nature of overseeing the league but stressed it is well worth the effort,[34] a sentiment that was shared by MB administrators in New Jersey. Malik remarked that he utterly underestimated the amount of work needed to coordinate league activities, thinking initially he would have nothing more than game-day responsibilities. Nevertheless, Malik said that he

---

[33] Muslim Basketball League website, Muslim Basketball League, http://www.hometeamsonline.com/teams/?u=MBLEAGUE&s=basketball (accessed 13 March 2015).

[34] Sulaiman Dadabhoy, personal interview, 12 April 2014, Norco CA.

and other MB administrators "love it," adding, "It's a lot of work, but I wouldn't trade it for anything else."[35] MB's Shaban showed a similar spirit, stating, "This is our passion. We're all working professionals. We all have family, and we do this because we believe that this is going to make a difference in the community."[36]

Digging more deeply into MBL, Dadabhoy discussed the delicate balancing act that he and other directors have attempted to perform between promoting league growth and preserving founders' two main goals, namely running a highly organized league and enabling the building of brotherhood. According to Dadabhoy, these goals have been "the two main things that we always want to make sure are there"[37] no matter what development the league has experienced, whether growing in number of teams, expanding to three divisions, or evolving from volunteer referees in the league's first year to the scenario of every MBL ref holding high school certification, including some who are college certified and two who are former NBA players. Dadabhoy pointed out that the ongoing goal of building brotherhood has itself been marked by growth, since MBL set out almost exclusively with players of South Asian and Arab descent but expanded to encompass an array of ethnicities, such as a team of Cham Muslims from Cambodia. MBL directors have cherished connecting Muslims of various ethnicities and races, and player Kareem Shahin commented on this league calling card by saying, "[I]n the Muslim Basketball League we have people from all races. We have Asians, Indians, Middle Easterners, Blacks, Whites—you name it, we have it: people from all over the globe."[38]

As another mark of resemblance with MB, MBL upholds a "no fighting, no cursing" policy. Dadabhoy made two links between this policy and bridging, first identifying its impact on non-Muslim referees, who appreciate officiating in a league that pushes the mute button on cursing and that has enforced a few lifetime bans on players for fighting, and second, suggesting that the "no fighting" rule can fight stereotypes associ-

[35] Essad Malik, personal interview, 1 May 2014, Parsippany NJ.
[36] Sami Shaban, personal interview, 1 May 2014, Parsippany NJ.
[37] Sulaiman Dadabhoy, personal interview, 12 April 2014, Norco CA.
[38] Kareem Shahin, personal interview, 11 April 2014, Fontana CA.

ating Muslims with violence. Dadabhoy proposed that non-Muslims may think nothing of physical altercations in other leagues, but upon seeing fighting in a Muslim league they will "automatically say, 'Oh, look at those Muslims.' That stereotype is always back there in some people's minds."[39] Because of where MBL games occur, Dadabhoy had more than just non-Muslim players in mind with these comments; he addressed the league's effect on non-Muslim onlookers as well. A former warehouse with thirty-four courts for volleyball, twenty-five for basketball, and nine for futsal, the Anaheim Sports Center is the largest indoor sports complex in the world. Playing during peak weekend evening hours, MBL draws dozens of gazes from non-Muslims in the arena, some of whom might not notice the words "Muslim Basketball League" on player jerseys but almost certainly cannot miss players gathering on one of MBL's five reserved courts to perform the salat prayer. For about fifteen minutes between games, once each evening, four of these courts stand empty while on the other court players who choose to join the salat form one or two long lines and touch their foreheads to the floor in prayer. Dadabhoy stated this sight piques many non-Muslims' curiosity, commenting that "people who are walking around, they'll stop, they'll look. I've had people ask questions. And the really cool thing is when kids come and ask questions. You'll see kids who are playing in their youth leagues—as young as ten years old, twelve years old—and they come and ask, 'What did you guys just do?'"[40] Dadabhoy called this "huge"[41] for introducing non-Muslims to Islamic practice and for igniting interfaith interaction, if only for a quick chat about the religious ritual that just covered the court.[42] Yet, as many spans as this on-court prayer

[39] Sulaiman Dadabhoy, personal interview, 12 April 2014, Norco CA.

[40] Ibid.

[41] Ibid.

[42] Hammad Choudhry, a physician who serves on the board of two Islamic schools in New Jersey, gave his perspective on how this type of occurrence can reduce Islamophobia. Presenting the scenario of a hypothetical pick-up game in which Muslims tell the non-Muslims they are playing with that they need to stop briefly to pray, Choudhry speaks from the non-Muslims' perspective and says, "Now they're praying and you've seen it, now you're not afraid of it. And you think, 'Well, that's

might help build, Dadabhoy placed even greater bridging significance upon non-Muslims' exposure to Muslim brotherhood. Dadabhoy talked about two MBL players who converted to Islam largely due to observing Muslim fellowship in the league. Though each had interest in Islam prior to joining MBL, what tipped both of their scales to convert was that "they saw the expanded brotherhood in MBL—something they didn't see at the mosque,"[43] which featured neither the league's ethnic and racial diversity nor its large number of similarly aged peers.

Following a game plan implemented by Muslim basketball leagues across America, MBL seeks to simultaneously appeal to both Muslims and non-Muslims, a dual focus apparent in its team names. On the one hand, Islamic terminology shapes some squad sobriquets, as teams such as One Ummah, Team Taqwa, and Just Duaa It[44] compete in the three competitive tiers, officially labeled the Makkah, Madeenah, and Jerusalem divisions. On the other hand, many MBL team names bear no Islamic references, including my personal favorites, Swish Kabobs, Skillz That Killz, and Your Worst Nightmare. Seeking to ensure a strong presence of both Muslims and non-Muslims, MBL nonetheless differs from MB by maintaining a Muslim to non-Muslim ratio, specifically three Muslims for each non-Muslim per team. Dadabhoy explained that the league started solely with Muslims, but in its second year, administrators chose to welcome players of all faiths in order to help them see "what Muslims are really like, outside what you hear on the media,"[45] and also in order to raise the overall level of play. Excited to have non-Muslims in the league, however, administrators decided to adopt a Muslim to non-Muslim ratio because they were concerned that the distinctively Muslim spirit of the league they desired to sustain might become sapped if Muslim players were a minority. Moreover, they hoped to stave off a situation in which Muslims would bring non-Muslim "ringers and have a full team

---

no big deal, so let's go play now'" (Hammad Choudhry, personal interview, 18 February 2014, Somerset NJ).

[43] Sulaiman Dadabhoy, personal interview, 12 April 2014, Norco CA.

[44] Ummah refers to the Muslim community, taqwa to God-consciousness, and duaa to intercessory prayer.

[45] Sulaiman Dadabhoy, personal interview, 12 April 2014, Norco CA.

of maybe just one Muslim" alongside non-Muslims who "weren't there for the brotherhood… They were there just to come beat everybody and go home."[46] A three-to-one ratio was judged a winning formula, though Dadabhoy pointed out one slight modification that was later made in response to an unforeseen problem in the league's three-division structure. With a few Division 1 teams stacked with elite players, some squads felt unable to hold their own and moved down to Division 2. The number of Division 1 teams diminished to six as a result, and so to reverse this trend MBL switched in 2014 to a two Muslim to one non-Muslim ratio for Division 1 only.

National Muslim Basketball Tour and IBall Academy

While MB and MBL are the nation's largest, Muslim basketball leagues have thrived in Charlotte, Dallas, Memphis, and other American cities. One of the biggest outside New Jersey and Southern California is in Orlando, where players first laced up their shoes to play in National Muslim Athletic Association tournaments in 2006. NMAA added spring, winter, and fall leagues in 2009, with most seasons since its infancy putting seventeen to twenty teams on the floor. NMAA's unique distinction is its separation of teams into a Muslim division, open to Muslims age eighteen and above, and an Interfaith division, welcoming any male eighteen or older.[47] Instead of enjoying a stay in Orlando, though, I would like to briefly depart from focusing on local leagues while still looking at Muslim American basketball organizations, dropping in on the National Muslim Basketball Tour (NMBT) and IBall Academy.

A national circuit of basketball tournaments, NMBT has hosted major events in Chicago, Houston, Los Angeles, and New York, capped

---

[46] Ibid. Haaris Ahmad, sports director of a mosque in Michigan, enjoyed a laugh while talking about the presence of non-Muslim "ringers" in Muslim basketball tournaments. Recalling a tournament in which Muslims invited the top high school basketball player in Toronto to play on their team, Ahmad said, "Invariably at Muslim tournaments you'll have guys coming in, they'll bring in guys and be like, 'He's interested in Islam.' But he's a ringer, so now what are you supposed to say?" (Haaris Ahmad, personal interview, 21 March 2014, Canton MI).

[47] National Muslim Athletic Association website, http://www.nmaa-us.org (accessed 8 May 2014).

off by a championship tournament involving the top teams from each of the four regional tourneys.[48] NMBT aims "to strengthen the Muslim community through service, educating both Muslims and people of other faiths about the religion of Islam through sports, and facilitating a better environment for youth to be active."[49] NMBT's roots go back to Chicago, where in 2010 a few friends fancied the creation of rivalries between Muslim teams from cities across the nation, along the lines of rivalries in the NBA. Co-founder Haron Saadeh, a Palestinian American born and raised in Chicago, discussed the original vision of connecting teams from different cities, saying at first he thought local leagues might feel uncomfortable with a nationwide newcomer stepping onto their territorial turf. He found instead that local league directors were pumped by the prospect of adding intercity action to established intraregional rivalries, and the directors were eager to join in NMBT's efforts to hold tournaments during gaps between their local league seasons. Saadeh expressed deep gratitude for this assistance, since NMBT tournaments require many helping hands. As many as forty-two teams, divided into advanced, intermediate, and high school levels, compete over a weekend, with breaks for prayer scattered throughout the athletic action. Additionally, twice during the weekend a local Islamic scholar delivers a half-hour talk that typically ties the theme of brotherhood to a current event, such as a lecture at a tournament shortly after the 2011 Japanese tsunami that revolved around the brevity of life and need to care for one's brother now instead of later.

As Saadeh described them, NMBT tournaments go beyond talking the brotherhood talk; they walk the brotherhood walk both on and off the court. Weekends usually include after-game dinners at players' homes, connecting tournament participants hailing from various cities. Saadeh values such gatherings for their promotion of Muslim fellowship

[48] In 2015 NMBT expanded to One! Athletics, adding football, volleyball, soccer, and softball to its sporting slate as well as offering youth sports camps in cities across the nation (One! Athletics website, http://oneathletics.org/ (accessed 14 March 2015)).

[49] "National Muslim Basketball Tour: About," http://www.nmbt.org/about (accessed 8 May 2014).

as well as for the sake of networking, remarking that there might be "a guy in Kansas City who is still going to school who meets a guy in Toronto who owns a business, and now they've become friends. They talk on Facebook, they exchange numbers."[50] Similar to MB and MBL, a hallmark of NMBT-inspired brotherhood is its racial and ethnic diversity. NMBT tournaments "enable people of different backgrounds to come together, meet new Muslims, and create new friendships,"[51] and Saadeh suggested that some players of different races and ethnicities would never interact with one another outside the tournament venue. After declaring that in NMBT tournaments "you'll have converts play against people who've been Muslims their whole lives, you'll have an Indonesian against an African American against a White guy against a Spanish guy and some Palestinians,"[52] he made the following comments about African-American Muslims from inner-city Chicago taking the NMBT floor with immigrant Muslims from an affluent Chicago suburb:

> For these people, if they didn't have this basketball or sports, they would never meet or talk. Let's be real. Other than basketball, they have nothing else in common. The guy from Naperville is not going to go down to the South Side of Chicago. There's no reason for him to go down there, and vice-versa. …Before you see them stepping on the court, you can see the differences—you see them dress a certain way, talk a certain way. But when they're on the court they're all wearing gym shoes, socks, shorts, and a t-shirt, and they all look the same. And they all love the game of basketball.[53]

With its Islamic lectures, breaks for prayer, and fostering of Muslim fellowship, NMBT has strong bonding intentions, yet bridging is an important part of the NMBT package, too. Tournaments were originally Muslim-only, but directors decided to adopt an allowance of two non-Muslims per team. Saadeh stated that a major draw for players of any faith is NMBT tournaments' combination of intense competition and high-quality hoops skills. He proclaimed, "We're a very competitive

---

[50] Haron Saadeh, personal interview, 18 March 2014, Rosemont IL.
[51] "National Muslim Basketball Tour: About."
[52] Haron Saadeh, personal interview, 18 March 2014, Rosemont IL.
[53] Ibid.

league. We offer cash prizes. We've had people who've played high school basketball, D-I, D-II college, people who've played overseas.... The atmosphere is great. You get real good basketball."[54] Saadeh presented this atmosphere as an eye-opener for some non-Muslim players who enter tournaments with a low estimation of Muslims' basketball ardor and abilities, but step off the court with a brand new view.

NMBT's dynamic duo of dawah paired with high-quality basketball also powers IBall Academy, a basketball training service that offers team and individual instruction to New Jersey youth. IBall Academy was jointly conceived by Maher Abuawad, a Palestinian American who played college basketball and participates in MB's first division, and his wife, Amnah Elbarrad. According to Elbarrad, IBall Academy seeks to "incorporate life lessons into basketball,"[55] which Abuawad illustrated by saying that while instructing trainees on the triple threat (the moment when a player receives a pass and must quickly decide whether to shoot, dribble, or pass), he might talk to them about "observing their environment, understanding options, understanding how to make quick decisions within a limited amount of time."[56] Abuawad's life lessons often do not refer directly to the Qur'an or Hadith, but with his belief that Islam is a complete way of life, Abuawad considers Islamic teaching to stand at the heart of any piece of instruction he provides. He declared, "Islam is not like: 'Alright, here's basketball, here's Islam.' No, you take Islam through everything."[57] For Abuawad, integrating Islam and basketball is a slam dunk, in part because of natural team chemistry between the two. For example, he identified an affinity between the discipline required to become a great basketball player and the discipline needed to pray five times a day, and he argued that developing the former discipline can contribute greatly to honing the latter. Abuawad added that by enabling players to practice Islamic virtues such as respect for others in the structured environment of the court, basketball habituates them to apply these values while facing any opponent in everyday experience. Abuawad also

---

[54] Ibid.
[55] Amnah Elbarrad, personal interview, 21 February 2014, Lawrenceville NJ.
[56] Maher Abuawad, personal interview, 21 February 2014, Lawrenceville NJ.
[57] Ibid.

connected basketball with boosting brotherhood, commenting that occasionally in his lessons he challenges Muslim racial and ethnic division by highlighting the importance of gelling as one unit on the court.

Dissimilar to other basketball organizations discussed in this chapter, as of our 2014 conversation, little if any bridging occurs directly through IBall Academy since it has involved only Muslim trainees. Abuawad hopes to instruct non-Muslims in the future, however, intending to work directly with public school basketball teams. This transition is likely to be as smooth as Abuawad's adroit ball-handling skills, considering his comfort with not explicitly referring to Islamic teaching in his life lessons as well as his passion for developing great players, a goal that knows no religious bounds. Abuawad puts this passion into practice by drawing on his own experiences at different levels of the game and also through a comprehensive program he uses with trainees. Abuawad gets this program rolling by conducting a player evaluation encompassing the following elements: strength of fundamentals; weaknesses; basketball IQ, court vision, and teammate awareness; understanding of individual intangibles; physical conditioning, movement, and endurance; and mental toughness and ability to make on-court adjustments. Based on evaluation results, he then offers individualized "Target Training" and "Target Learning" programs to account for player deficiencies and to transform weaknesses into strengths.[58]

Muslim Athletic League

I round out this chapter in Boston, where Muslim Athletic League (MAL) founder Odsen Piton has big dreams to establish community athletic centers throughout the nation and the world, envisioning them as a Muslim version of the YMCA. This objective may be far from actualized, since MAL activities as of 2015 occur in the Boston area alone, but MAL's impact is locally deep even if not yet nationally or internationally wide. As I sat with the Haitian-born Piton at a pizza shop topping off a Sunday afternoon filled with four hours of MAL games, he described his Brooklyn upbringing and his founding of the league. Piton

[58] "IBall Academy: Basketball Training Overview," IBall Academy, http://www.iballacademy.org (accessed 8 May 2014).

described sports as a way for him to stay out of trouble while growing up in poverty without a father figure, and after converting to Islam in college, he wanted to make sports available as a way to drown out calls of illicit allures to youth. Piton mentioned that the shadow of 9/11 also served significantly in setting MAL in motion. As he explained in a newspaper interview, Piton and friend Ahmad Polad started organizing informal sporting events among youth "in an effort to reach out to non-Muslims who were…wary of them."[59] These athletic gatherings were seeds from which MAL blossomed.

With its motto, "Connecting a Diverse and Talented World through Sports," MAL organizes soccer, flag football, and baseball activities for men and boys and has plans to include soccer, volleyball, and general fitness for women and girls. At the sporting hub of this Boston association, though, is undoubtedly basketball, including tournaments for boys and a league for men. Piton proclaimed that "basketball is our forte,"[60] especially the Athletic League for All Men's League, which since 2010 has included a winter season and summer all-star team. League games are highly competitive and feature a few former college players as well as players who could hold their own in college arenas across the nation. I was struck by the league's level of on-court intensity, with at least one technical foul handed out in each of the four games I observed, two players ejected for shoving in one game, and Piton stepping onto the court to assist the referees in diffusing a dispute dangling on the verge of a major altercation in another. Although opposed to fighting in the league, Piton is thrilled by its fiercely competitive nature and high talent level, recognizing that these characteristics enhance the league's appeal. Aiming to amplify the league's attractiveness to current and future participants further, Piton puts players' names on jerseys, posts statistics on Facebook, holds an all-star game and skills competitions, doles out prizes for Player of the Week, and occasionally places

[59] Paul Leighton, "Muslim League Promotes Tolerance through Sports," http://www.salemnews.com/
local/x546350755/Muslim-league-promotes-tolerance-through-sports (published 29 December 2009; accessed 24 April 2014).
[60] Odsen Piton, personal interview, 9 March 2014, Cambridge MA.

game footage on YouTube, as he has done to showcase a high school player's skills against adult opponents in the league.

Piton's efforts have appealed to an array of individuals, with teams including African-American Muslims and Muslims of Somali, Arab, South Asian, and Bosnian descent. League rosters also include a large number of non-Muslims, much to Piton's delight. Whether unveiling his vision to hold an annual interfaith basketball tournament on September 11 or expressing his excitement about non-Muslims on MAL teams, Piton makes it clear as day that he is a bridge-builder at heart. Like most other Muslim American sports administrators, for Piton this aspect of dawah is based not on formal presentation of Islamic teaching, but on connecting non-Muslims with Muslims through the fun, familiar venue of sports. Piton speaks against preaching to non-Muslim players, concerned it might push them away from Islam. He explained, "I grew up a non-Muslim, and I remember in my days if somebody tried to preach to me, it might turn me off. ...I'm not here trying to preach to anyone but rather try to instill some of the values that Islam instilled in us, which are human values: respect one another, care for one another, help one another, give back to the community."[61] Striving from MAL's dawning days to create a welcoming environment for non-Muslim players, Piton recalled it was difficult at first to get non-Muslims to come, since many were nervous about playing in a Muslim league. A few, though, entered the league and, according to Piton, told their friends, "These guys are good people. They're peaceful."[62] Little by little, non-Muslim reluctance morphed into excitement, to the tune of non-Muslims making up about eighty percent of all players in the league.

While the adult basketball league has been MAL's most fully flowering sports program, Piton is highly devoted to cultivating athletic activities for inner-city youth. He professed that these activities are "beyond just sports. ...For my youth basketball program I try to teach the kids, 'Hey, whatever you need, let me know. I can try to reach out to other organizations.'"[63] Complementing his comments, a complete picture of

[61] Ibid.
[62] Ibid.
[63] Ibid.

Piton's concern for Muslim and non-Muslim youth appears on MAL's website, which lists the following youth sports program goals:

—Provide at-risk youth a platform to demonstrate their God-given athletic talents as well as the opportunity to network with diverse and talented individuals.
—Help youth develop skills they can apply in everyday situations, learn sportsmanship, and learn to be themselves while engaging society with confidence.
—Teach youth social responsibility, how to live healthy lives, and the importance of making smarter life choices which in the end will keep them out of trouble and away from drugs and gangs.
—Prevent youth and young adults from radicalizing.[64]

In line with these goals' intention to affect lives not only on the court or field, but off as well, MAL prizes community service, which Piton described as an essential piece of Islamic practice. Both youth and adult league participants are beneficiaries of this service. Quite a few players, for instance, have received assistance from Piton in crafting their resumes and developing job skills. Furthermore, youth and adult participants are providers of this service. Piton encourages players to dive head-first into MAL efforts such as serving food at homeless shelters. Much of this community work takes place under the auspices of MAL Cares, which provides services ranging from holding basketball fundraiser tournaments for disaster relief, to providing backpacks and school supplies for children in need to bestowing the Community Difference Maker Award honoring Boston-area volunteers.

[64] "Muslim Athletic League: About Us," http://malusa.org/about-us/ (accessed 8 May 2014).

8

Revivalist Organization Athletic Activities

As many Muslim Americans would call it, their religion is receiving blows from a two-fisted attack. Islamophobia is doing its damage, but a widespread understanding of Islam held by Muslims themselves is also capable of inflicting serious injury. In our conversation at the New Jersey branch headquarters of the Islamic Circle of North America, Ibrahim Jaaber expressed concern about a tendency to bifurcate human experience into religious and secular realms. As demonstrated by his decision to bid adieu to pro basketball due to what he identified as irreconcilable differences with Islamic values, Jaaber subscribes to the view that neither basketball nor anything else should be tucked away into a so-called secular realm. For Jaaber, Islam is a complete way of life, pertaining just as fully to basketball as to prayer or fasting. He bemoans that many Muslim Americans do not share this view, placing sports and other activities they regularly enjoy outside Islamic parameters. Jaaber stated that as young Muslim Americans disconnect their religion from significant aspects of their lives, they lose interest in Islam. According to Jaaber, the need is acute; steps must be taken to reverse the trend of Muslim youth thinking about Islam "as though it had something missing"[1] and as if it were divorced from pursuits such as sports that constitute major pieces of their weekly calendar and their personal identity.

From the standpoint of those who share Jaaber's conviction that Islam is a complete way of life, Muslims must recognize that Islam vitally intersects with any interest they have and with any activity in which they participate. Thus, Native Deen, 3ILM, and other revivalist Muslim American hip-hop groups bust rhymes that refer explicitly to Islamic principles, not only to inculcate these ideals via a musical genre that courses through many young Muslims' veins, but also to proclaim that

---

[1] Ibrahim Jaaber, personal interview, 18 February 2014, Somerset NJ.

Muslim youth should not dissociate a type of music they love from the religion they follow.[2] Thus, Muslim gamers can play a video game such as Abu Saleh in which their character must negotiate practicing Islam while assailed by temptations,[3] not only to apply this skill to their own lives, but also to learn to place gaming right alongside praying under the umbrella of Islam. In some cases, the outcome of subsuming every interest or activity under an all-encompassing Islamic canopy involves invoking a label of unacceptability by Islamic standards. A vulgarity-laced hip-hop song or a video game dripping with bloodshed at nearly every turn is destined to get a big thumbs-down from a large number of Muslims. Similarly with sports, situating every aspect of athletics within the purview of Islam might result in deeming a particular athletic activity impermissible, just as Jaaber responded to his pro basketball sojourn in Lithuania. On the other hand, as seen in multiple examples in this book, it also results in many sports activities being embraced as a vibrant component of Islamic experience.

From American sea to shining sea, such embrace of athletic activity appears in associations I am calling Muslim American "revivalist organizations." Contrary to Muslim basketball leagues, sports do not comprise these organizations' central activity, and in some cases sports may not have held a glimmer in founders' visionary eyes. Nonetheless, in each of these organizations, sports have become a prominent aspect of the complete way of life of Islam, whether in the form of late-night pick-up basketball games drawing a handful of students to a university gym or of all-day events swarming with over a thousand individuals competing in an athletic menagerie. Like any example of Muslim American sports, much

---

[2] Muslim Americans have different views regarding the acceptability of listening to hip-hop music, largely because of a longstanding disagreement among Muslims over whether music, or certain forms of music, is halal (permissible) or haram (impermissible) (Suad Abdul Khabeer, "*Rep That Islam*: The Rhyme and Reason of American Islamic Hip Hop," *Muslim World* 97 (2007): 128–30). Abdul Khabeer points out that many Muslim Americans "who favor the religious sanctioning of hip hop draw analogies between hip hop and poetry within the Islamic tradition" (ibid., 130).

[3] "Abu Saleh (CD) Arcade Game," http://www.islamicbookstore.com/ abus-alcdarga.html (accessed 14 March 2015).

of the motivation to organize these athletic activities centers simply upon a fancy to have fun. At the same time, though, revivalist organizations also often arrange sports activities for the purpose of dawah, seeking to propel Muslim Americans towards deeper piety and stronger fellowship, and to connect non-Muslims with Muslims in post-9/11 America.

Muslim Students Association

A key character in American Islamic revivalism's seminal era, the Muslim Students Association (MSA) was founded by students primarily in scientific and technical fields at the University of Illinois at Urbana-Champaign. The MSA's first national conference in 1963 drew students who had come to the United States from India, Pakistan, Iran, Turkey, Saudi Arabia, Egypt, and other nations. Many attended colleges and universities in American locales with no mosque or otherwise organized Muslim community, and so the MSA provided unique opportunity for Muslim fellowship in addition to fortifying foreign students' commitment to Islam in a majority non-Muslim land. Since its Illinois inception, a prevailing MSA theme has been Islam as a total way of life, based upon the Qur'an and the example of Muhammad. This theme was forged in the crucible of revivalist thinkers from Islamic lands, especially Sayyid Qutb and Mawlana al-Mawdudi,[4] but it was greatly shaped by its American surroundings. Kambiz GhaneaBassiri notes that while some MSA founders were affiliated with Mawdudi's Jama'at-i Islami or, like Qutb, had Muslim Brotherhood connections, this does not mean that founders "agreed with every action these organizations undertook. Such an understanding misleads one to think of the MSA as an outreach of a foreign organization and overlooks the significant influence of the American context on the development of the MSA."[5] Moreover, although revivalist characteristics have endured over the decades throughout MSA expansion to hundreds of college and university campuses, these characteristics have manifested themselves in a wide spectrum of ways. Zareena

---

[4] In its early years, the MSA publication *Al-Ittihad* ("Unity") regularly included articles by Qutb and Mawdudi (Kambiz GhaneaBassiri, *Competing Visions of Islam in the United States: A Study of Los Angeles* (Westport CT: Greenwood Press, 1997) 26).

[5] GhaneaBassiri, *A History of Islam in America*, 266.

Grewal asserts that amidst its revivalist roots, the MSA "quickly evolved into an umbrella institution, not reflective of any one specific strain of Islam or even of Islamist political ideology."[6] Revivalist emphases on Islam as a complete way of life and on the importance of dawah infuse the lyrics of MSA refrains, but they are set to a variety of American-inflected melodies at MSA chapters across the nation.

Consistent with such variety, some MSA chapters organize sports activities whereas others do not. Within the former stands the University of North Carolina at Chapel Hill MSA, which coordinates Sportsfest, an annual fundraising event with basketball and flag football tournaments for men and for women. Bringing multiple MSA chapters to Chapel Hill, the 2015 Sportsfest amassed a generous donation toward educational efforts for underprivileged Muslim women in Zanzibar.[7] Another large-scale MSA event including athletic competition takes place in Texas, where MSA chapters across the Lone Star State come together for the Texas MSA Showdown. As suggested by the website for its ninth annual version in 2015, a desire to promote bonding permeates Showdown. MSA members are told to expect to meet "Muslims from all across Texas as you build unity, school spirit, and your imaan [faith]."[8] The weekend-long gathering comprises more than just sports, as competitors go head to head in categories such as film, extemporaneous speaking, poetry, and Qur'an recitation. Yet, for many of its participants, totaling over 600 in 2014, Showdown's lifeblood is its tournaments in men's and women's basketball, men's flag football, and women's volleyball.

Besides major events incorporating multiple chapters, MSA athletic activities take place at the individual chapter level. Boston University MSA president Amir Ali fondly described his chapter's MSA All-Star Weekend, a basketball bash featuring a three-point shootout, skills challenge, and all-star game. True to the basketballization of American Is-

[6] Grewal, *Islam Is a Foreign Country*, 138–39.

[7] "UNC MSA Sportsfest," University of North Carolina Muslim Students Association, http://www.uncmsa.org/#!sportsfest/c17et (accessed 14 March 2015).

[8] "MSA Showdown," Muslim Students Association Lone Star Council, http://www.msa-texas.org/#!msa-showdown-2015/c8mg (accessed 13 March 2015).

lam, All-Star Weekend is just one way in which basketball shapes Boston University MSA culture, at least for many of its male members. Ali proclaimed that basketball is "engrained in our religious life."[9] He and his MSA pals pray the fajr (early morning) salat at 5:30 on Saturday mornings and then head to a campus gym and play basketball, often for about four hours. Basketball is also a popular nighttime activity for MSA members, especially on Friday and Saturday nights when they seek out an alternative to the campus drinking and partying scene. Looking back on his college days, Chris Blauvelt stated that among his University of Michigan MSA friends, playing basketball "was basically what we always did on Friday and Saturday night."[10] Reminiscent of Shabana Mir's observation of Muslim college students seeking out "alternative freedoms" as substitutes to alcohol-centered entertainment,[11] these Friday- and Saturday-night basketball games enable young Muslims to adhere to their religious beliefs instead of capitulating to campus social norms that conflict with Islamic interdictions against alcohol. Choosing the jump shot over the shot glass, they avoid alcohol in an environment where it readily flows. Furthermore, as Blauvelt proposed, weekend nighttime basketball empowers young Muslim men to turn their backs to hegemonic conceptions of college student masculinity drenched in drinking. Blauvelt asserted that for Muslim students who play basketball on Friday and Saturday nights, there is no need to "feel like you're any less of a man, because it's a strenuous, physical activity. It's competitive, so it's a way of still being a man but not giving in to peer pressure."[12] Unlike classmates who measure their manhood by knocking back twelve-ounce bottles, MSA students can maintain their sense of masculinity by knocking down three-pointers.

Participants in individual chapter MSA sports activities are fre-

[9] Amir Ali, personal interview, 7 March 2014, Boston MA.

[10] Chris Blauvelt, personal interview, 19 March 2014, Detroit MI.

[11] Mir devotes a chapter of *Muslim American Women on Campus* to a variety of responses to campus alcohol consumption and partying. Some Muslim American female students join fully in this alcohol culture, while many others do not and therefore seek out "alternative freedoms and models of 'healthy,' integrated Muslim American youth identities" (Mir, *Muslim American Women on Campus*, 51).

[12] Chris Blauvelt, personal interview, 19 March 2014, Detroit MI.

quently Muslim friends who have known each other for a significant period of time, but these activities also initiate connections between Muslims on campus. Ali recounted his Boston University MSA's first function of the 2013–2014 academic year, which ended up including an impromptu football game he considers to be extremely influential in getting a few freshmen involved in his MSA chapter. Ali opined, "When you sit in a room and you bring everybody together, it's kind of awkward at first. Nobody knows each other. But if you put a ball in their hands...you're in a familiar space."[13] Taking this to heart, Ali suggested at the beginning of the school year event that MSA members and Muslims new to the university play football together. He recalled the scene:

> Everybody's yelling, screaming. Everybody feels like it's their showcase to shine. It's their time to show that they're significant. They're good at this. They're a leader. You become vocal. You're going to say, "Go over there. Watch out for him. Go deep, slant route, post route, whatever." So you're talking, and it's not within the context of trying to create awkward conversation knowing somebody, but it's more like, "Let's try and win this game together." And you make a catch—quick high-five. That brings people together. It does a great job of ice-breaking.[14]

In other instances of MSA athletic activity, ice gets broken between Muslims and non-Muslims. University of California-Los Angeles MSA activities director Wali Kamal pointed out that non-Muslim students occasionally participate in informal basketball, soccer, football, and cricket games that members of his chapter cobble together. Mentioning that the main motivation of these games "isn't necessarily to break down barriers" but to have fun, Kamal stated that bridging may nonetheless result as "a corollary."[15] Elsewhere on some campuses, bridging forms the motivational nitty-gritty of particular MSA athletic activities. University of Delaware MSA president Madinah Wilson discussed her chapter's 2014 Islam Awareness Week, which featured a basketball tournament along with events such as an interfaith dinner and presentation about women in

[13] Amir Ali, personal interview, 7 March 2014, Boston MA.
[14] Ibid.
[15] Wali Kamal, personal interview, 11 April 2014, Los Angeles CA.

Islam.[16] Though double-dipping as a charity fundraiser, the tournament was arranged largely in order to connect non-Muslim students with Muslims on the court and supply them with a favorable view of a religion they may have previously seen in a negative light. Drinking further from sports' bridging well, Delaware MSA Awareness Week included a screening of *Fordson: Faith, Fasting, Football.* With its dramatic portrayal of high school athletes engaging in the distinctively Islamic practice of fasting during Ramadan amidst the familiar American context of pursuing excellence on the football field,[17] the documentary about the Dearborn team is well equipped to highlight the harmony between the two words in the label "Muslim American."

Islamic Circle of North America and Muslim American Society

Shortly after the MSA's founding, the Islamic Circle of North America (ICNA) became the new neighbor on the American Islamic revivalist block. Established in 1968 by South Asian immigrants, ICNA "initially focused on educating its growing membership about Islam, the goal being to adhere to Islamic values amongst a religiously diverse community."[18] ICNA has picked up a number of programs and projects over the years. Its website proclaims that nearly half a century after its birth, ICNA now works to

[16] Madinah Wilson, personal interview, 19 February 2014, Newark DE.

[17] According to the film website, the documentary follows "a predominantly Arab-American high school football team from a working-class Detroit suburb as they practice for their big cross-town rivalry game during the last ten days of Ramadan, revealing a community holding onto its Islamic faith while they struggle for acceptance in post 9/11 America" ("*Fordson: Faith, Fasting, Football* and the American Dream," http://www.fordsonthemovie.com (accessed 24 April 2014)). The film's director is Chicago-area Muslim Rashid Ghazi, who saw tremendous bridging potential in documenting the troubles and triumphs of football players at a primarily Muslim high school. Ghazi has proclaimed, "In America, sports have probably done more to break down racial tension and misunderstanding than anything else" (quoted in Joshua Haddow, "There's a Muslim Football Team at a High School in Michigan," Vice Media, http://www.vice.com/read/fordson-faith-fasting-football-rashid-ghazi (posted 31 January 2012; accessed 24 April 2014)).

[18] "About ICNA," Islamic Circle of North America, http://www.icna.org/about-icna (accessed 14 March 2015).

establish connections between Islam and the public, collaborating with numerous Muslim organizations to reach this end. ICNA also works closely with many national interfaith organizations for the betterment of society. By focusing on self-development, education, outreach, and social services, ICNA has cemented its place as a leading grassroots organization in the American Muslim community.[19]

Among its largest programs are ICNA Relief, developed to provide humanitarian and social services for underserved communities in the United States, and WhyIslam?, spawned especially to teach non-Muslims about Islam. Often taking its message to the masses in packed public places such as shopping malls or Times Square, WhyIslam? has used major sporting events as springboards to encourage non-Muslims to consider turning to Islam. Near New Jersey's MetLife Stadium, Super Bowl XLVIII spectators were greeted by a billboard displaying Why-Islam?'s phone number under the words "Life Is Not Just a Game." Later the same year, WhyIslam? representatives traveled to Brazil for the World Cup, where they wore t-shirts that posed the question "What's Your Goal?" along with the WhyIslam? phone number.

ICNA's relationship with sports goes well beyond tying proselytization efforts to major athletic events. At the core of ICNA's Young Muslims program reside NeighborNets, weekly gatherings comprising a halaqah (talking circle) followed by a social activity. Especially for male attendees, this latter component oftentimes revolves around basketball or another sport. In Atlanta, the local ICNA branch is affiliated with Marjaan, a group that relies heavily on sports to boost piety and fellowship among Muslim youth. Marjaan was launched in 2007 by young Atlanta Muslims dismayed by "the lack of participation, the lack of belonging, and the lack of knowledge present within the Muslim Youth community," as well as by the influence of "peer pressure to engage in illicit relationships with women, drugs, and gangs."[20] The Arabic word marjaan means "precious gems" or "jewels," reflecting founders' conviction that Muslim youth "are all precious jewels, jems [*sic*], pearls, yet each one of

---

[19] Ibid.

[20] "Marjaan: About Us," http://www.marjaan.org/about-us/ (accessed 29 April 2014).

us needs to be found under the scope of Islam to be polished and groomed to become valuable assets to society."[21] Marjaan founders chose sports, specifically basketball and flag football tournaments, to function as their primary polishing wheel. Basketball has been Marjaan's number-one sport since day one, with annual hoops tournaments drawing around thirty teams, divided into thirteen- through seventeen-year-old as well as eighteen-and-above age groups, to face off in preliminary and playoff rounds punctuated by breaks for prayer and a religious lecture.

In the array of ICNA athletic activities, none comes close in size to ICNA-New Jersey's annual Muslim Sports Day. Descending upon two adjacent middle schools that offer abundant indoor and outdoor athletic space, over a thousand men, women, and youth compete in basketball, volleyball, soccer, cricket, karate, track and field, table tennis, tennis, and badminton tournaments,[22] held alongside amusements such as carnival rides, sack races, tug of war, and a baby crawling race. ICNA-New Jersey began hosting Muslim Sports Day in 2012, before which the event was coordinated by the organization Islamic Games and was known as Islamic Games Northeast. In retirement since 2012, Islamic Games held supersized sporting get-togethers inspired by the following objectives:

—To foster better relationship between Muslims and other Americans through sports

—To execute professional sports and athletic events

—To organize Muslim athletes, coaches, officials, and sports events

—To promote athletics skills within the Muslim community

—To develop higher appreciation for sports among Muslims[23]

---

[21] Ibid.

[22] More specifically, events are broken up by age and gender as follows: basketball (male: 10–13, 14–17, 18 and up; female: 10–13, 14 and above), volleyball (male: open; female: under 13, 14 and above), soccer (male: 10–13, 14–18, 19–35, 36 and above; female: 10–13, 14–18), cricket (male: open), karate (male: various age groups; female: various age groups), track and field (male youth 100m, 200m, 400m, 800m, 1500m; female youth 100m, 200m), table tennis (male: open; female: open), tennis (male: 15–18, 19 and older; female: 15–18, 19 and older), and badminton (male: all ages; female: all ages).

[23] "Islamic Games: About Us," http://www.islamic-games.com/ (accessed 24 April 2014). Islamic Games planned to host regional games in the United States that

Displaying his high regard for the first objective, national chairman Salaudeen Nausrudeen declared that Islamic Games events were open to members of all faiths because "it is critically important that...other Americans see Muslims as Americans, too."[24] This bridging legacy abides in ICNA-New Jersey's Muslim Sports Day vision. Estimated by event coordinator Mogheera Nagra at five to ten percent and concentrated mostly in basketball, the non-Muslim presence may be relatively small, but Nagra and fellow organizers have big aspirations to provide non-Muslim participants with a profoundly positive understanding of Islam.[25] Yet, despite this deep bridging desire, there is no mistaking that at least in terms of number of individuals affected, bonding rules the Muslim Sports Day roost. A distinct Muslim flavor fills the fields and gyms throughout the day. Signs saying "Do Not Litter" followed by the Hadith statement "Cleanliness Is Half Emaan [Faith]" bestrew the middle schools' grounds, smells from food stands serving South Asian and Arab cuisine pungently permeate the premises, and the day's Muslim tang is tasted most recognizably shortly after 1 P.M., when tournaments for each sport temporarily come to a halt for the salat prayer. With hundreds of athletic shoes behind them, 2014 Muslim Sports Day participants and spectators formed long lines and prostrated on large blue tarps laid out on the grass after listening to requests to help fund WhyIslam? World Cup dawah efforts in Brazil and to support families devastated by fighting in Syria. The event's Muslim stripes are further exhibited by the ever-present sight of women in hijab, as female participants, making up thirty to forty percent of Muslim Sports Day athletes, heed the event regulation that "Islamic Dress codes are expected—if you can pray in it,

---

would culminate at a National Islamic Games. In its brief history, Islamic Games were held only in New Jersey and Michigan.

[24] Quoted in Ahmed Mohamed, "Michigan Hosts Large Muslim American Sports Event,"

http://iipdigital.usembassy.gov/st/english/article/2009/08/200908191642352sademahom4.323977e-02.html#axzz2t8TEsPfh (posted 20 August 2009; accessed 24 April 2014).

[25] Mogheera Nagra, personal interview, 22 February 2014, Somerset NJ.

you can play in it!"[26] Hijab is also on display by way of booths at the bazaar. Vendors such as Urban Modesty (featuring the catchy slogan "If You Got Modesty, We Got You Covered") peddle their sartorial splendor next to book publishers, jewelry sellers, and stands advertising online Islamic studies programs and shariah-compliant investment firms.

Like ICNA, the Muslim American Society (MAS) is a grassroots revivalist organization with branches across America. With a mission "to move people to strive for God consciousness, liberty, and justice and to convey Islam with utmost clarity,"[27] MAS describes itself as a "charitable, religious, social, cultural, educational, and not-for-profit organization. It is a pioneering Islamic organization, an Islamic revival, and reform movement that uplifts the individual, the family, and the society."[28] A fraternal relationship has blossomed between ICNA and younger brother MAS, which was born in 1993, twenty-five years after ICNA's first breaths. Members of each organization have assembled annually since 2002 at the joint ICNA-MAS national convention. Family resemblance between the two siblings extends into the realm of sports, as MAS efforts to put its conception of Islam as a complete way of life into practice entail integrating sports activities within weekly gatherings and coordinating sports leagues and athletic events. Sports enjoy high billing in a number of MAS Youth divisions.[29] The San Diego division, for example, hosts annual basketball and flag football tournaments for young men and, in 2014, inaugurated May Madness, a basketball tournament for female

---

[26] "Muslim Sports Day: Rules," Islamic Circle of North America–New Jersey, http://msd.icnanj.org/index.php?option=com_content&view=article&id=174&Itemid=2 (accessed 8 May 2014).

[27] "About MAS," Muslim American Society, http://www.massandiego.org/ index.php?option=com_content&view=article&id=13&Itemid=69 (accessed 14 March 2015).

[28] Ibid.

[29] MAS Youth presents itself as "a hub for youth who aspire to fulfill all their potential and who are not satisfied with occasional and/or nominal participation in Islamic (community) activities/functions: those who subscribe to the belief that reform (enjoying what is good and forbidding what is evil) is an essential part of Islam and is both mandatory and necessary, and requires collective and organized efforts" ("MAS Youth," http://www.massandiego.org/index.php?option=com_content& view=article&id=16&Itemid=30 (accessed 13 March 2015)).

players. Most MAS Youth San Diego tournament participants are high-schoolers, but the group arranges sports activities for a younger set as well, including a ten-week basketball clinic for aspiring hoops stars aged six to thirteen. A few thousand miles from San Diego, athletes converge upon Tampa, where the local MAS Youth division has been hosting members of several MAS chapters at the multi-sport MYathlon since 2003.[30] Divided into Rookie (age nine to twelve), Junior (twelve to fifteen), Senior (sixteen to eighteen), and Pro (nineteen and up) Divisions, male and female competitors vie for tournament supremacy in basketball, soccer, flag football, and volleyball. Along the lines of ICNA-New Jersey's Muslim Sports Day, in which male participants play in one middle school and females in the other, gender separation is emphasized at each MYathlon. A rule declares that "no one of the opposite gender will be allowed in the courts or fields during the weekend tournaments for the comfort of other players, including parents and coaches."[31] As another commonality with Muslim Sports Day, while MYathlon welcomes non-Muslim competitors, the vast majority of participants are Muslims, leading MYathlon pride of place to fall upon bonding. Organizers proclaim that

> as servants of Allah (SWT) [*subhanahu wa ta'ala*, meaning "glory to Him, the exalted"], all that we do should be in striving to attain His Pleasure. Therefore, whether it is during your team preparations, your games the day of, or even just your down time, try to take some time out to refresh your intentions—after all, MYathlon's main purpose is to strengthen the bonds of brotherhood and sisterhood for the sake of Allah (SWT).[32]

Recognizing young Muslims' passion for sports and believing that playing together can strengthen inclinations for praying and staying together, MAS Youth leaders detect huge bonding potential in major events such as MYathlon and in sports activities at the local division level.

---

[30] MY stands for MAS Youth. MYathlon was formerly known as the MAS Olympics.

[31] "MAS Tampa MYathlon," http://www.mastampa.org/MYathlon/ (accessed 8 May 2014).

[32] Ibid.

Muslim Youth Community Center

Similar to the nationwide revivalist organizations already discussed in this chapter, sports activities play an important dawah role in a few revivalist organizations that operate exclusively in one particular geographical area. A prime example is the Muslim Youth Community Center (MYCC), founded in 2008. Though MYCC hopes to one day franchise facilities across America, complete with basketball courts, swimming pools, outdoor athletic fields, fitness areas for men and for women, daycare, seminar rooms, auditoriums, banquet halls, and more, as of 2015 its functions are found within New Jersey state lines. MYCC's mission is to "serve local communities by providing a venue for communal programs that promote Muslim values to people of all ages, faiths, and backgrounds,"[33] and its programs encompass four realms: community engagement, family services, learning and professional development, and recreational activities. During its rather brief history, MYCC has made headway in the first three realms. Its New Jersey Islamic Speakers Bureau, for instance, trains and arranges for Muslims to give presentations about Islam in public schools and libraries, and MYCC partners with charitable organizations such as Smile, which runs a food pantry out of a Northern New Jersey mosque and seeks to expand its reach throughout the Garden State thanks to MYCC's helping hand. MYCC's bread and butter, though, has been its programs in the recreational activities realm. Along with MYCC Sports Youth basketball and volleyball leagues for boys and for girls, MYCC oversees the adult leagues Muslim Basketball and Jersey Association of Muslim Sports (JAMS), which includes flag football, softball, soccer, and cricket leagues. JAMS softball is a particularly big hit, with around 300 players taking their swings on New Jersey diamonds during the 2014 season.

Taking JAMS, Muslim Basketball, and MYCC Sports Youth as a whole, roughly thirty percent of participants are non-Muslims, giving MYCC athletic activity ample opportunity to impact non-Muslims' conceptions of Islam. The organization's website announces an aspiration to

---

[33] "MYCC: About," Muslim Youth Community Center, http://www.myccnj.org/about/ (accessed 8 May 2014).

bridge what it calls the "Muslim/Non-Muslim Gap," saying, "For far too long, Islam has been seen as 'the other religion'... [MYCC] extends an open invitation to people of all creeds to come enjoy our services and programs and allows the Muslims to give back to their communities."[34] Along with their eagerness to bridge this gap, MYCC organizers are keen to deal with gaps within the Muslim community. Demonstrating a focus on bonding coexisting with its bridging concentration, MYCC adds to its "Muslim/Non-Muslim Gap" description by presenting four gaps as major roadblocks to Islamic piety and fellowship. More substantively than any other artefact I have discovered, the statements that describe each gap encapsulate what I heard from a large number of Muslim American athletic organizers as they discussed concerns that galvanize their bonding gusto. Thus, I quote these statements in their entirety in order to shed light on what fuels the motivational motor for bonding not only in MYCC sports, but in dozens of Muslim athletic activities across America:

> Age Gap: Our generation are the children of immigrant parents. Between the two generations exists a culture, language, and even, understanding gap. A few years from now, the masjids [mosques] will be run by the youth of today, and if this generation doesn't identify with the masjids, our masjids will be nothing more than hollow structures. MY Community Center offers a whole suite of services and programs that can be enjoyed by the older generation as well as the younger generation, bringing them together not only for spiritual, but also for recreational purposes.
>
> Ethnicity Gap: So many of our masjids are geographically close to one another, but operate as silos. They often become branded as the "Pakistani masjid" or "Arab masjid" or "African-American masjid." MY Community Center knocks down these subtle, yet very real, racial barriers and allows the communities to unite as one.
>
> Religiosity Gap: The masjid have long been known as spiritual centers—a place for worship and nothing more. Unfortunately, 90% of the Muslims in America do not regularly attend prayers or programs at the masjid. What better way than to use sports, recreation, humanitari-

---

[34] Ibid.

an services, civic engagement, etc. to bring people together—regardless of where they may lie on the religiosity spectrum?

Accommodation Gap: For far too long, our currently existing institutions have failed to address the needs of our sisters. From sports to cooking classes, to pre- and post-natal counseling, our sisters will finally have services dedicated to them and allow them to stay active in an environment built around the Islamic principle of modesty.[35]

A Muslim in his forties might complete a pass to a Muslim half his age on the flag football field, or an African-American Muslim might set a pick for an Afghan Muslim teammate on the basketball floor. A Muslim outfielder who prays five times a day might exchange a high-five with a Muslim teammate who rarely prays, or a Muslim woman might enjoy her first chance ever to play volleyball with Muslim sisters in a gym isolated from the presence of men.[36] In each case, sports step into a gap identified by MYCC. Enabling Muslims to connect with a wide array of fellow followers of Islam as well as with non-Muslims on a regular basis, athletic activity forms a fundamental part of MYCC's vision to "develop a strong, healthy community of Muslims that weaves seamlessly into the American fabric while still maintaining its sacred values."[37]

Seeking to bring this vision to fruition, MYCC has carved out a particularly distinctive plot in Muslim American athletic terrain with its MYCC Sports Youth basketball league. Comprising twelve boys' teams in its inaugural 2013 season, the league grew to twenty-two boys' teams and five girls' teams the following year. A few squads are mosque-based, but the majority come from New Jersey Islamic high schools, making the league an unprecedented opportunity for Islamic school basketball teams to compete against one another in an organized association. Ibrahim Omar, who co-founded the league during his junior year at an Islamic school, explained that he and his friends were frustrated by his school's slim athletic pickings in comparison to local public schools. Omar stated

---

[35] Ibid.

[36] MYCC's Muslimah Athletics "was created to strengthen the bonds of sisterhood while participating in health and fitness activities in a modest and Islamic environment. Activities include Pilates, yoga, Zumba, volleyball, and much more" (ibid.).

[37] Ibid.

that before the league's formation, his school "didn't have any organized sports at all. We would have these bush-league basketball tournaments that we would join—not a real roster, no set practices. It's something that irked me, and it's also something that when I would tell people I go to Islamic school, they were like, 'Oh, I would go to Islamic school, but you guys don't have sports, so that's not something I want to get involved in.'"[38] Supplying new access to athletic activity for Islamic school students, the league has been received with great acclaim. Omar gushed that when the league began, "the response was amazing. Kids loved it. They just loved the fact that now they had a chance to play in an organized league with refs and a schedule and play-offs and a trophy at the end of the year."[39] Players also relish the prospect of participating in All-Star Weekend, featuring a three-point contest and skills competition in addition to an all-star game. As a further perk for the cream of the crop, the league has caught the eye of college recruiters, who otherwise would identify Islamic school diamonds in the rough only through basketball camps or summer travel teams. Comparing getting noticed by recruiters before and after the genesis of the league, Al Ghazaly High School player Anas Najib proclaimed, "Being in an Islamic school, you're bottled in, and you can't do that. You don't have the chance. This league, it's a big step forward."[40] While Islamic school boys have been pumped up about the league, Omar suggested that girls may be even more thrilled. He remarked that Islamic school girls "have never had a platform where they can compete like this. Some guys played in rec leagues before, AAU teams—the girls have never had this platform because they've never been provided with the opportunity to have that intimacy and that privacy that they need to play, so this is a first for them, having organized basketball. So they were extremely excited."[41] In the process of breaking athletic opportunity ground, the league has also broken ground in bringing together Muslim youth throughout New Jersey. MYCC administrator Sami Sha-

[38] Ibrahim Omar, personal interview, 1 May 2014, Parsippany NJ.

[39] Ibid.

[40] Quoted in Stanmyre, "New Jersey Islamic Students See Basketball League Taking Shape."

[41] Ibrahim Omar, personal interview, 1 May 2014, Parsippany NJ.

ban declared that the league contains teams from Muslim communities that, prior to playing together, were never "connected in a systematic way. These are communities that have existed for thirty years in New Jersey within ten, twenty miles of each other. ...Through this, they're coming together."[42] Besides this particular promotion of bonding, league administrators encourage teammates to work together in practicing the Islamic principle of charity. Shaban described a league food drive that ventures to feed 100 families during Ramadan, with the team collecting the most food scoring a private session with former basketball pro Mahmoud Abdul-Rauf.

Muslim Interscholastic Tournament

In the same vein as what MYCC Sports Youth basketball has provided for Islamic school athletes, the Muslim Interscholastic Tournament (MIST) has furnished high-schoolers with an abundant supply of kindling to ignite their competitive fires. MIST competitions are "geared towards bringing high school students together from around the nation to develop leadership, communication, and other creative skills, all while gaining a deeper understanding of Islam and Muslims."[43] MIST's story starts in 2002, when University of Houston freshman Shazia Siddiqi drew upon her experiences in art and speech competitions to create an event intended to strengthen connections among young Muslims while providing them with fun and challenging activities. An individual from the Washington, D.C. area learned about the initial event in Houston and started a D.C. MIST the next year, and the movement soon proliferated. MIST has grown to hold regional tournaments in Atlanta, Boston, Chicago, Detroit, Houston, Nashville, New York, Philadelphia, Southern California, Toronto, and Washington, D.C., with winners from each regional gathering advancing to an annual national tournament. Organized around a different theme each year—such as "American-Muslim Identity" or, in 2015, "The Clarity of Sincerity: From Outer Perceptions to Inner Reflections"—MIST tournaments include work-

[42] Sami Shaban, personal interview, 1 May 2014, Parsippany NJ.

[43] "MIST: About," Muslim Interscholastic Tournament, http://www.get-mistified.com/about/ (accessed 8 May 2014).

shops and talks that relate to the annual theme. Depending on the region, MIST tournaments involve up to thirty-one different competitions, divided into six categories:

> Category One, Knowledge and Quran: Knowledge Test 1, 2, 3, and 4; Brothers Quran Recitation Level 1 and 2; Sisters Quran Recitation Level 1 and 2; Tafseer [Interpretation] Test
>
> Category Two, Arts: 2D Art; 3D Art; Fashion Design; Graphic Design; Photography
>
> Category Three, Writing and Oratory: Extemporaneous Essay; Extemporaneous Speaking; Original Oratory; Poetry; Prepared Essay; Short Fiction; Spoken Word
>
> Category Four, Bracket Competitions: Debate; Brothers Improv; Sisters Improv; Math Olympics; MIST Bowl
>
> Category Five, Group Projects: Business Venture; Brothers Nasheed [Islamic song]/Rap; Sisters Nasheed/Rap; Research in Action; Science Fair; Scrapbook; Short Film; Social Media
>
> Category Six, Sports: Brothers Basketball; Sisters Basketball

With youth vying for prizes and for spots in the national tournament, MIST's competitive aspect is "what keeps it exciting,"[44] according to D.C. region coordinator Adam Kareem, who contrasted MIST tournaments to similar-size Muslim gatherings centered around religious lectures. Kareem expressed that the latter type of gathering is valuable for Muslim youth, but "because it doesn't require as much involvement from the people who attend, there's always going to be a limit on how effective I think it can be and how much people really invest themselves into it."[45] For MIST, on the other hand, participants get ready weeks in advance, pouring themselves into preparation and then into the tournament itself.

As displayed by the list above, MIST competition goes far beyond just sports. Basketball was included the first year specifically for the purpose of generating male interest. MIST organizers nailed a three-pointer with this inclusion; basketball has been a major reason why male participants have flocked to MIST tournaments. Organizers felt that basketball

---

[44] Adam Kareem, personal interview, 20 February 2014, Alexandria VA.
[45] Ibid.

players would miss out on what MIST had to offer if their experience took place on the court alone, and so basketball is MIST's lone competition containing a stipulation that participants must register for at least one other event. Detroit region coordinator Faisal Chaudhry addressed this rule, saying that "for a lot of the basketball kids, I feel like they just want to do sports and then they kind of want to get out of there. But we force them to do something else. …It gets them out of their comfort zone, but they're still comfortable. It's still a safe environment, so they can express themselves."[46] Illustrating this last point, Chaudhry proudly noted a basketball player who one year took first place in fashion design.

Many basketball competitors participate in MIST activities on consecutive weekends, since some regions hold their basketball tournament the weekend before all other competitions due to facility issues. In the Detroit region, 150 of the 442 MIST competitors in 2014 took part in the full-day basketball tournament at Henry Ford Community College, whereas every other event occurred the following weekend at Wayne State University, which is cost-prohibitive in basketball court rental. In the Atlanta region, on the other hand, basketball takes place on the same weekend as other competitions, which Atlanta coordinator Salma Stoman stated is necessary because competitors come from a number of Southern states and often travel much greater distances than participants in other regions.[47] The Atlanta region allocates Friday solely to basketball. From 3 o'clock in the afternoon until around midnight, boys play their preliminary and final round games in one gym and girls in another. Separated from male onlookers and officiated by female referees, girls go head to head without headscarves, donning t-shirts and shorts.

As they compete on the MIST basketball floor, participants team up with fellow members of their public or Islamic high school. MIST specifies that participants represent their school and compete against other schools in all events, not only in group contests such as basketball or business venture, but also in individual competitions in which students gain points for their school team. MIST included mosque-based teams initially in D.C., but D.C. organizers shifted to MIST's original purely

[46] Faisal Chaudhry, personal interview, 20 March 2014, Detroit MI.
[47] Salma Stoman, phone interview, 21 April 2014.

school-centric model in order to connect Muslim youth with fellow Muslims at their high school and to bring more non-Muslims into a Muslim environment to help them learn about Islam. According to Kareem, this shift had its share of critics. Coaches of successful mosque-based teams were reluctant to break up their squads, and many doubted that public high schools could supply enough participants to form a team. In time, though, the response became resoundingly positive, as the shift accomplished what it set out to do. Chaudhry asserted that, especially through basketball with its teams of ten or so players, MIST has facilitated Muslim schoolmate friendships that most likely never would have blossomed otherwise. Chaudhry suggested that a MIST basketball roster typically "crosses the borders between age, grade, and class within the high school. When you're in high school the freshmen stay to themselves. But with basketball the varsity senior guys are playing with the freshmen guys."[48] Furthermore, MIST basketball rosters sometimes cross borders between religions. MIST's arms are open wide to embrace non-Muslim participation in any event, consistent with founders' ambition to provide non-Muslim high-schoolers with an understanding of Islam that contrasts sharply with negative conceptions they have encountered in post-9/11 America. Occasionally, a non-Muslim participant is extremely successful in an assortment of MIST competitions. Stoman commented that although non-Muslims will probably not do as well as Muslims in a religious-based competition such as Qur'an recitation, the array of events not centered on Islamic knowledge enables a situation such as what took place in her Atlanta region, where a Jewish competitor finished third in the overall individual points standings.

Excitement about non-Muslim involvement was a recurring theme in conversations with coordinators, yet I heard even more about bonding than bridging, perhaps a product of the fact that over ninety percent of participants at most MIST tournaments are Muslims. As described by coordinators, through basketball or any other competition, MIST is chock full of power to strengthen young Muslims' attraction to Islamic piety and their camaraderie with Muslim peers. Kareem professed:

[48] Faisal Chaudhry, personal interview, 20 March 2014, Detroit MI.

I think MIST is so great because it's just a lot of fun. That's what brings a lot of the high school youth out, because it's like, "I'm enjoying myself and being Muslim." And I think MIST is one of the first experiences that a lot of high-schoolers have where the two can intersect. Because I feel like it's so common when it comes to religious endeavors that it's always taught or approached in a very dry, in a sort of right and wrong, yes and no way, where it doesn't encourage creativity or personal expression. And it's just not very fun. And I think when we take that away from Islam it's a disservice to it, but also it paints this picture that isn't very attractive to young people.[49]

University of Delaware student Madinah Wilson concurs that MIST is a potent force in stimulating young Muslims' piety. She proclaimed that the Philadelphia area MIST tournament "has been awesome," adding that "students who I've never seen go to the mosque"[50] are now praying at the mosque because of personally transformative MIST experiences. As for boosting camaraderie, MIST's school-centric model is not its only feature that nurtures relationship building among Muslim youth. D.C. region coach Joshua Salaam pointed out that when regional winners move on to the national competition, they compete on a regional team with students they previously faced off against, making them "friends as opposed to archrivals."[51] Moreover, MIST brings together Muslims of various ethnicities and races, creating further opportunity for young Muslims to interact with fellow Muslims they might never associate with apart from MIST. Chaudhry identified the Detroit MIST event as "the most diverse Muslim conference I've ever been to,"[52] considering its sizable African-American constituency, mostly from the city, joined by scores of participants of Arab and South Asian descent, primarily from the suburbs. Chaudhry noted the rarity of interracial gathering among metro Motor City Muslims, and he distinguished MIST's racial diversity with what he has seen at Muslim youth camps, where exorbitant fees

[49] Adam Kareem, personal interview, 20 February 2014, Alexandria VA.
[50] Madinah Wilson, personal interview, 19 February 2014, Newark DE.
[51] Joshua Salaam, personal interview, 19 February 2014, Herndon VA.
[52] Faisal Chaudhry, personal interview, 20 March 2014, Detroit MI.

typically mean that South Asian or Arab Americans from affluent families make up the majority of attendees.[53]

In MIST's capacity to foster connections among Muslim youth, perhaps none is as valuable as a connection involving an individual who is the only Muslim at her or his school. Chaudhry suggested that linking these students with Muslim peers is crucial in order to help them not feel alone in their commitment to their faith. He declared, "We don't want kids to think that being different is a bad thing. ...They're the only Muslim in their high school, so not only do they feel different, they feel isolated. ...We try to combat that isolationism."[54] One combat tool at coordinators' disposal is the right to waive the school-based team rule for these particular students, since without enough schoolmates to form a team, they may feel discouraged to participate otherwise. Stoman explained that in the Atlanta region, students from high schools without enough competitors to form a team are combined with others in the same boat to make up a squad comprising multiple schools from one geographical area. In step with Chaudhry's comments, she argued that providing this opportunity can cultivate deeply meaningful relationships for young Muslims who have felt isolated in their faith. Stating that "it's a lot of pressure" to be the only Muslim in a school, Stoman explained, "You're automatically different, and then you always have to justify the difference as well as trying to have to justify why you're not different."[55] For these students who feel like black sheep in their school, MIST is a welcome field filled with members of their own religious flock.

[53] Chaudhry noted that Detroit MIST's registration fee is $35, and every year approximately $1,000 is given in financial aid. About ten percent of Detroit MIST participants receive either full or partial financial assistance (ibid.).

[54] Ibid.

[55] Salma Stoman, phone interview, 21 April 2014.

9

Mosque Athletic Activities

Azhar Ghani conjured up a scene that he prefers would fade to black. A father and coordinator of youth sports activities at a Southern California mosque, Ghani is concerned that Muslim youth may know the mosque solely as a place of religious instruction and prayer. Ghani encouraged me to "imagine a world" without sports or any other social activity at the mosque, where youth "just came in, did their prayers, and left."[1] Ghani views this scenario as perilous for young Muslims' faith, since they may easily become bored at the mosque and may internalize a split between a sacred world of the mosque and a secular sphere of sports and other activities they enjoy. Seeking to prevent youthful disenchantment with the mosque and to thwart an adoption of a sacred vs. secular worldview that runs afoul of regarding Islam as a complete way of life, Ghani and many other American mosque leaders turn to sports to help keep these threats at bay. Ghani spoke glowingly of youth playing sports at the mosque and taking a time out to pray. He said the "ability to do that is awesome,"[2] because it encourages young Muslims to engage diverse aspects of their lives at the mosque and to place every facet of their existence under the all-encompassing umbrella of Islam. Like Ghani's mosque in Southern California, mosques throughout the United States are giving Muslims the opportunity to play and pray, with sports serving a vital role in the mosques' mission of strengthening piety and fellowship. Many of these mosques' athletic activities include non-Muslim participants also, therefore promoting not only bonding, but bridging as well.

[1] Azhar Ghani, personal interview, 12 April 2014, Thousand Oaks CA.
[2] Ibid.

Mosque Athletic Activities: An Overview

Sports activities arrived on the American mosque scene near the end of the twentieth century. A *Houston Chronicle* article discusses basketball games at Houston-area mosques in the early 1990s, noting that leaders "took notice of the sport's appeal and propelled it further—endorsing it, improving the courts, and strategically using it as a hook for youth programs. 'Pizza and basketball' fliers brought in the masses, and a short religious talk was thrown in the mix."[3] The article quotes Houston imam Isa Parada, who declared that basketball "works great. They're there to play ball, but when the time comes, they pray."[4] Moving into the twenty-first century, Boston University student Amir Ali talked about sports drawing youth to his Massachusetts mosque, which holds a Friday evening halaqah (talking circle) featuring a religious talk and discussion about the lesson. After the halaqah, youth head outside to play basketball and football games that Ali characterized as "very competitive but very friendly."[5] Ali described these games as "a way to keep on meeting up with your friends" at the mosque and added, "Even to this day, we're all at different colleges, but we all go back to the mosque just because we want to play basketball and football together."[6] Ali's account of mosque sports activities promoting fellowship among youth reflects a common theme I heard in interviews, and occasionally this theme was accompanied by the insight that sports facilitate the transcending of differences among young people at a mosque. Ghani stated that along the lines of what develops in schools, cliques form among mosque youth. Ghani believes that "sports are a good way to break down those barriers,"[7] especially by assigning players to teams in a way that members of different cliques need to interact with one another as teammates. In many cases,

---

[3] "Basketball a Slam-Dunk for Area Muslims," http://uhdnews.uhd.edu/news/stories.aspx?articleid=302&zoneid=1 (published 4 June 2012; accessed 22 April 2014).

[4] Ibid.

[5] Amir Ali, personal interview, 7 March 2014, Boston MA.

[6] Ibid.

[7] Azhar Ghani, personal interview, 12 April 2014, Thousand Oaks CA.

barriers broken down by mosque sports activities pertain to ethnicity or race. Denis Stankovski of the Muslim Association of the Puget Sound near Seattle adjudges his mosque's youth soccer program to hold significant sway in enabling Muslim youth to overcome "any stereotypes that are in a culture and to spend time with each other irrespective of their backgrounds."[8] Rizwan Butt expressed a similar vision of athletic activities at the Easton Phillipsburg Muslim Association in Pennsylvania, where he considers the youth to have become role models for adults of the mosque community. Differentiating between the older generation and the youth of his mosque, Butt proclaimed, "We see the fact that the barriers that some of us come with culturally—cultural barriers, ethnic barriers, economic barriers, social barriers—they don't have that. So when they are together, you really feel humbled by the fact that these young kids are showing us how to be a Muslim ummah—how to be together."[9] Butt attributes a great deal of importance to mosque athletic activities in fostering this scenario, asserting that the youth's "togetherness in sports has translated into a greater benefit in many, many different levels,"[10] including modeling the ideal of Muslim unity across racial and ethnic lines.

Though sports-related bonding at American mosques typically involves *playing* sports, *watching* sports may bring youth to the mosque and help strengthen fellowship. Northeastern University student Omar Abdelkader spoke with excitement about imam Suhaib Webb's ability to attract young Muslims to the Islamic Society of Boston Cultural Center. According to Abdelkader, one of Webb's strongest connections with youth involves watching televised Boston Celtics games in the mosque with a throng of young basketball lovers.[11] Demonstrated further by his one-on-one basketball game against imam Siraj Wahaj of Brooklyn, which has earned high billing in Muslim American athletic lore, Webb is among a cohort of American imams who wear an adoration of sports on their sleeve. Amir Ali of Boston University lauded the close relationship

---

[8] Denis Stankovski, phone interview, 24 April 2014.
[9] Rizwan Butt, personal interview, 4 May 2014, Easton PA.
[10] Ibid.
[11] Omar Abdelkader, personal interview, 10 March 2014, Boston MA.

between imam Omar Suleiman and New Orleans Saints coach Sean Payton, and Ali celebrated the tendency of some imams to sprinkle their Friday sermons with athletic allusions and lace their lectures at nationwide Muslim gatherings with risible references to intercity sports rivalries.[12]

In contrast to this picture of mosque leaders enthralled with sports, however, I was told in quite a few interviews that many older individuals in leadership positions see no value in holding athletic activities at their mosques. Over the course of a convivial evening in which I enjoyed delicious biryani and rousing table tennis matches in his parents' home, Sohaib Jaffer explained that he started the Michigan Muslim Sports League (MMSL) in response to elders of his mosque finding no benefit in offering sports for mosque youth. Jaffer portrayed these leaders as saying, "If you want to play sports, you do it on your time. You don't need to come here and do it. This is a prayer hall, or we're going to do lectures here, or we don't have enough money. We have budgets for other stuff that we're concerned about."[13] Jaffer lamented that because of this mindset, a number of youth no longer attend his mosque, a trend he hopes to reverse through the MMSL and by one day raising enough funds for a mosque community center containing basketball courts and a fitness facility, in addition to a library, lecture hall, and other amenities to promote religious instruction. Whereas Jaffer spoke from his perspective as a Muslim in his twenties about elders not valuing sports in the mosque, a mosque leader about four decades older than Jaffer addressed this issue further. Roshan Shaikh touched on the absence of organized athletic activities at many American mosques, including his own in New York, which hosts a wide range of services and activities for its large congregation and local community but has no coordinated athletic offerings.[14] Shaikh commented that leaders "who are in the fifties and sixties and seventies" in age frequently "have no idea" about the merit in offering sports at mosques,

---

[12] Amir Ali, personal interview, 7 March 2014, Boston MA.

[13] Sohaib Jaffer, personal interview, 20 March 2014, Ypsilanti MI.

[14] Mosque attendees and non-Muslims in the neighborhood occasionally gather outside the mosque for informal games of basketball and cricket.

and he stated that "religion and sports have not been aligned properly"[15] by older immigrants from Islamic lands. Standing as an additional obstacle to sports activities at mosques, older leaders may attribute little importance to supporting youth programs of any kind at their mosque. Omar Malik, a youth leader at a Detroit-area mosque, expressed disappointment that most Muslim communities do not back mosque youth work as a full-time profession. He contended that "unless you're a doctor, engineer, or IT guy, naturally in our cultures it's like, 'Well, you're a nobody,'"[16] and therefore financially supporting a mosque youth worker does not even appear on some mosque communities' radar screens. Malik dreams of a day when Muslims across the United States will consider a youth worker to be "as important as imam of the mosque,"[17] and when they will no longer pour money into constructing a new mosque building while apportioning scant resources to the mosque's youth. If this day fails to arrive, Malik surmises, Muslim Americans will find themselves with strikingly beautiful mosque buildings but with an equally striking paucity of young people inside.

From the perspective of some Muslim Americans who organize mosque sports activities, those who fail to find value in these activities not only perform a major disservice to mosque youth; they also fall short of Muhammad's example of making the mosque a multifunction facility that offers a panoply of activities beyond just prayer and religious instruction. Explaining why soccer, basketball, and table tennis are played at his North Carolina mosque, Abderrazak Kitsy said that the mosque is "not just a place for worship," since Muhammad's mosque in Medina was a

[15] Roshan Shaikh, personal interview, 21 February 2014, Bay Shore NY.

[16] Omar Malik, personal interview, 21 March 2014, Warren MI. Sadek Hamid notes a similar trend in the United Kingdom, commenting, "While Muslim youth work may have much to offer, there still remains a number of practical challenges in communities where there is still little understanding of the value of youth work as a profession and a preference towards encouraging children into prestigious careers such as medicine, law, and science" (Sadek Hamid, "Mapping Youth Work with Muslims in Britain," in *Youth Work and Islam*, ed. Brian Belton, 82–97 (Dordrecht: Springer, 2012) 96).

[17] Omar Malik, personal interview, 21 March 2014, Warren MI.

"place for everything."[18] Kitsy stated that leaders of his mosque are "try-ing to follow the Prophet's legacy and have the mosque for everything,"[19] including sports. Talha Ali, president of a Chicago-area mosque, asserted that based on Islamic tradition, sports should be considered "part of the holistic set of services"[20] that a mosque provides its community. Ali ex-panded on this comment by placing spiritual, educational, physical, and social aspects under this holistic canopy and then identifying sports as "an avenue of physical development as well as social development."[21] Considering that sports often draw Muslims to the mosque, where they may engage in prayer and religious instruction, athletic activities are also connected with a mosque's spiritual and educational, in addition to its physical and social, aspects.

Judging from anecdotal evidence from interviews, a conviction that sports activities occupy an important position within the life of a mosque appears to be held by a large number of Muslims throughout the United States, albeit not as widespread among older Muslim Americans. Reli-ance on this anecdotal evidence alone, though, provides only a vague sense of the prevalence of athletic activities at mosques across the nation. Seeking more clarity in the form of gauging the percentage of American mosques that offer some sort of sports activity, I performed an unscien-tific study of mosque Internet sites in April 2014. My searches located a total of 594 active American Sunni and Shia mosque websites,[22] of which 129, or 21.7%, mentioned at least one athletic activity at the mosque. I acknowledge that my study has its shortcomings. I am left only to specu-late, for example, about the presence of sports activities at mosques with no website or with websites I failed to locate, and I realize that some sites I found may not refer to sports activities that are indeed held at the mosque. Nonetheless, I propose as an estimate that approximately one-

---

[18] Abderrazak Kitsy, phone interview, 23 April 2014.

[19] Ibid.

[20] Talha Ali, phone interview, 5 March 2014.

[21] Ibid.

[22] My searches began with typing the name of a state followed by the word "mosque" into a Google searchbox. I went through the first twenty pages that ap-peared for the ten most populous states in the nation, and I went through the first ten pages that appeared for the remaining forty states plus the District of Columbia.

fifth of all American mosques offer some sort of athletic activity. As for popularity of sports played at these mosques, the following list indicates the number of mosques that host a particular sport:

Basketball:	60
Soccer:	46
Martial arts:	32
Volleyball:	22
Table tennis:	14
Cricket:	9
Badminton:	8
Swimming:	7
(Flag) football:	5
Archery:	4
Tennis:	3
Boxing:	2
Wrestling:	2
Racquetball:	1

According to my investigation, forty-five mosques offer only one sport, forty-eight host two to four different sports, and ten mosques organize five or more. (Twenty-six websites failed to specify, often referring generically to "sports activities.") Fifty-seven mosques noted having sports activities for youth, thirty-three having sports for both youth and adults, and none having sports for adults only. (In this matter, thirty-nine websites did not specify.) Furthermore, though many mosques may have simply chosen not to refer to gender in identifying their sports activities on their website, it may be worthwhile to point out that twenty-two mosques mentioned organizing athletic activities for female members of their community.

Considering the basketballization of American Islam and soccer's prime position in the ancestral homelands of many Muslim Americans, I was hardly surprised to see these two sports top the chart above, but before learning the lay of the American mosque athletic land, I had not expected to find martial arts taking the third spot. Yet, whether karate, judo, taekwondo, or some other style, scores of Muslim Americans sing martial arts' praises, especially accentuating their benefits for youth. According to Javed Khan, who got into karate as a teen in India and has been teaching the sport to youth at a New Jersey mosque since 1999, many of these benefits pertain to physical conditioning. Khan argued that whereas in some sports individuals are "only training one or two muscle parts of their body, one or two reflex actions," in karate "they're training their whole body, their legs, their arms, their vision, their stomach, hand and eye coordination."[23] Sufu Hashim, a martial arts instructor for over forty years, matched Khan's enthusiasm about martial arts' physical perks. The African-American convert to Islam converted a basement room of the Islamic Society of Western Massachusetts into a martial arts gymnasium, where he aims to help overweight youth shed excess pounds and to enable young students to bulk up muscle mass. Besides addressing physical benefits, both Khan and Hashim connected martial arts with the development of discipline, respect, and other character traits. Khan maintained that martial arts provide youth with "a lot of confidence, social presence, and responsibility."[24] Hashim claimed that training in martial arts can counteract what he deems a detrimental tendency among Muslim immigrant parents to teach their children to passively accept being wronged by peers, in order not to perpetuate stereotypical associations between Muslims and violent actions. Hashim remarked that while he generally esteems a "nice, calm character" in everyday affairs, he prizes "the need to be aggressive"[25] in the martial arts setting, which can equip otherwise timid youth to stand up for themselves when necessary. He stressed, however, that this aggression must not transfer into unprovoked belligerence outside the martial arts setting, since this would contradict Islam's emphasis on peace and its acceptance of violence only in the case of defending oneself or others.

Neither Hashim nor Khan devotes class time to formally instruct students in Islamic teachings, but both care deeply about exemplifying Islamic principles to those under their tutelage and making sure nothing in their classes conflicts with these principles. Khan pointed out a poten-

---

[23] Javed Khan, personal interview, 18 February 2014, South Brunswick NJ.
[24] Ibid.
[25] Sufu Hashim, personal interview, 7 March 2014, West Springfield MA.

tial conflict he chooses to avoid, which involves similarity between traditional bowing in karate and prostration during the salat prayer. Though
he draws heavily upon a number of karate traditions, one he has kicked
out of his karate classes is the act of students kneeling and bowing down
to show their instructor respect. Khan explained, "I will go to my home
dojo and I will do that because I know what the intent is, but I don't do
it" in classes at the mosque because it can be easily misconstrued as a substitute to bowing to God and, therefore, an action that "clashes with the
Islamic way."[26] Khan's decision to refrain from this tradition is motivated
by concern that it would deter Muslim parents from sending their children to do martial arts at the mosque. He believes this would entail a
huge loss for these youth, not only because they would miss out on karate's physical and character development rewards, but also because of the
link Khan identifies between karate at the mosque and bonding. Echoing
numerous other voices heard in this chapter, Khan puts great stock in the
power of athletic activities to attract youth to the mosque, where they can
grow in personal piety and fellowship with Muslim peers. He commented, "Kids now get really bored. They don't want to go to the mosque because they say, 'All we do there is religious studies. There is nothing ben-
eficial, nothing exciting happening over there.'"[27] Khan contends that a
martial arts class can remedy this situation, implanting within young
Muslim minds an association between the mosque and an activity they
look forward to engaging in every week.

ADAMS and MCWS

As reflected in the results of my website study, sports offerings at American mosques encompass a wide spectrum. At one mosque, a weekly
youth basketball game constitutes the extent of its athletic calendar. At
another mosque, men, women, and youth can choose from a smorgasbord of leagues, tournaments, and pick-up games. Providing a taste of
the latter, I turn my attention to two mosques where jump shots and
goals are woven into their fabric alongside daily prayers and weekly sermons. I begin in the outskirts of the nation's capital, where a multi-

[26] Javed Khan, personal interview, 18 February 2014, South Brunswick NJ.
[27] Ibid.

flavored sports menu forms one segment of a vast array of events held at the All-Dulles Area Muslim Society (ADAMS). Among the nation's largest mosque communities, comprising over 6,000 families, ADAMS regularly engages in community service and interfaith dialogue. ADAMS is home to one of the D.C. area's biggest Boy Scout and Girl Scout programs, but nothing draws youth to its facility like its extensive list of athletic offerings. As I learned from youth director Joshua Salaam and volunteer youth worker Sajjad Ahmad, sports are a cherished means of bonding and bridging at ADAMS, demonstrated by the fact that the inclusion of a spacious gymnasium was a top priority when ADAMS's new mosque building was constructed in Herndon, Virginia. Within these gym walls and on fields outside, ADAMS youth sports include basketball, football, soccer, and cricket leagues, complemented by clinics in these sports. Worlds apart from mosque communities that affirm little worth in youth work, the ADAMS Youth calendar is crammed with events,[28] and ADAMS has put its money where its mouth is by investing in Salaam as its youth director. A member of the African-American Muslim hip-hop trio Native Deen, far and away American Islamic hip hop's best-known group,[29] Salaam is an instantly recognizable role model for ADAMS youth, many of whom have immersed themselves in Native Deen's rhythmic calls to embrace Islamic piety and take pride in Muslim identity.[30] Salaam is passionate about sports and their capacity to enhance ADAMS's effect upon the lives of both Muslims and non-Muslims,

---

[28] "ADAMS Youth," http://www.adamsyouth.net/ (accessed 28 April 2014).

[29] In claiming that Native Deen is the "best-known group" in American Islamic hip hop, I should note that I am following Suad Abdul Khabeer's distinction between American Islamic and American Muslim hip hop. He writes, "I use the term Islamic rather than Muslim to distinguish a genre of hip-hop music and culture created by American Muslims that seeks to comply with Islamic religious standards and practices whose current and primary audience is Muslims. For example, Islamic hip hop may restrict the types of musical instruments used, generally does not employ expletives, and frequently refers to issues of doctrinal import" (Abdul Khabeer, *"Rep That Islam,"* 125–26).

[30] For more on Native Deen and its link to Muslim identity, see Steven Fink, "For the Best of All Listeners: American Islamic Hip Hop as Reminder," *Journal of Religion and Society* 14 (2012), http://moses.creighton.edu/jrs/2012/2012-14.pdf (accessed 13 March 2015).

young and old alike. In addition to its youth sports programs, ADAMS draws a large number of adults to its gym and athletic fields. Reflecting on adult athletic activities he has seen during his seven-year tenure at ADAMS, Salaam named Sunday football games, pick-up basketball two or three nights a week, a basketball league, and inter-mosque soccer games that feature family and friends of players shouting support for their mosque's team. Ahmad noted that badminton is the most popular sport at ADAMS among community elders, and the mosque has also held golf outings. Rounding out its sporting collection, ADAMS organizes swimming sessions for girls and women on Saturday and Sunday mornings at an indoor community pool, which, during these mornings, is isolated from any male presence (an online announcement states, "WARNING: Male lifeguard enters pool area at 12 sharp!"), and ADAMS hosted the Indonesian martial art silat for many years until the class outgrew the gymnasium.

Salaam and Ahmad applauded the high degree of competitiveness and athletic ability demonstrated in ADAMS leagues and clinics. Salaam declared that although he does not make winning the focus for youth in league games, he does promote "extremely tough competitiveness."[31] Ahmad proudly pointed out that youth who have participated in ADAMS leagues and clinics have gone on to play for Division 1 and 2 college basketball and football teams. On one level, Salaam and Ahmad's enthusiasm about this competitiveness and skillfulness is simply an outpouring of their zest for sports. On another level, it manifests a realization that the higher the quality of its sports program, the greater the number of Muslim and non-Muslim athletes who will come to ADAMS to participate. League teams commonly include non-Muslim players, some of whom show up at ADAMS three times a week for league games and pick-up play. Non-Muslim youth gain exposure to Islam not only by entering a mosque and interacting with Muslim teammates, but also through short talks that Salaam or another ADAMS leader often gives before league games. Turning his attention to Muslim youth, Salaam professed that "there's a lot of people who are attracted to sports that may not be attracted to other aspects of the faith," and for these individuals

---

[31] Joshua Salaam, personal interview, 19 February 2014, Herndon VA.

"sports become a connector"[32] to the mosque, from which they might otherwise stay away. Ahmad articulated another common theme related to sports-related bonding, namely that athletic activities unite Muslims across ethnic and racial lines. Ahmad stated,

> When we get on a basketball court or a football field or a soccer field, we are a cohesive unit. I think that's critical because one of the things we pride ourselves on at ADAMS is we're an extremely diverse community. If you go to any of our open gym nights like Tuesday nights when youth play, there's probably half a dozen to a dozen nationalities that are out there, and just to bring those kids together is critical.[33]

Functioning as a microcosm of the united global ummah ideal, what transpires in the ADAMS gymnasium is considered by mosque leaders to be a tremendously important supplement to what takes place in its prayer hall.

In America's heartland, the Muslim Community of the Western Suburbs (MCWS) is in the same league as ADAMS when it comes to providing a huge collection of sports activities. A glance at the following athletic listings on the Campus Events Calendar in April 2014 offers a window into sports' prominent place at this Detroit-area mosque:

Fri., April 25: Basketball, HS Boys at 4:30 P.M.; Basketball, Men's at 10:30 P.M.

Sat., April 26: Basketball, Men's at 12:30 A.M.; Badminton, Men's at 7:00 A.M.; Sunna Saturday Gym at 1:00 P.M.; Soccer, College Men's at 4:30 P.M.

Sun., April 27: Badminton, Men's at 7:00 A.M.; HS Boys Basketball Tournament at 2:00 P.M.; Volleyball, Men's at 8:30 P.M.

Mon., April 28: Basketball, MS Boys at 6:30 P.M.; Floor Hockey, Men's at 9:00 P.M.

Tues., April 29: Badminton, Men's at 5:00 P.M.; Basketball, Men's at 10:30 P.M.

---

[32] Ibid.
[33] Sajjad Ahmad, personal interview, 19 February 2014, Herndon VA.

Wed., April 30: Basketball, Men's at 12:30 A.M.; Upper Elementary Girls
   Basketball at 6:00 P.M.; Middle School Girls Basketball at 7:00
   P.M.; Floor Hockey, Women's at 8:00 P.M.
Thu., May 1: Volleyball, Men's at 8:00 P.M.[34]

Impressive as this list might be, MCWS sports director Haaris Ahmad named even more athletic activities at his mosque, including cricket,
a running club, and an Ultimate Frisbee league. Many MCWS sports
activities are specifically for women and girls. One of the mosque's most
popular sports for women is floor hockey, introduced because of the large
percentage of MCWS female congregants who grew up not playing organized sports. MCWS sports coordinators concluded that compared to
other sports such as basketball or volleyball, the floor hockey learning
curve would be minimal for these athletic neophytes. MCWS also invests
heavily in youth sports, especially basketball. Court times are booked for
multiple age groupings, separately for boys and for girls. Saturday youth
gatherings pair religious instruction sessions with basketball and other
sports, such as mixed martial arts or table tennis in the mosque basement's 4,000-square-foot lounge. Ahmad argues that for some youth
who play sports at MCWS, one of the greatest benefits they receive relates to their self-image. He proposed that creating "a base level of skill
in sports is a good way of boosting confidence, and people gravitate to
you and respect you when they see you in a context where you're excelling."[35] Ahmad cited his daughter as an example, associating her proficiency in basketball with a greater sense of self-confidence, which carries
over into not feeling "pressured to do anything against her faith"[36] in the
presence of non-Muslim peers.

As described by Ahmad, MCWS athletic facilities are bursting at
the seams. Members of the MCWS community are eager for even more
athletic activities at the mosque but are hindered by space constraints,
and so Ahmad and other leaders are trying to raise funds for a supple-

---

[34] "MCWS Campus Events Calendar," http://mcws.org/home (accessed 28
April 2014).

[35] Haaris Ahmad, personal interview, 21 March 2014, Canton MI.

[36] Ibid.

mentary gym and more outdoor athletic space. Currently playing in the mosque parking lot, MCWS cricket buffs are calling for a field for their sport, and Ahmad noted that expanded facilities would enable more non-Muslims to participate in MCWS sports activities. Ahmad highly encourages MCWS members to invite non-Muslims to join them in sports at the mosque, provided these guests agree to abide by the rules of "no fighting and no swearing" and to dress in accordance with mosque norms. Ahmad recalled that, unfortunately, the "no fighting" rule has been violated in the heat of mosque competition. He recounted a physical altercation at an MCWS basketball tournament that resulted in serious injury, assistance from the police, and a decision to place a hiatus on tournaments at the mosque. This decision was not made rashly; the brawl was the straw that broke the camel's back after MCWS leaders had been noticing tournament competitiveness reaching the brink of getting out of hand. Tournaments have been reinstated at the mosque, but because the on-court fracas involved players from outside the MCWS community, Ahmad and other leaders are now more selective about who may participate. In an attempt to welcome outsiders but also prevent another melee, players must now be either individuals from the MCWS community or friends and acquaintances of these individuals.

Youth of Ummah and Sunnah Sports

ADAMS and MCWS are among a short list of American mosques that provide a wide selection of sporting opportunities for adults. More common is an assortment of sports solely for youth, such as what is served up at another Detroit-area mosque, the Islamic Organization of North America (IONA). With over 100 regular attendees, IONA's Youth of Ummah (YOU) program features religious instruction on Thursday evenings and Saturday afternoons, along with basketball, football, and soccer leagues after the Saturday instruction session. YOU is the brainchild of Omar Malik, who somehow finds time to pour himself into the group despite a full-time information technologies and programming position at General Motors. Malik is a firm believer in the strong capacity of sports to bring youth to the mosque, which he described as an alienating environment for many young Muslims unless it includes athletic activities. Malik pronounced that the typical experience in which they remove their shoes, sit down on the mosque carpet, and quietly listen to a talk about Islamic teachings is not going to cut it for young, energetic Muslims. Initially, Malik attempted to attract youth to the mosque by way of overnight gatherings, skits, and team-building activities, but he found that these ventures fell short. He concluded that a successful mosque youth program requires putting sports "in the mix, otherwise it's not going to work."[37] As Malik views it, sports play such a vital role in mosque youth programs not only because athletic activities meet young Muslims' desire to unleash their boundless energy, but also because sports can overturn their expectation that they will be disregarded by older Muslims at the mosque. Malik hopes to help youth shed this presumption, which he maintains can occur as he and other older members of the mosque community take the court or field as teammates of young Muslims. Amidst building these relationships, Malik asserts, Muslim youth who had previously shunned Islamic piety begin "coming to the mosque and asking you their tough questions and starting to have more faith in their religion... Some of them don't pray and all of a sudden they start praying more."[38]

Yearning to get youth excited about coming to the mosque, Malik has devised an incentive-based system that he integrates into YOU sports activities. YOU members earn points for attending Thursday-evening religious talks, participating in community service projects, and giving group presentations on religious topics. Malik keeps a weekly chart that shows each participant's percentage representing his involvement in these three activities. Those who fall below sixty percent are required to sit out five to ten minutes of league games, which, according to Malik, strongly motivates YOU members to take part in the religious talks, community service, and group presentations. Malik declared, "Instead of us always preaching to them, they automatically step up their game. They want to play, and also in that indirectly they start learning about Islam and they start enjoying it."[39] Among those who play in YOU leagues on a regular

[37] Omar Malik, personal interview, 21 March 2014, Warren MI.
[38] Ibid.
[39] Ibid.

basis, some are selected to become group leaders based on their exemplary demonstration of Islamic virtues. Malik portrayed competitive sports as if they possess x-ray powers, revealing an individual's true inner character. He stated,

> If you want to produce new future leaders, sometimes they might look religious, but when you put them on the basketball court, you get to see the real personality. We believe you can't really show your faith until you're tested. A lot of people might sound nice in a mosque—it's just natural. But when you put them on a basketball court and intense situations happen, you really see what they're all about. Are they going to start swearing, cussing, badmouthing?[40]

Malik's motivation to keep swearing and badmouthing out of the game is in part due to bridging desires, since the eyes and ears of non-Muslim teammates are highly attuned to Muslims' actions. Non-Muslims make up about ten percent of YOU basketball, football, and soccer rosters, and as he suggested in the following comments, YOU's bridging scope includes not only non-Muslim players, but onlookers as well: "We're in the middle of the park—let's say all of a sudden forty people are bowing down in prostration to God—and we've seen neighbors just standing and watching. It's a really amazing scene from that point of view."[41] Curious bystanders have approached YOU athletes to inquire about their prayer, giving some of these onlookers the first chance in their lives to interact with Muslims. The significance of these interactions in IONA's hometown of Warren may be particularly great, considering that residents of this Detroit suburb sought to deep-six IONA's 2006 plans to build its new mosque in their town.[42] In an environment where Muslims are commonly considered unwanted threats, residents who engage in conversation with YOU Muslims may seriously question this consideration and perhaps become inspired to do their own

[40] Ibid.
[41] Ibid.
[42] A neighborhood association complained to the city Planning Commission that the proposed mosque was in violation of zoning regulations. The Planning Commission initially agreed but reversed its course after a city attorney argued that this decision lacked legal grounds (Howell, "Muslims as Moving Targets," 165).

part in chipping away at Islamophobic walls in their community.

Unlike YOU, with its predominantly high school age membership, another sports program at a Midwestern mosque is composed of elementary and middle school youth. Based at the Islamic Foundation mosque in the suburbs of Chicago, Sunnah Sports was launched in 2013 and sky-rocketed a year later to an average weekly attendance of 150–200, about one-fifth of whom are girls. As stated on its website, Sunnah Sports

> is a youth program that is uniting and maturing hearts in the love of Allah, Rasulullah [Prophet Muhammad], his family, his companions, and the Awliya [saints] through brotherhood, companionship, and sportsmanship. Sunnah Sports seeks to inspire the youth in developing a personal relationship to God while fostering the principles of Islam in their hearts such as: good character, honesty, service, respect, and personal development.[43]

Embossed upon these references to love, a personal relationship with God, and character development is a heavy imprint of Sufism,[44] the mystical dimension of Islam that has greatly shaped Sunnah Sports founder Hussain Jilani's understanding of his faith. As a waiter loaded our table with a scrumptious Pakistani spread, Jilani touched on his ambition to start Sunnah Sports, which was sparked by a hajj pilgrimage conversation with individuals who encouraged him to start some sort of program for Muslim American youth. Stimulated by this conversation and a conviction that children, beginning at "a very young age, need to feel like the mosque is their home,"[45] Jilani began welcoming youth to the Islamic Foundation mosque every Friday evening for Sunnah Sports. Each week, over the course of four hours, children assemble for salat prayers, eat dinner, and listen to a short religious talk, but mostly they

---

[43] "Sunnah Sports: About," http://sunnahsports.com/about/ (accessed 8 May 2014).

[44] For information on Sufism, see William C. Chittick, *Sufism: A Beginner's Guide* (London: Oneworld, 2007); Carl W. Ernst, *Sufism: An Introduction to the Mystical Tradition of Islam* (Boston: Shambhala, 2011); and Seyyed Hossein Nasr, *The Garden of Truth: The Vision and Promise of Sufism, Islam's Mystical Tradition* (New York: HarperOne, 2007).

[45] Hussain Jilani, personal interview, 17 March 2014, Villa Park IL.

play sports. Basketball is Sunnah Sports's number-one athletic activity, complemented by football, cricket, dodgeball, kickball, badminton, archery, and wrestling. Jilani's fondness for giving youth a variety of experiences suffuses Sunnah Sports, from this polychromatic sporting lineup to the weekly dinner, where children might titillate their taste buds with hummus and falafels one Friday evening and tacos and quesadillas the next.

While Jilani made it clear that mosque doors stand wide open to children of all faiths, the large majority of Sunnah Sports participants are Muslims. According to Jilani, one of the greatest contributions Sunnah Sports can make to young Muslim lives is to cultivate the regular habit of prayer, which he claims to be more difficult for Muslim children in the United States than in Islamic countries where the salat prayer dictates daily societal structure. Jilani's bent for bonding also lays stress upon reciting the Qur'an. He gives candy to Sunnah Sports participants in accordance with the level of recitation they achieve. Yet, throughout our conversation, the theme to which Jilani consistently gravitated was helping youth grow in Islamic character traits, especially love. Jilani stated that, whether during his brief talk before dinner or in the midst of a basketball game, "That is what we aim to really imbibe in them—how to love, and to be selfless, and to be thinking of others, not to think of yourself."[46] From Jilani's Sufi perspective, the seeds of love can beautifully blossom anywhere; a Friday-evening dodgeball game is not only tons of fun, but also an invaluable occasion to love one's teammates and opponents and become further equipped for a lifetime of love for all of humanity.

The Khoja Community

Along with their commitment to athletic activity, ADAMS, MCWS, IONA, and the Islamic Foundation share the characteristic of ethnic diversity. Some American mosques with sports programs, on the other hand, are composed almost exclusively of one ethnic group, such as the Salahadeen Islamic Center, a Kurdish mosque in Nashville. Coupling education with sports activities, the Kurdish Achievers program goes

[46] Ibid.

back to the 1980s, started as a joint effort between the mosque and the local YMCA to curtail the formation of gangs by Kurdish youth who faced harassment in their new Tennessee home. When it comes to sports at mosques of predominantly one ethnic group, the athletically active Khoja community is in a league of its own. With their forebears converting to Islam centuries ago in South Asia before settling in East Africa,[47] most Khojas adhere to the Nizari Ismaili branch of Shia Islam,[48] but a significantly sized Khoja minority separated from Nizari Ismailism in the late nineteenth and twentieth centuries to join the Twelver branch, Shia Islam's largest.[49] For these Twelver Shia Khojas, or Khoja Shia Ithna-Asheris,[50] sports at mosques and nationwide gatherings are much more than a casual hobby. Khizer Husain, a board member of American Muslim Health Professionals, upholds the Khojas as a model community for other Muslim Americans in response to the federal government's "Let's Move Faith Communities" healthy-living initiative. Husain proclaims, "The Khojas are a stand-out community in terms of their use of sports to promote physical well-being and to renew social and cultural bonds."[51]

---

[47] For centuries, Indians from Gujarat sailed down the East African coast in *dhows* (sailships) during North Eastern monsoons. Among these Indians were young Khoja traders seeking to engage in commerce and trade, and after settling in East Africa, they formed a Khoja Shia Ithna-Asheri community, or jamaat. They invited family and friends from India to join them in East Africa, and this Khoja community is now spread in over forty countries, including the United States and Canada ("History of the Khoja Shia Ithna-Asheries," The World Federation of Khoja Shia Ithna-Asheri Muslim Communities, http://www.world-federation.org/Misc/ KSI+History/ (accessed 28 April 2014)).

[48] The Nizari make up the second largest branch of Shia Islam, with an estimated 15 million Nizari living in over twenty-five nations. Among other distinctions from the larger Twelver Shia branch, the Nizari view the Aga Khan as their Imam, or divinely appointed spiritual guide.

[49] Listed as over 100,000 on the World Federation of Khoja Shia Ithna-Asheri Muslim Communities website, the Twelver Shia Khoja community forms a small fraction of the estimated 150 million Twelver Shias around the globe.

[50] Ithna-Asheri Khojas maintain a relationship with the larger Twelver Shia community but also retain their own organizational framework.

[51] Quoted in "Muslim Sports Tournament Expected to Draw 2,000 to Orlando in 2012,"

He continues to say, "You'd be hard-pressed to find a Khoja congregation where 'East African' volleyball games don't fill the evenings. The mosques' own gyms have become one-stop shops to pray and play!"[52]

One of many Khoja congregations that fits Husain's description to a "t" is the Shia Ithna'asheri Jamaat of New York (SIJNY), located just outside New York city limits on Long Island. SIJNY houses Union Sports Club for volleyball, Jaffery Sports Club for soccer, and Long Island Tennis Club. While the tennis club is small in number, the membership of Union and Jaffery reflects the premier sporting position of volleyball and soccer for Khoja Americans and Khojas around the world. Notably, volleyball at SIJNY and in other Khoja communities differs from the sport with which most Americans are familiar. In the East African version, teams may touch the ball only once to return it unless the first touch is hit into the net, which allows a teammate to set the ball to another who can spike it. Containing other differences from international volleyball, such as the use of a harder ball and a lack of positional rotations, East African volleyball has been a SIJNY fixture since the 1970s. Games were initially played outdoors, but with the birth of Union Sports Club in 1982, contests were moved indoors, enabling volleyball to become a year-round SIJNY sport unaffected by New York climatic vagaries. Union involves both adults and youth, with Friday-night volleyball a weekly highlight for the latter. This Friday-night time slot was chosen quite intentionally, since it provides SIJNY youth with a fun activity at the mosque during a prime time when they might be socializing in a manner inconsistent with Islamic principles elsewhere. Also connecting youth to the mosque, Jaffery Sports Club offers Jaffery Juniors for five-through seventeen-year-old soccer players, in addition to its men's teams, which have taken the field since the mid-1980s. A Jaffery squad competes in an adult county recreation league, and Jaffery teams have won a slew of tournaments including the Khoja Ithna-Asheri Supreme Council championship in Tanzania in 2006. Many Jaffery members play with

http://www.letsmove.gov/blog/2011/11/16/muslim-sports-tournament-expected-draw-2000-orlando-2012 (posted 16 November 2011; accessed 21 April 2014).

[52] Ibid.

non-Muslims on teams outside the club, enjoying opportunities to raise awareness about Islam as they unite across religious lines between the lines of the soccer field. Speaking from his personal experience, Jaffery member Mustafa Dinani declared, "Even if you have a language barrier, that goes away. If you have a cultural barrier, that goes away. All you care about is soccer, playing a good game, and scoring a goal. A goal is the same, so all those barriers fall."[53]

Turning to another Khoja community, the Jaafari Islamic Center near Minneapolis hosts athletic activities every day of the week, offering East African volleyball, soccer, football, and badminton for males and badminton for females. Sports pace the pulse of mosque community life for a number of Jaafari youth, which became abundantly clear in conversations with three young mosque sports committee members. At some point in each conversation, I heard a variation on a similar theme, namely that sports draw youth to the mosque and therefore keep them away from sinful pursuits. College student Hassan Mulla proclaimed, "Sports has pretty much been my life. That's what really has kept me connected with my community. ...It's pretty much kept me in line—not going astray."[54] Citing pressure upon youth in his mosque community to transgress Islamic norms due to the allurements of drugs, alcohol, and sex, Komail Lakha stated, "If you come to the mosque and you play your sports and you're with your Muslim friends that don't peer pressure you into doing that kind of stuff, it really makes a big difference. ...You're staying away from any kind of peer pressure and you're being closer to your religion as a result."[55] According to high school senior Maythum Mehdi, mosque sports activities are especially salubrious for Muslims like himself who attend a high school with very few Muslim students. With this scenario making Muslim teens more susceptible to conform to low moral standards, Mehdi suggested, some high-schoolers at Jaafari "fall off quite a bit from coming to the mosque,"[56] but this trend can be reversed by the enticement of mosque-based volleyball and other athletic

[53] Mustafa Dinani, personal interview, 22 February 2014, Mineola NY.
[54] Hassan Mulla, personal interview, 26 April 2014, Brooklyn Park MN.
[55] Komail Lakha, personal interview, 26 April 2014, Brooklyn Park MN.
[56] Maythum Mehdi, personal interview, 26 April 2014, Brooklyn Park MN.

activities. Jaafari sports occasionally attract non-Muslims, through events such as an interfaith basketball tournament. Mehdi pointed out that an interfaith East African volleyball tournament would be tough to pull off because of outsiders' lack of familiarity with the sport's unique rules, but plans are in the works to expand the Jaafari interfaith athletic menu with a soccer tournament comprising teams from a variety of religious institutions.

Like SIJNY and Jaafari, Al Ahad Islamic Center in Allentown, Pennsylvania keeps its attendees athletically active, but my discussion of sports involving this Khoja mosque focuses on two particular annual occurrences that unite Muslims throughout the Allentown area, or Lehigh Valley. The first takes place during Ramadan, when individuals from Al Ahad get together with congregants of three Sunni mosques for volleyball and soccer tournaments. Serving as a sharp contrast to headline-grabbing Sunni-Shia strife in the Middle East, former Al Ahad president Mohammed Khaku pronounced that these Sunni mosques and Al Ahad "are one voice. We are all united. ...We are all first Muslims."[57] This harmony fills the Ramadan air, as about 500 Sunnis and Shias play their volleyball and soccer contests until 2 or 3 o'clock in the morning, along with table tennis, video games, Islamic Jeopardy, and other amusements. Khaku portrayed a festive atmosphere at these late-night gatherings, after which participants often eat breakfast and then sleep in order to fortify

[57] Mohammed Khaku, personal interview, 4 May 2014, Allentown PA. Khaku's statement mirrors harmonious Sunni-Shia relations that occur in other American locations. Mustafa Dinani, for example, said about playing soccer with Sunnis, "There's never been a problem. When we go to tournaments...we go together sometimes. We play on the same team. There's a lot of respect for one another, appreciation for one another" (Mustafa Dinani, personal interview, 22 February 2014, Mineola NY). As another example, Sally Howell discusses the Imams Coordinating Committee (ICC), formed initially in 2006 in response to the Muhammad cartoon controversy precipitated by a Danish newspaper. Comprising both Sunni and Shia leaders, the group issued its Muslim Code of Honor, essentially a pledge to promote civility between Sunni and Shia communities in the Detroit area. Its final point proclaims, "We encourage all Muslims living in the United States to emphasize their commonality in accordance with God's statement, 'Hold fast, all together, to the rope of God and be not divided among yourselves'" (Howell, "Muslims as Moving Targets," 155).

themselves to fast for the rest of the new day. A similarly congenial environment typifies Muslim Family Fun Day, a yearly event that has brought together all four Lehigh Valley mosque communities since 2008. Including tournaments in volleyball, soccer, cricket, basketball, and taekwondo, as well as carnival rides and a culinary hodgepodge pandering to a plethora of palates, Family Fun Day is advertised as "a first step towards a long-term vision of working together for the greater good as well as a means to develop mind, body, and friendship through sports."[58] Besides boosting bonding by strengthening ties between Sunni and Shia Muslims, the event promotes practicing the Islamic principle of charity. Money raised at Fun Day has been donated to tsunami relief, support of Palestinians in Gaza, assistance for orphans in Iraq, and an expansion project at a local Islamic school. Furthermore, sports tournaments and other Fun Day activities are open to non-Muslims, which led Khaku to declare, "We look to be more active in the community and socialize with different groups in the Lehigh Valley, and events like this lift the spirits of young Muslims whose religion is negatively stereotyped. We are building bridges between all faiths."[59]

Joining Friday-night volleyball games, Family Fun Day, and other local events, the Khoja athletic calendar is dotted with nationwide gatherings, such as a 2012 tournament in Orlando that saw over 500 participants go head to head in volleyball, soccer, basketball, golf, tennis, and badminton, or a 2011 competition that brought sixteen men's volleyball and twenty-five women's badminton teams to Minnesota. Volleyball tournaments pitting teams from Khoja mosques across the nation are circled especially boldly on many Khoja calendars. Typically held three times a year at different Khoja community locations, volleyball tournaments include one day of round-robin play followed by a second day of quarterfinal, semifinal, and final-round action. Mehdi of Jaafari rendered an exciting scene that made me wish I could play in the next tournament.

---

[58] Quoted in "6th Annual Muslim Family Fun Day—Allentown USA," http://www.world-federation.org/Secretariat/Articles/Archive/6th_Annual_Muslim _Family_Fun_Day_Allentown_USA.htm (posted 28 August 2013; accessed 8 May 2014).

[59] Quoted in ibid.

He described stepping onto a court in Orlando surrounded by 500 screaming spectators, calling it "unbelievable" and an "amazing experience."[60] According to Jaafari's Lakha, each volleyball tournament contains strong rivalries between sides that have met in previous tournaments and highly anticipate the opportunity to get revenge for a prior defeat or to gain the laurels of victory once again. Yet, amidst this intense competition, a strong sense of camaraderie between opponents prevails. Fierce on-court foes enjoy deep friendship before and after locking horns on the court. These tournaments essentially function as Khoja reunions, preserving ties within a diasporic community for players and spectators alike. Among these spectators are community elders who regularly interacted back in the day in East Africa, but now in the United States get to meet infrequently outside the tournament venue. Albeit not a common phenomenon, another type of connection might be made; marriage matches have germinated over the course of a volleyball weekend. Lakha addressed this possibility, saying that a bachelor playing in a tournament might meet an older man from a different Khoja community, and "if you have a good conversation with them they could suggest that you talk to their daughter"[61] and make a marriage proposal.

Though East African volleyball is the most popular sport at Khoja nationwide gatherings, soccer falls not too far behind, especially since the 2012 formation of Umoja Games. Headed by a committee of representatives of Khoja communities across the United States and Canada, Umoja Games is "an organization formed to reignite the once very prominent passion for soccer and develop a grass-roots approach to building a sustainable program that would benefit current and future generations of the Shia Muslim faith."[62] The organization built upon Umoja Championships coordinated by SIJNY's Jaffery Sports Club by holding its first tournament for men and youth in Orlando in 2013, and it added a women's tournament in Allentown in 2014. As I learned from founder Mustafa Dinani, leaders have been especially eager to develop the Umoja

[60] Maythum Mehdi, personal interview, 26 April 2014, Brooklyn Park MN.

[61] Komail Lakha, personal interview, 26 April 2014, Brooklyn Park MN.

[62] "Umoja Games: About Us," http://www.umojagames.org/about-us/ (accessed 8 May 2014).

Academy, which they inaugurated at the 2014 Allentown tournament. Leaders' vision for the academy features clinics to be held at cities throughout North America, in which young players receive instruction from professional coaches free of charge. As a consequence of a belief that "the combination of good academic performance and enthusiasm for sports, in particular soccer, are recipes for a well-rounded individual that can go on to achieve much greater feats,"[63] a further foundational fragment of this vision is the bestowal of academic scholarships for clinic participants. The academy aims to invest in Khoja youth on multiple levels while strengthening fellowship within the Khoja community. The Umoja website proclaims that the academy "brings with it a robust program tailored for each age group so that they can hone their footballing skills, gain a deeper understanding of the sport as well as increase the love for the game. On a much more global level, the Academy will bring together our community, irrespective of geographical locations, and allow everyone, kids and parents alike, to foster new long-lasting relationships."[64]

[63] "Umoja Games: Academy," http://www.umojagames.org/academy/ (accessed 8 May 2014).
[64] Ibid.

10

Islamic School Athletic Activities

Should a public university in Michigan foot the bill for footbaths that enable Muslim students to perform ablutions before the salat prayer? Should a Nebraska meat-packing plant meet its Muslim employees' demands to be granted time off for prayer breaks without loss of pay? Should a prison in Ohio be required to serve Muslims serving jail time food that falls in line with Islamic dietary regulations?[1] Questions regarding the extent to which accommodations should be made for Islamic beliefs and practices have at times put interpretation of the First Amendment to the test and have caused some Americans to denounce Muslims as outsiders with unwarranted accommodation appeals. A few of these instances have centered upon athletic activity, such as the setting aside of Harvard gym time exclusively for women discussed in an earlier chapter. An additional athletic accommodation issue that, unlike the Harvard hubbub, lay largely under the national media radar involved Muslim students in physical education classes at American public schools. For the multitude of Muslims who believe their religion necessitates gender separation during athletic activity, except at very young ages, the structure of American public school physical education is discordant with Islamic norms. Thus, in its "You've Got a Muslim Child in Your School" bro-

---

[1] See Tamar Lewin, "Some U.S. Universities Install Foot Baths for Muslim Students," *New York Times*, http://www.nytimes.com/2007/08/07/world/ americas/07iht-muslims.4.7022566.html?_r=0 (published 7 August 2007; accessed 13 March 2015); "70 Who Quit Over Prayer Time Return to Work," http://www.nbcnews.com/id/18869414/ns/us_news-life/t/who-quit-over-prayer-time-return-work/#.VQNFoLFOmM8 (published 25 May 2007; accessed 13 March 2015); and Andrew Welsh-Huggins, "Ohio Removes Pork from Prison Menus in Nod to Muslim Inmates," http://cnsnews.com/news/article/ohio-removes-pork-prison-menus-nod-muslim-inmates (published 5 October 2011; accessed 13 March 2015).

chure, the Islamic Society of North America asked public school admin-istrators throughout the nation not to require their Muslim students to participate in physical education, swimming, or dancing classes as typi-cally arranged at American public schools. The brochure enjoined:

> Alternative meaningful education activities should be arranged for them. We urge you to organize physical education and swimming clas-ses separately for boys and girls in accordance with the following guide-lines: a. Separate classes should be held for boys and girls in a fully cov-ered area. b. Only male/female instructors for the respective group. c. Special swimming suits which will cover all the private parts of the body down to the knee. d. Separate and covered shower facilities for each student.[2]

A lack of such provisions occasionally precipitates a great deal of angst for young Muslim Americans, especially female students. In her study of Yemeni American girls at a Dearborn public high school,[3] Loukia Sarroub reports, "Although only three semesters of gym were required at Cobb, some girls enrolled in the class for four years, failing it each time because they did not dress in gym clothes or participate in class. This situation was exasperating for both them and their teachers."[4] Sarroub's findings illuminate the experience of numerous young Muslim women who struggle to navigate their way through the American public school physical education system.

The reach of these findings, however, needs to be circumscribed. A generalized portrait of all young Muslim Americans concluding it impos-sible to reconcile their religion with their public school P.E. class would

---

[2] Quoted in Eck, *A New Religious America*, 285–86.

[3] Sarroub selected this school ("Cobb" is a fictionalized name) for her study not only because of its large Muslim population, but also because she "learned that the school and its students were experiencing difficulties adjusting to one another as the number of Arabic-speaking students increased" (Loukia K. Sarroub, *All American Yemeni Girls: Being Muslim in a Public School* (Philadelphia: University of Pennsylva-nia Press, 2005) 24). Throughout her book, Sarroub seeks to substantiate her claim that "[l]iving in two worlds was both difficult and constraining for the Yemeni American Muslim girls. These students…struggled to negotiate their Yemeni and American selves in various contexts" (ibid., 23).

[4] Ibid., 34.

warrant a failing grade. This picture can feed the ever-lurking Islam vs. America clash mentality, and it would drown out Muslim youth testimony of profoundly positive involvement in American public school physical education. Ideally, comprehensive coverage of Muslim American athletic activity would unveil various nuances that lie within Muslim American participation in public school physical education and athletic programs. My interest is piqued by the prospect of making such discoveries some day in the future, but as of now, my explorations of Muslim experience in school physical education and extracurricular athletic activities, which form the nucleus of this chapter, have focused on full-time private Islamic schools.[5]

Islamic Schools and Islamic School Athletic Activities: An Overview

A precise number of full-time Islamic schools[6] in the United States at any given time is nearly impossible to pinpoint, considering the periodic popping up of new schools and the occasional closure of older ones. The most comprehensive attempt to estimate this number took place in 2009, when Islamic Schools League of America founder Karen Keyworth determined the approximate figure to be 235.[7] Keyworth gauged the total number of children in these schools at 32,000, leading her to conclude that about four percent of all Muslim American children attend full-time Islamic schools.[8] As suggested by this low percentage, scads of Muslim

[5] The sole exception is Fordson High School in Dearborn, discussed in my section on fasting in chapter 4.

[6] I would like to point out a distinction between full-time schools, which like the public school day typically are in session Monday through Friday mornings and afternoons and which cover a wide array of academic subjects, and weekend schools, which usually take place a few hours on Saturday or Sunday and focus on religious education.

[7] Karen Keyworth, "Islamic Schools of America: Data-Based Profiles," in *Educating the Muslims of America*, ed. Yvonne Y. Haddad, Farid Senzai, and Jane I. Smith, 21–37 (New York: Oxford University Press, 2009) 28. Keyworth also found that "fully 45 percent of Islamic schools are completely independent entities. Another 29 percent are connected to a mosque but make decisions very autonomously. Only 21 percent of Islamic schools are actually governed by a mosque" (ibid., 32–33).

[8] Ibid., 28.

American parents choose not to send their children to Islamic schools, preferring public schools or homeschooling for a variety of reasons.[9] Moreover, other parents would opt for Islamic schooling but are financially prohibited from doing so. For those parents who select Islamic schooling, once again a spectrum of reasons comes into play. Yvonne Haddad and Jane Smith write in *Educating the Muslims of America* that Islamic schools "provide alternative education for character development; protect children from stereotyping and taunting; offer Islamic alternatives to such social ills as premarital sex, drugs, and violence; and allow children to avoid public school curricula that may in some way be prejudiced against Islam."[10] Though too diverse to be completely encapsulated by one conceptual framework, many factors that motivate the choice for Islamic schooling can be subsumed under the notion of "moderate separatism." This concept articulates an argument that Islamic schooling is especially well equipped to prepare children not only to grow in knowledge of their religion, but also to blossom in self-awareness and the ability to engage with society outside the Islamic school setting.[11] Ac-

[9] Samana Siddiqui identifies among these reasons the following characteristics of some Islamic schools: poor organization, high staff turnover, subpar academic standards, and fostering of insularity (Samana Siddiqui, "Muslim Schools vs. Public Schools," Islamic Circle of North America, http://www.icna.org/muslim-schools-vs-public-schools/ (posted 14 December 2009; accessed 13 March 2015)).

[10] Yvonne Y. Haddad and Jane I. Smith, "Introduction: The Challenge of Islamic Education in North America," in *Educating the Muslims of America*, ed. Yvonne Y. Haddad, Farid Senzai, and Jane I. Smith, 3–19 (New York: Oxford University Press, 2009) 5.

[11] Jasmin Zine explains "moderate separatism" by writing that "early childhood and elementary education in religiously based schools can actually encourage greater knowledge of self without compromising the knowledge of others, and this knowledge of others may occur in sites other than schools or through transition to common schooling in higher grades" (Jasmin Zine, "Safe Havens or Religious 'Ghettos'? Narratives of Islamic Schooling in Canada," in *Educating the Muslims of America*, ed. Yvonne Y. Haddad, Farid Senzai, and Jane I. Smith, 39–65 (New York: Oxford University Press, 2009) 43–44). Zine notes coming across this concept in Jeff Spinner-Halev, "Extending Diversity: Religion in Public and Private Education" (paper presented at the Canadian Centre for Philosophy and Public Policy Conference "Citizenship in Diverse Societies," University of Toronto, Toronto, October 1997).

cording to the website of New Jersey's An-Noor Academy, not all Islamic schools are up to the task of outside engagement. The website identifies what it calls "defensive" Islamic schools, suggesting that by striving "to 'shield' and 'protect' the children from harmful influences that are antithetical to the Islamic system,"[12] these schools tend to breed insularity. Dissatisfied with the defensive model, An-Noor evinces a strong preference for what it labels "proactive" Islamic schools. Declaring that these institutions aim "to nurture the intellectual, emotional, social, and spiritual growth of Muslim children with the hope of producing confident, competent individuals who can go out into American society and contribute positively without compromising their Islamic beliefs and practices,"[13] the proactive model falls in line with the concept of moderate separatism.

Whether defensive or proactive, or better described by some other label, each Islamic school in America is likely to face some sort of significant challenges in providing its students with athletic activities. One obstacle was explored in an earlier chapter, namely the mindset of many first-generation immigrant parents that the value of athletics pales in comparison to the worth of academics in setting their children up for successful American futures. Unaware that I would hear multiple iterations of this idea in later interviews, I initially encountered it from Patrick Fitzpatrick, a physical education teacher who converted to Islam while coaching the Algerian men's national basketball team. Stating that administrators at the prekindergarten-through-twelfth-grade Al-Rahmah School in Baltimore decided to place greater emphasis on its physical education program upon his arrival at the school, Fitzpatrick claimed this decision was met with "more pushback"[14] from parents than would be the case at a public school. Fitzpatrick asserted that from the perspective of quite a few Al-Rahmah parents, school "is for education, you get degrees, you earn money."[15] Math and science factor firmly into

---

[12] "About An-Noor Academy," http://www.annooracademy.com/About/ general-information (accessed 21 April 2014).

[13] Ibid.

[14] Patrick Fitzpatrick, personal interview, 20 February 2014, Baltimore MD.

[15] Ibid.

this equation; physical education and extracurricular athletic activities do not. Possessing this mindset, some parents who serve on Islamic school advisory boards are loath to see precious funds apportioned to physical education and sports programs. Especially at the many Islamic schools in fledgling stages where a healthy school budget remains a dream rather than a reality,[16] athletics are frequently relegated to a subpar status amidst higher school priorities. Abir Catovic recounted the history of Noor ul-Iman (NUI) in New Jersey, a prekindergarten-through-twelfth-grade institution that is atypical among American Islamic schools both in terms of its large enrollment, with approximately 600 students, and its longevity, having been around since 1993. The NUI athletic director commented that her school is also rather distinct among Islamic schools due to its afterschool sports offerings and strong commitment to physical education. This high prioritization of athletics, however, was a long time coming. Beset by fiscal constraints, NUI had no extracurricular athletics until its tenth year, concentrating on developing resources in areas such as science and Qurʻanic studies instead. NUI's early stages resembled what I found at Bright Ascension, a Southern California institution. As of 2013–2014, its second year of existence, this prekindergarten-to-eighth-grade school enrolling forty students lacked the wherewithal to hire a physical education teacher and to construct a playground or sports field. Diagnosing these deficiencies as her school's "major hindrance," principal Aniqa Janjua said, "If we had a proper playground, we'll have more students. When parents come in…that's the first thing they look at: 'You don't have a playground. You don't have sports equipment.'"[17] While some of these parents may emphasize academics above athletics, they nonetheless see a nearly complete lack of athletic resources as a stop sign in their drive to locate the optimum schooling option for their offspring.

With a full-time male physical education teacher for boys and full-time female physical education instructor for girls, along with afterschool

---

[16] According to Keyworth's study, most Islamic schools "are still very young and have not yet been in existence long enough that they can adequately be assessed as to the quality of education provided" (Haddad and Smith, "Introduction: The Challenge of Islamic Education in North America," 12).

[17] Aniqa Janjua, personal interview, 10 April 2014, Fontana CA.

high school and middle school basketball and soccer teams for boys and for girls, NUI has progressed since its first decade to the opposite end of the Islamic school sports spectrum compared to an institution such as Bright Ascension. Nonetheless, NUI's athletic program is not out of the financial challenge woods. Catovic commented that NUI is unable to pay its coaches, making it difficult to find qualified individuals who can take on this commitment and leaving Catovic stretched to her limits as coach of all four NUI girls teams in the 2013–2014 academic year. Catovic also lamented that NUI does not have funds for a soccer field or indoor basketball court. Although grateful that the local parks and recreation department permits NUI soccer teams to use one of its fields without a fee, Catovic regrets that NUI basketball teams must rent a gym for practices, which increases the burden of fundraising on players and their families. Catovic identified a different type of challenge in not having a gym, suggesting that some of her students are intimidated to play at an opposing school with its own court. Catovic declared that when these players see another school's home court, at least for a while "it's like total defeat. It's a psychological thing."[18] Even for Islamic school teams that have their own gym, the situation may fall far short of ideal. IBall Academy director Maher Abuawad remarked that quite a few Islamic school administrators seem to be satisfied with a substandard gym for their school. He stated, "A lot of these principals are new to the culture in the sense of basketball being important to the kids, so they buy these facilities but don't think that a gym is important."[19] Abuawad cited one particular example in which a building purchased to house an Islamic school included a gym with a less-than-regulation-size court and hazardous conditions for players. Abuawad's wife, Amnah Elbarrad, built on her husband's concern, commenting that "it's embarrassing" for a college recruiter or someone else from outside the Islamic school community to "see a gym like that."[20]

The absence of an indoor basketball court may create headaches at NUI, but Catovic displayed her sanguine personality through a story that

---

[18] Abir Catovic, personal interview, 1 May 2014, Monmouth Junction NJ.

[19] Maher Abuawad, personal interview, 21 February 2014, Lawrenceville NJ.

[20] Amnah Elbarrad, personal interview, 21 February 2014, Lawrenceville NJ.

placed a positive spin on this lack. Catovic recollected her friendship with the athletic director of St. Peters High School, who invited NUI to use his school's gym as its home court. Due to financial hardship, the Catholic school was forced to close, but Catovic's deep appreciation of this act of interreligious generosity endures, just as she remains touched by the athletic director giving NUI all of St. Peters's basketballs after his school permanently shut its doors. These interfaith acts of kindness stand poles apart from what transpired in Texas, where an Islamic school received the cold shoulder from an athletic association made up mostly of Christian schools. Founded in the 1970s, the Texas Association of Private and Parochial Schools (TAPPS) has mushroomed to a membership of over 300 schools, including a few Jewish institutions. In 2010 TAPPS mulled over but eventually declined granting membership to Iman Academy SW, a Houston Islamic school with a well-established soccer team. TAPPS's application process for the school featured a specially concocted questionnaire with queries including the following:

> Historically, there is nothing in the Koran that fully embraces Christianity or Judaism in the way a Christian and/or a Jew understands his religion. Why, then, are you interested in joining an association whose basic beliefs your religion condemns?
>
> It is our understanding that the Koran tells you not to mix with (and even eliminate) the infidels. Christians and Jews fall into that category. Why do you wish to join an organization whose membership is in disagreement with your religious beliefs?[21]

Some questions were not as loaded to connect the school with a version of Islam that categorically condemns non-Muslims, yet others seemed to imply that Islam not only looks down upon other religions, but seeks to eradicate their presence. The school was asked, for example,

---

[21] Quoted in Travis Waldron, "Texas School Sports League Asks Muslim School If It Wants to 'Eliminate The Infidels,' Denies Its Membership Application," Think Progress, http://thinkprogress.org/justice/2012/03/14/443807/texas-school-sports-league-asks-muslim-school-if-it-wants-to-eliminate-the-infidels-denies-its-membership-application/ (posted 14 March 2012; accessed 21 April 2014).

"What is your attitude about the spread of Islam in America? What are the goals of your school in this regard?"[22] Adding insult to injury, TAPPS surveyed member schools to get their opinion of an Islamic school joining the league, and sixty-three percent expressed opposition. Iman Academy SW administrator Cindy Steffens responded to TAPPS's rejection of her school by proclaiming, "We know our kids are just as American as their kids. We just wanted to play ball."[23] Spurned by fellow Americans, students at this Islamic school continue to play ball, but not under the auspices of the Lone Star State's largest religiously affiliated athletic league.

Despite low parental appraisal of athletics, inadequate financial resources, anti-Islamic sentiments, or any other obstacle, major athletic emphases can be found in certain American Islamic schools. Some place exceptionally high value on physical education, some provide an array of afterschool sports activities, and others feature a combination of these two scenarios. In almost every case, these schools have been in existence for at least a decade, have reached a healthy financial state, and have developed a critical mass of parents and staff buying into the idea that healthy living is an important Islamic principle that needs to be highlighted in a holistic Islamic school education. Abeer Odeh of Detroit-area Crescent Academy addressed this idea, describing ways in which her school strives to instill upon students the merits of healthy living. Odeh mentioned Crescent Academy's extracurricular sports programs for boys and for girls, its special athletic events such as a girls' swim night and boys' lock-in at a local sports complex, and its uncommon decision to have recess at the middle school level, each of which reflects an aspiration to underscore the importance of exercise and taking care of one's body. Odeh went on to say that the concept of balancing the mental, spiritual, and physical realms of life, which she and other school staff consider to be a fundamental Islamic principle, is integrated throughout Crescent

---

[22] Quoted in Mary Pilon, "Before Games, Religious Questions," *New York Times*, http://www.nytimes.com/2012/03/03/sports/in-texas-islamic-schools-face-tough-road-to-participation.html?_r=0 (published 2 March 2012; accessed 21 April 2014).

[23] Quoted in ibid.

Academy's curriculum.[24] Unlike Islamic schools that focus upon the mental and spiritual but not the physical, Crescent Academy makes athletic activity an integral part of Islamic schooling alongside subjects such as math or Qur'anic studies.

Orange Crescent School

An additional characteristic of quite a few Islamic schools with a major athletic emphasis is the jumpstarting of this emphasis by one particular individual at the school. This description aptly applies to Orange Crescent School (OCS) in Southern California, a kindergarten-through-eighth-grade school founded in 1983 by the Islamic Society of Orange County. OCS contains a commitment to physical education unlike any other Islamic school I have encountered. Such a commitment requires the support of a small army of administrators, teachers, and parents, yet there is no question that one man has been both the initial visionary and commanding officer. From the first e-mail reply I received to our interview that could have continued for hours, my interactions with physical education instructor Khaldoun Dahhaj have made me feel as if calling him "passionate" about his job would be a major understatement. A first-generation immigrant from Jordan, the fifty-something-year-old Coach K is licensed by the West German athletic federation to coach both soccer and track and field, sports with which he is clearly enamored. Yet, with even more gusto than that accompanying his comments about these sports, Dahhaj expressed enthusiasm about his students. He declared that his dedication to physical education at OCS is "about those children. That's what I believe, always believed, and always will believe in it. I will fight my way to make things happen for them… With the support I have from the community, we are doing a great job here, and it's all about those kids—having fun and becoming healthier day by day. And it makes you want to do more."[25] Surrounded by trophy-lined shelves and stacks of sports equipment in his office, Dahhaj piled story upon story about OCS physical education offerings and their benefits for students, stopping at one point to take me outside to look at a banner declaring

---

[24] Abeer Odeh, personal interview, 19 March 2014, Canton MI.
[25] Khaldoun Dahhaj, personal interview, 11 April 2014, Garden Grove CA.

OCS a "School Fitness Winner" in Arnold Schwarzenegger's Governor's Challenge for Physical Fitness. Coach K proudly asserted that some parents have chosen OCS because of its physical education program, which he described as a significant source of publicity for the school. This athletic advertisement has been airing since 2001, when Dahhaj enrolled his child in OCS preschool. Searching for signs of athletic life at the school, he was deeply disappointed by what he saw. Dahhaj recalls girls having no involvement in sports and boys "just playing basketball and running around."[26] Feeling personally compelled to take on the task of building OCS athletics nearly from scratch, Dahhaj successfully appealed for a physical education teaching position. Dahhaj stated that he began with just one basketball and one soccer ball, but once school parents "saw my involvement and what I was able to bring, they really were generous enough to accommodate anything I would ask."[27] This comment elicited a further round of stories, featuring parents who helped Dahhaj raise funds to purchase track and field equipment, a shoe store-owning father who donated dozens of shoes, and a parent who paid for the installation of an artificial turf soccer field.

Crediting administrative and parental support he has received over the years, Dahhaj enumerated the mélange of athletic activities he has instituted at OCS. Early on, he brought table tennis, basketball, and soccer tournaments to the school. First came the table tennis tourney, including both students and teachers. Next was basketball, with teams at each grade level, separated by gender, taking two months to complete preliminary and playoff rounds. Coach K mentioned basketball, soccer, volleyball, flag football, tennis, badminton, tee-ball, and softball as standard P.E. class fare, and he added that "track and field is major here. ...You name it, every single event in track and field was introduced—we're still doing it—except for the high jump and pole vault due to lack of resources"[28] and the hammer throw due to safety concerns. As fruit of Dahhaj's labor, a six-lane track encircles the school parking lot, where students devote one month of P.E. to sprints, relays, hurdles, and long-

[26] Ibid.
[27] Ibid.
[28] Ibid.

distance running, followed by a month of field events. This track was one of multiple sites of a flurry of activity throughout the OCS campus during the 2014 edition of Sports Day, an annual event that coincides with the school's Spirit Day and its participation in the national Jump Rope for Heart program. Giant inflatables, omnipresent popsicles, and a watermelon-eating contest caught my eye, but athletic events formed the flesh of the day's proceedings. Containing standard sporting activities such as basketball and soccer, each Sports Day also features a new athletic element incorporated by Dahhaj. In 2014 he introduced what he called the Iron Student/Teacher Challenge, containing a prescribed formula of push-ups, sit-ups, and distance running for students and for staff. Girls and female staff were fully involved in the day's athletic panoply, a reflection of the reality that few accomplishments provide Dahhaj with as much pleasure as what he and female P.E. teachers Narmeen Ramjan and Leila Dakelbab have done for girls' sports at the school.[29] Whereas girls and sports were virtually an oxymoron before his arrival, Dahhaj insists that sports for girls are now equally important as they are for boys at OCS. Girls and boys enjoy the same sports, playing together up to third grade and separately in most sports in fourth grade and above. An OCS visitor might see Coach K leading boys in basketball in one area of school grounds and then move on to observe the school's female physical education teacher instructing hijab-wearing girls in soccer. The visitor might also notice older boys and girls on the same court for volleyball, pitted against one another. Dahhaj explained that since volleyball is not a contact sport like basketball or soccer, and because teams are separated by a net, he finds it compatible with Islamic principles to have boys and girls of any age play volleyball against each other. Regardless of age or gender, OCS students are left with no doubt that physical activity is an essential piece of their Islamic school education, which further encompasses emphasis on healthy nutritional choices. Dahhaj gives students extra points

---

[29] Dahhaj requested that I note these two women's tireless efforts in enhancing athletic opportunities for girls at OCS. Ramjan is a certified nurse who taught P.E. for girls at OCS from 2007–2009, and Dakelbab held this same position from 2010–2013, during which she pursued postgraduate education to become vice principal of the school (Khaldoun Dahhaj, personal e-mail to author, 1 March 2015).

in their physical education grade if they can exhibit evidence of healthy eating, and he has made OCS a soda-free campus, captaining a campaign to clear out soda vending machines that had been in place for years.

Muslim Community Center Full Time School

Their winter weather may be as different as night and day, but OCS and the Muslim Community Center Full Time School (MCC-FTS) have a lot in common. Similar to OCS, this Chicago-area institution is a kindergarten-through-eighth-grade school that places an extremely high priority on athletic activities largely because of one particular member of the school family. A talented basketball and football athlete during his own school days, second-generation Indian American Habeeb Quadri stirred his zeal for sports together with his conviction that physical fitness enhances academic performance into a pot he unveiled at MCC-FTS, where he serves as principal. MCC-FTS has grown considerably since its humble 1990 beginnings, when it enrolled twenty-five students in kindergarten and first and second grades. As of 2014–2015, its enrollment stands at nearly 600, with twice as many staff members as its initial number of students. Under Quadri's guidance, its sports program has burgeoned as well. Students may whet their athletic appetites with afterschool programs in boys' basketball, girls' basketball, boys' soccer, girls' volleyball, a running club, and a girls' kickboxing and tae-bo club. This sporting lineup is stamped with Quadri's imprimatur, mixing the principal's principles regarding strong athletic programs in any school setting with his desire to foster the well-being of Muslim youth. Quadri conducts workshops for public schools about the needs of Muslim students and travels throughout the nation as one of Muslim Youth North America's most popular speakers. Co-author of a book that discusses struggles commonly confronting Muslim youth,[30] Quadri aspires both to challenge and to encourage young Muslim Americans, and as he sees it, a vibrant MCC-FTS athletic program is one way to make this aspiration a victorious reality.

---

[30] Habeeb Quadri and Sa'ad Quadri, *The War Within Our Hearts* (Leicestershire, UK: Kube Publishing, 2009).

Echoing a popular American Islamic school theme, Quadri stated that before coming to MCC-FTS, academics were held in high esteem but athletics were not. Quadri commented, "When I got here there was a gym teacher who wasn't certified, but parents were like, 'Don't worry. As long as you're doing academics, you're doing enough. Kids just need to run around.'"[31] Since Quadri's arrival, P.E. at the school has changed dramatically, from an afterthought receiving negligible resources to a critical curricular component in which teachers trained in physical education instruction introduce students to a variety of sports while focusing on skill development, fitness, sportsmanship, and other important aspects of athletic participation. Like Dahhaj at OCS, Quadri is adamant that Muslim girls get to experience the school's athletic opportunities just as fully as boys. He exuberantly proclaimed that MCC-FTS is the first Islamic school to receive a grant from the GoGirlGo! Women's Sports Foundation, started by retired tennis star Billie Jean King. This grant has enabled MCC-FTS to expand its afterschool athletic menu for girls, and to separate girls from boys in physical education classes beginning in third grade rather than sixth grade as before, a change that Quadri associates with giving girls greater self-confidence. Quadri returned to this notion of developing self-confidence through sports multiple times during our conversation, and at one point he suggested that watching, not just playing, sports can contribute to this development for MCC-FTS students. A school outing each year involves a local sporting event such as a University of Illinois-Chicago basketball game, and frequently the beginning of a salat prayer period coincides with the athletic event. Quadri said that in this situation, he might declare to students, "OK, guys, we're watching this game, and how do we pray?"[32] He then explained, "We'll take them to a corner—we'll take ten at a time—to show that you can still practice your faith even in a setting where it might be uncomfortable."[33] Though some students may get cold feet, Quadri greets this experience warmly for the sake of their growth in self-confidence as followers of Islam.

[31] Habeeb Quadri, personal interview, 17 March 2014, Morton Grove IL.
[32] Ibid.
[33] Ibid.

New Horizon Schools

Quadri had plenty of company in linking Islamic school sports with strengthening young Muslims' piety. In multiple interviews, I heard variations on the argument that, by demonstrating the vital importance of not just the spiritual and intellectual aspects of Islamic education but the physical as well, students receive a lasting lesson in viewing Islam as a complete way of life, and they become more attracted to Islam since it elevates fun physical activity to an exalted level. Even more frequently in conversations, though, associations made between bonding and Islamic school sports pertained to strengthening Muslim fellowship. From a P.E. class's first whistle to its closing bell, or on the afterschool basketball practice court and soccer game field, Muslim youth interact with Muslim peers and teachers in myriad meaningful ways, building new relationships and tightening existing ones with fellow followers of their faith. Laughing together in the school gym or encouraging one another after a deflating defeat, Muslim camaraderie can congeal through Islamic school athletic activities.

Bridging may also occur through Islamic school sports, but much more rarely than bonding since in the Islamic school setting Muslims are seldom playing with or against non-Muslims. In Southern California, however, two schools stand outside the norm, as students have plenty of opportunity to interact with non-Muslims in athletic leagues in which each institution is the sole Islamic school member. Both schools are part of the New Horizon system, initially crafted by Islamic Center of Southern California (ICSC) hands. One of California's largest mosques, ICSC proclaims that the "emergence of an American Muslim identity is its prime goal."[34] This aim spilled over into the shaping of New Horizon schools, which identify one of their hallmarks to be a commitment to help each student develop "a positive identity as an American Muslim."[35] As New Horizon-Pasadena (NHP) principal Amira al-Sarraf explained,

[34] "The Islamic Center of Southern California: About Us," The Islamic Center of Southern Californina, http://icsconline.org/aboutus (accessed 25 April 2014).

[35] "New Horizon School Pasadena: Mission & Goals," New Horizon School Pasadena, http://www.newhorizonschool.org/pages/about_us/missiongoals (accessed 25 April 2014).

a popular pathway her school pursues to promote this identity is to stress that students possess both American rights and American responsibilities. Al-Sarraf commented that she wants her students to be "balanced and productive human beings that recognize their important role as Americans—how they can take advantage of the opportunities they have living here and do their part to improve their communities and their societies. Their faith is an integrated piece in that."[36] Distancing themselves from an insular approach to Islamic education, New Horizon schools strive for students, under the guidance of Islamic principles, to be thoroughly engaged with American society. An Islamic school team competing in an interscholastic league with non-Muslim opponents fits hand in glove with this ambition.

Opening its doors in 1984 as the original member of the New Horizon family, NHP's 2014–2015 enrollment of 200 students spans preschool through eighth grade. For much of its history, NHP middle school students could unleash their pent-up energy at an afterschool sports club, where they engaged in athletic activities among themselves plus a few informal games against other schools sprinkled into the mix. In 2013 NHP upped its interscholastic sports game. Middle school boys now participate in flag football and basketball, and middle school girls in volleyball and basketball as members of the Foothill League. Principal al-Sarraf coached the volleyball team in its initial Foothill League season, which she described with a grin as an opportunity for her girls to grow in character since they failed to win a single match. Al-Sarraf used the team's struggles on the scoreboard to try to transform players' perspective on the meaning of winning, exhorting them that "winning isn't about the points at the end of the game."[37] She explained, "When I saw this student improve and make every serve over the net, as opposed to last game where they missed most of their serves, that's a win. ...It's helping kids to strive for those goals and to compete to improve themselves."[38] Al-Sarraf's winless season strengthened her desire for NHP athletes to "find a healthy balance on how competition can be a force of good in helping

---

[36] Amira al-Sarraf, personal interview, 10 April 2014, Pasadena CA.
[37] Ibid.
[38] Ibid.

us strive for excellence, without that feeling of worth being tied to the score at the end of the game,"[39] but instilling this point of view has not come easily since it clashes with a common mindset among students and parents. Al-Sarraf cited one parent in particular as a case in point. In response to NHP players frequently finding themselves on the short end of the Foothill League scoring stick and feeling down as a result, this parent sent al-Sarraf an e-mail encouraging her to consider ending NHP's affiliation with the league. Al-Sarraf strongly disagreed.

Another league-related rub for some NHP parents has been its absence of soccer. Including a large percentage of first-generation immigrants, NHP parents tend to favor soccer over basketball and football. Al-Sarraf commented that on days when the school hosts soccer activities for students, NHP parents flock to the field to watch and socialize. On the other hand, as she remarked, "That same culture is not as strong around those other sports. So when we have a basketball game or flag football game, we just don't get as much of our parent population—either parents of the kids who are on the team, or just school population, going out to the game."[40] Al-Sarraf hopes to see this state of affairs change, reaching a point where school spirit surrounds the court or field and NHP parents outnumber visiting team parents at NHP home games. The principal proclaimed that football "has a really strong role in American culture in many American schools, and that is just not something that we have yet built up."[41] Wanting to construct this American cultural edifice within the NHP community, al-Sarraf was pleased to point out that for its first Foothill League season, NHP brought in coaches who were born in the United States and attended schools where football games enjoyed pride of social place. From al-Sarraf's perspective, such an effort to get NHP students and parents more excited about football is an extremely worthwhile investment, for the sake not only of boosting school spirit, but facilitating bridging as well. Al-Sarraf commented that coming to an Islamic school may unnerve some parents of other Foothill League teams, and so NHP staff concentrate on making

[39] Ibid.
[40] Ibid.
[41] Ibid.

them feel welcome in what may initially feel like threatening territory. She said that staff members "talk to them so they don't necessarily feel like we're strange," but she added that she would "love to have more of our parents doing some of that outreach."[42] Al-Sarraf believes this wish will come to fruition as more and more NHP parents get hooked on football and basketball and come out for games at the school.

While interfaith connections via the Foothill League may be relatively slow in coming for parents, NHP students have been rubbing shoulders with non-Muslim peers through the league on a regular basis. These interactions have entailed a few unexpected twists and turns. Al-Sarraf recollected her team's first league volleyball game, before which the opposing coach asked al-Sarraf if NHP players would like to join their Christian school opponents in a pre-game prayer. Al-Sarraf recalled, "For a moment I had a little bit of panic because I wasn't sure what they were going to say in the prayer. I have a responsibility to figure out what our kids are going to feel comfortable with."[43] She opted to accept the invitation, telling her players something to the following effect: "We're going to say a prayer. If everything she says you agree with, as far as how it matches up with our faith, then you're praying for that. But if there's a point where she says something you don't agree with...just know that that's not what you believe."[44] As it turned out, the opposing coach ended her prayer in the name of "Jesus our Lord," thereby expressing a belief at odds with the Islamic view that, though a prophet worthy

---

[42] Ibid.

[43] Ibid.

[44] Ibid. Muslim Basketball League player Kareem Shahin discussed making the opposite decision as al-Sarraf while playing in a Southern California Christian basketball league, but spoke highly of league members' response. Shahin explained that during pre-game prayers, he and a Muslim friend "just step aside, because they're doing it in the name of the Lord Jesus Christ. We just step aside, and people have no problem with it whatsoever" (Kareem Shahin, personal interview, 11 April 2014, Fontana CA). Shahin's experience differs from that of four Muslim football players at New Mexico State University, who filed a lawsuit against their coach for religious discrimination after he dubbed them "troublemakers" for objecting to reciting the Lord's Prayer in a team huddle after practices and before games. The university ended up settling the case out of court (Coakley, *Sports in Society*, 537).

---

of great respect, Jesus is not to be worshiped. Al-Sarraf recognizes this situation may have temporarily flummoxed her volleyball flock, but she cherishes the enduring effects of young Muslims and Christians praying together and making a memorable interreligious connection at a very impressionable stage of their lives.

Founded nearly two decades after NHP, New Horizon-Irvine (NHI) had a 2014–2015 enrollment of 197, almost identical to its older New Horizon sibling, albeit with sixth as its highest grade level as opposed to eighth at NHP. As a further sibling similarity, in 2013 NHI also joined an interscholastic athletic league in which it is the only Islamic school member. NHI fifth- and sixth-graders participate in the Developmental Sports League, playing against Christian schools, a Jewish school, and private schools of no religious affiliation. The league offers boys' flag football and girls' volleyball in the fall, boys' and girls' basketball in the winter, and co-ed soccer in the spring. NHI principal Dina Eletreby highly esteems her school's involvement in the league, linking it to an unprecedented sense of school pride. She remarked that "having a team that plays other schools really added an entire dimension. It was something we were looking to bring for a while."[45] During NHI's early years, Eletreby saw a need to concentrate on more pressing matters than sports, but as core academic subjects became more established and other initial priorities were fulfilled, she searched for ways to enrich students' experience at the school. Questioning how students could be given "a sense of connection to the school beyond just parents wanting them to be here,"[46] an afterschool sports program jumped out as an answer. According to Eletreby, implementing this answer has resulted in more than stoking school spirit fires, since it has kindled bridging as well. Calling it an unintended but "very positive consequence"[47] of joining the Developmental Sports League, Eletreby highlighted the fact that league games bring non-Muslim parents to an Islamic school, which, like al-Sarraf, she avowed can play an important role in reducing non-Muslims' fear of Islam. In reference to these parents coming to NHI, Eletreby pronounced,

[45] Dina Eletreby, personal interview, 9 April 2014, Irvine CA.
[46] Ibid.
[47] Ibid.

"I think there's great benefit in that, in terms of the community just coming and seeing that we're a regular school and being welcomed within our school environment, and for them to see that our parents are cheering their kids on the same way that they do. Even if we moved or shifted their thinking by adding one additional alternative about Islam, that's a very significant and positive thing."[48] Especially in regard to parents who previously have never crossed paths with a Muslim and whose conceptions of Islam have been molded by images of violent extremists and essentialist caricatures of the faith, what may simply appear to be a chance for fifth- and sixth-graders to play sports can mean much more than what meets the eye.

Joining my conversation with Eletreby, school athletic director, coach, and physical education teacher David Rutledge expanded on the theme of bridging through the Developmental Sports League. Rutledge propounded that NHI players often feel extra responsibility for their on-court or on-field behavior because they represent a religion that is often viewed negatively,[49] and according to Rutledge, they have responded to this pressure with flying colors. As an example, he mentioned playing at the league's Jewish school and noticing that the scorekeepers were extremely pleased when NHI players went over to the bench to shake their hands and thank them at the conclusion of the game. Rutledge is a non-Muslim, but he is passionate about challenging Islamophobia and takes great pleasure in seeing his students take on this task. The Australian sports enthusiast expressed, "We've won games by one point, and we've come from behind—all those real sporty moments and accomplishments—but far and away my proudest moments"[50] have been when NHI

---

[48] Ibid.

[49] I heard a similar sentiment from a coach of a mosque-based youth soccer team who declared, "There is an additional challenge that we put on them, like 'Because now people perceive you as a Muslim, it puts an additional responsibility on you in terms of behavior'—and sometimes in the heat of the moment with sports, maybe you don't agree with the referee or something. It's not like a regular team. People will pay more attention. At the same time, we're trying not to make it such a big deal, but we do focus on the way we play soccer—our attitude with people, our cheerfulness for everybody" (anonymous phone interview, 22 April 2014).

[50] David Rutledge, personal interview, 9 April 2014, Irvine CA.

players shake hands with individuals from the opposing school or help non-Muslims view Islam more positively through league games in other ways. Rutledge remarked, "You really feel like games are won and lost and it's fun at the time, but things sort of move on after that," whereas his players' actions that promote bridging are what "stays with people, and they're the type of things that are really everlasting."[51]

[51] Ibid.

Conclusion

I was warned. I was told that daytime driving on Southern California freeways came with a heavy heaping of impenetrable gridlock, but I held out hope that I might catch a break. With the clock past morning rush hour, I thought I might just make it to the campus of UCLA in about forty-five minutes after wrapping up my interview at Orange Crescent School forty-three miles away. Pleased by a promising outset in Orange County, a Los Angeles logjam rudely greeted me on the 405 freeway. I ended up taking my seat with two members of UCLA's MSA chapter an hour later than planned, still frustrated and frazzled from what felt like an interminable sixty minutes of being swallowed up in a brutal bottleneck. During this hour, I bounced back and forth between aggravation and appreciation, peeved by the traffic but placated by the patient reassurance I received in each phone update to my waiting interviewees. Cheerful refrains of "No worries" and "We know what traffic is like on the 405" were music to my ears. As I continue to feel toward all eighty-five individuals who took their time to share their insights and experiences with me, I was deeply grateful to these UCLA students. I appreciated their willingness to carve out a chunk of their busy school day, and I felt thankful for their kindness in insisting that I not fret due to my tardy arrival. For this particular interview, I had one more reason to be especially grateful; it wrapped up with words I very much needed to hear. Wali Kamal ended his reflections on sports activities in his MSA chapter by declaring, "Sports—as much as it is a tool for building community, brotherhood, things like that—at the end of the day, it's just fun."[1] Focused throughout my research on athletic activities' resulting effects, Kamal's stress upon sports' intrinsic pleasures above their instrumental functions raised a red flag regarding the possibility of overemphasizing the significance of sports for Muslim Americans. Contrary to a picture I may have constructed of Muslim Americans heading en masse to play sports first and foremost due to bonding and bridging desires, a reminder

[1] Wali Kamal, personal interview, 10 April 2014, Los Angeles CA.

was welcome that such a picture is a distorted image. In countless cases, a stronger motivation leads Muslim Americans to play sports. The love of the game, the pursuit of fun, or the joy of competition may sit in the driver's seat motivating Muslim American athletic activity. Bonding and bridging may be the furthest thought from some athletically engaged Muslim Americans' minds, and in some cases any bonding or bridging that results via Muslim American athletic activity may be an unintended effect.

Intentional or not, however, bonding and bridging resulting from Muslim American athletic activity are shaping American Islam, scoring highly significant ramifications along the way. Particularly from a revivalist perspective, the payoff of more Muslims growing in devoutness and of strengthening the unity of the ummah is immeasurable, finding its currency in eternal reward. Personally standing outside the Islamic faith tradition, I prefer to let Muslims themselves take the lead in commenting on the importance of this bonding reward, and so I turn to the significance of bridging instead. Does it really matter if non-Muslims acquire positive views of Islam through playing sports with Muslims? My reply to this question centers on the notion of American pluralism and Muslims' place within it. Challenging a common conceptualization that places Muslims outside of American society, bridging promoted by sports can play a significant part in increased acknowledgement of Muslims' complete, unequivocal membership within a pluralistic America.

Lauded in certain American circles, the vision of a pluralistic America is, of course, vilified in others. A few minutes of tuning in to certain talk radio shows or of browsing websites overflowing with xenophobia leave no doubt that many Americans view pluralism as a pernicious ploy to rip America apart at its seams. Stentorian voices reject pluralism and opt instead for the melting pot, with its call for the removal of cultural differences in the intense homogenizing heat of Anglo-conformity. Initially popularized in 1908 by Jewish playwright Israel Zangwill, who hoped for a New World end to Old World ethnic and religious feuds,[2]

---

[2] The hero of Zangwill's play *The Melting Pot* is a young Russian Jew named David, who proclaims upon eyeing the immigrant assemblage at Ellis Island, "America is God's Crucible, the great Melting-Pot where all the races of Europe are melt-

the melting pot image quickly seared itself into American consciousness and found expression in innumerable ways. At the Ford Motor Company, for example, the auto manufacturer followed nine months of English and assimilation classes for newly arrived immigrant workers with a dramatic ceremony of symbolic rebirth. Descending into a giant pot while clothed in variegated native European garb, workers emerged in American clothes holding American flags after the pot was stirred.[3]

As Ford and many other Americans regarded melting pot flames to be vital for their nation's preservation and prosperity, some argued that a bright American future is contingent on extinguishing this fire. In 1915 a fellow Jewish American expressed his deep-seated dissent with Zangwill's melting pot ideal. Sociologist Horace Kallen made his position crystal clear in the title of his article "Democracy Versus the Melting Pot." Casting Zangwill's vision as inherently incompatible with democratic values, Kallen favored a portrayal of America as a symphony orchestra, featuring harmony of various cultures' distinctive tones rather than an idealized monophonic Anglo-American timbre. In Kallen's orchestra, each player could relish the opportunity to hear his ethnic instrument's particular beautiful sounds while simultaneously experiencing the euphonious enchantment of diverse tones coming together in mellifluous accord. Kallen gave this orchestra the label "cultural pluralism" and emphasized the importance of responding to ethnic diversity by way of active engagement. Beyond mere acknowledgement of difference, and light years apart from the melting pot ideal, Kallen's orchestra welcomes the retaining of deep cultural commitments while one instrumental section seeks to actively understand another. Moreover, this orchestra's audience should settle in their seats and get ready for a performance that never ends. Unlike the melting pot's eagerness to expedite the eradication

ing and re-forming! ...Germans and Frenchmen, Irishmen and Englishmen, Jews and Russians—into the Crucible with you all! God is making the American!" (quoted in Eck, *A New Religious America*, 54–55).

[3] According to anthropologist Franz Boas in a 1910 report before Congress, the melting away of immigrant differences included not only cultural aspects, but physical elements as well. Boas's "Changes in Bodily Form of Descendants of Immigrants" described a purportedly growing brain capacity and bodily size as well as lightening of hair color of Jewish and Sicilian immigrants.

of heterogeneity, the pluralistic orchestra recruits a vast array of instrumentalists from each new generation, as its encounter with diversity involves an inexhaustible supply of mutual enrichment.[4]

Writing nearly a century after Kallen, Diana Eck emphasizes *religious* diversity in the twenty-first-century edition of the American pluralistic orchestra. Eck declares that this many-hued religious menagerie "requires participation, and attunement to the life and energies of one another."[5] This statement provides a trophy-winning description of what takes place in Muslim basketball leagues, mosque sports programs, and other local Muslim American sports settings where athletic energies of non-Muslim and Muslim Americans intersect, fostering fuller non-Muslim acknowledgement and understanding of Muslims' deeply rooted residence within American society. Attuning their lives on the court or field with Muslim teammates, non-Muslims may think differently not only about Islam, but also about America, reimagining it as a nation where Muslims have every right to enjoy the same benefits of citizenship that non-Muslims call their own. In this reimagined America, a repeat of post-9/11 violation of Muslim American civil liberties would be considered unacceptable. If another violent act is perpetrated on American soil by Islamic extremists, Christians, Jews, atheists, and others would demonstrate extremely solid support for Muslims' full rights as fellow Americans. In this reimagined America, non-Muslims would view Muslim Americans unequivocally as compatriots, not because Muslims' religious commitments have become charred beyond recognition in melting pot fire, but in part because these commitments are recognized for their countless contributions to the beautiful sounds of a pluralistic American orchestra.

I hold no illusion that every American will be swept up by this pluralistic wave. Some will do everything in their power to fight its force and will pour fuel on the fire to melt away Muslim distinctiveness in Ameri-

[4] This description is similar to Bruce Lawrence's conception of America as a kaleidoculture, in which "each part makes the whole more vivid, more colorful, more capacious without exhausting the limits for contest and for experiment, for challenge and for change" (Lawrence, *New Faiths, Old Fears*, 140).

[5] Eck, *A New Religious America*, 70.

ca. My argument in this book has not entered the realm of inevitability, as if Muslim athletic activity comes with a money-back bonding and bridging guarantee. I have, though, sought to raise bonding and bridging as potential athletic aftereffects carrying highly significant stakes for both Muslim and non-Muslim Americans. From my standpoint, as someone whose innumerable encounters with Muslim kindness leave me excited about Muslim American sports' potential for bridging, I stake my hopes especially on more and more Americans unabashedly welcoming Muslims as full members of a pluralistic American orchestra without requiring them to prove they are "good Muslims" who deserve a seat on the symphony hall stage.[6]

Even among those Americans who prefer to listen to a pluralistic orchestra than to witness the melting pot's flames, many may not yet be willing to admit Muslim instrumentalists. Imprinted with lasting 9/11 images and daily headlines trumpeting the devastating deeds of ISIS, Boko Haram, or the latest version of a violent strain of Islam, a deeply engrained perception of Muslims as threats rather than assets to Ameri-

---

[6] Mahmood Mamdani argues that after 9/11, President Bush "seemed to assure Americans that 'good Muslims' were anxious to clear their names and consciences of this horrible crime and would undoubtedly support 'us' in a war against 'them.' But this could not hide the central message of such discourse: unless proved to be 'good,' every Muslim was presumed to be 'bad.' All Muslims were now under obligation to prove their credentials by joining in a war against 'bad Muslims'" (Mahmood Mamdani, *Good Muslim, Bad Muslim: America, the Cold War, and the Roots of Terror* (New York: Pantheon, 2004) 15). Along these lines, Andrew Shryock discusses what he calls "penitential rites of citizenship," in which Muslims must counteract the burden of proof against them and show they are indeed "good Muslims" and therefore worthy of being accepted as American citizens. Shryock writes that Muslims are required to "engage in these corrective, penitential rites of citizenship even (or especially) when one has no connection to 'bad' Arabs or 'bad' Islam. Only *after* these rites of belonging have been performed does minoritized citizenship (racialized, ethnic, exemplary, provisional, or exceptional) become possible" (Andrew Shryock, "The Moral Analogies of Race: Arab American Identity, Color Politics, and the Limits of Racialized Citizenship," in *Race and Arab Americans Before and After 9/11: From Invisible Citizens to Visible Subjects*, ed. Amaney Jamal and Nadine Naber, 81–113 (Syracuse NY: Syracuse University Press, 2008) 107–108).

can society may lead to doubt that Muslims do indeed belong in the orchestra. Stepping into this space of skepticism, Muslim American athletic activities have a priceless contribution to offer America as it progresses further into its future. As non-Muslim Americans learn about retired NFLer Az Hakim's organization to assist children of incarcerated parents, or about the Boston-area Muslim Athletic League's charity basketball tournaments to raise funds for individuals of all faiths, many may move closer to being convinced not only that Muslims deserve a seat in the pluralistic American orchestra, but that they are supremely talented to make it more beautiful. As non-Muslims experience the magnanimity of Muslim teammates and opponents firsthand in a Muslim Students Association flag football game or a mosque basketball league, Islamophobic walls that have denied Muslims complete access to the symphony hall stage may sustain major damage and eventually crumble.

Bibliography

Print Sources

Abdo, Geneive. *Mecca and Main Street: Muslim Life in America after 9/11*. New York: Oxford University Press, 2006.

Abdul Khabeer, Suad. "*Rep That Islam*: The Rhyme and Reason of American Islamic Hip Hop." *Muslim World* 97 (2007): 125–41.

Ahmed, Akbar. *Journey into America: The Challenge of Islam*. Washington DC: Brookings Institution Press, 2010.

Alba, Richard, and Victor Nee. *Remaking the American Mainstream: Assimilation and Contemporary Immigration*. Cambridge MA: Harvard University Press, 2003.

Aldousari, Badi. "The History and the Philosophy of Sport in Islam." Unpublished M.A. thesis, Ball State University, 2000.

Alvesson, Mats. *Interpreting Interviews*. Los Angeles: Sage, 2011.

Amara, Mahfoud. *Sport, Politics, and Society in the Arab World*. New York: Palgrave Macmillan, 2012.

Apuzzo, Matt, and Adam Goldman. *Enemies Within: Inside the NYPD's Secret Spying Unit and bin Laden's Final Plot Against America*. New York: Touchstone, 2013.

Bakalian, Anny P., and Mehdi Bozorgmehr. *Backlash 9/11: Middle Eastern and Muslim Americans Respond*. Berkeley: University of California Press, 2009.

Baker, William J. *Playing with God: Religion and Modern Sport*. Cambridge MA: Harvard University Press, 2007.

Baldassaro, Lawrence. "Before Joe D: Early Italian Americans in the Major Leagues." In *The American Game: Baseball and Ethnicity*, edited by Lawrence Baldassaro and Richard A. Johnson, 92–115. Carbondale IL: Southern Illinois University Press, 2002.

Barrett, Paul M. *American Islam: The Struggle for the Soul of a Religion*. New York: Picador, 2008.

Bazzano, Carmelo. "The Italian American Sporting Experience." In *Ethnicity and Sport in North American History and Culture*, edited by George Eisen and David K. Wiggins, 103–16. Westport CT: Greenwood Press, 1994.

Borish, Linda J. "Women, Sport, and American Jewish Identity in the Late Nineteenth and Early Twentieth Centuries." In *With God on Their Side: Sport in the Service of Religion*, edited by Tara Magdalinski and Timothy J. L. Chandler, 71–98. New York: Routledge, 2002.

Boyd, Todd. *Young, Black, Rich, and Famous: The Rise of the NBA, the Hip Hop Invasion, and the Transformation of American Culture.* New York: Doubleday, 2003.

Brinkmann, Svend. *Qualitative Interviewing.* Oxford: Oxford University Press, 2013.

Cainkar, Louise A. *Homeland Insecurity: The Arab American and Muslim American Experience after 9/11.* New York: Russell Sage Foundation, 2009.

Caldwell, Deborah. "A Basketball Player Finds Peace." In *Taking Back Islam: American Muslims Reclaim Their Faith*, edited by Michael Wolfe, 228–32. Emmaus PA: Rodale, 2002.

———. "Muhammad Ali: The Reassuring Face of American Islam." In *Taking Back Islam: American Muslims Reclaim Their Faith*, edited by Michael Wolfe, 146–49. Emmaus PA: Rodale, 2002.

Cavanaugh, Jack. *The Gipper: George Gipp, Knute Rockne, and the Dramatic Rise of Notre Dame Football.* New York: Skyhorse Publishing, 2010.

Chittick, William C. *Sufism: A Beginner's Guide.* London: Oneworld, 2007.

Coakley, Jay. *Sports in Society: Issues and Controversies*, 10th edition. New York: McGraw-Hill, 2008.

Collins, Mike. "Leisure Studies and the Social Capital Discourse." In *Sport, Leisure Culture, and Social Capital: Discourse and Practice*, edited by Mike Collins, Kirsten Holmes, and Alix Slater, 155–66. Eastbourne: Leisure Studies Association, 2007.

Cottrell, Robert C. *Icons of American Popular Culture: From P. T. Barnum to Jennifer Lopez.* New York: Routledge, 2009.

———. *Two Pioneers: How Jackie Robinson and Hank Greenberg Transformed Baseball—and America.* Dulles VA: Potomac Books, 2012.

Curtis IV, Edward E., editor. *The Columbia Sourcebook of Muslims in the United States.* New York: Columbia University Press, 2008.

———. *Muslims in America: A Short History.* New York: Oxford University Press, 2009.

Davies, Douglas J. *An Introduction to Mormonism.* New York: Cambridge University Press, 2003.

Demerath, Nicholas J., and Philip Hammond. *Religion in Social Context: Tradition and Transition.* New York: Random House, 1969.

Dolan, Jay P. *The American Catholic Experience: A History from Colonial Times to the Present.* Garden City NY: Doubleday, 1985.

Doyle, David Noel. "The Remaking of Irish America." In *Making the Irish American: History and Heritage of the Irish in the United States*, edited by J. J. Lee and Marion R. Casey, 213–52. New York: New York University Press, 2006.

Duina, Francesco. *Winning: Reflections on an American Obsession.* Princeton: Princeton University Press, 2011.

Dwork, Deborah. "Immigrant Jews on the Lower East Side of New York: 1880–1914." In *The American Jewish Experience*, edited by Jonathan D. Sarna, 102–17. New York: Holmes & Meier, 1986.

Eck, Diana. *A New Religious America: How a "Christian Country" Has Now Become the World's Most Religiously Diverse Nation.* San Francisco: HarperSanFrancisco, 2001.

Ernst, Carl W. *Sufism: An Introduction to the Mystical Tradition of Islam.* Boston: Shambhala, 2011.

Ewing, Katherine Pratt, and Marguerite Hoyler. "Being Muslim and American: South Asian Muslim Youth and the War on Terror." In *Being and Belonging: Muslims in the United States since 9/11*, edited by Katherine Pratt Ewing, 80–103. New York: Russell Sage Foundation, 2008.

Feezell, Randolph. *Sport, Philosophy, and Good Lives.* Lincoln: University of Nebraska Press, 2013.

Fink, Steven. "Fear Under Construction: Islamophobia Within American Christian Zionism." *Islamophobia Studies Journal* 2/1 (2014): 26–43.

Freedman, Lew. *DiMaggio's Yankees: A History of the 1936–1944 Dynasty.* Jefferson NC: McFarland, 2011.

Gerdy, John R. *Sports: The All-American Addiction.* Jackson: University Press of Mississippi, 2002.

GhaneaBassiri, Kambiz. *Competing Visions of Islam in the United States: A Study of Los Angeles.* Westport CT: Greenwood Press, 1997.

———. *A History of Islam in America: From the New World to the New World Order.* New York: Cambridge University Press, 2010.

Gorn, Elliott J., and Warren Goldstein. *A Brief History of American Sports.* Champaign: University of Illinois Press, 2004.

Grewal, Zareena. *Islam Is a Foreign Country: American Muslims and the Global Crisis of Authority.* New York: New York University Press, 2013.

———. "Lights, Camera, Suspension: Freezing the Frame on the Mahmoud Abdul-Rauf-Anthem Controversy." *Souls: A Critical Journal of Black Politics, Culture, and Society* 9/2 (2007): 109–22.

Haddad, Yvonne Y., and Jane I. Smith. "Introduction: The Challenge of Islamic Education in North America." In *Educating the Muslims of America*, edited by Yvonne Y. Haddad, Farid Senzai, and Jane I. Smith, 3–19. New York: Oxford University Press, 2009.

Hagee, John. *In Defense of Israel.* Lake Mary FL: Frontline, 2007.

———. *Jerusalem Countdown: A Warning to the World.* Lake Mary FL: Frontline, 2006.

Hammersley, Martyn, and Paul Atkinson. *Ethnography: Principles in Practice*, 3rd edition. London: Routledge, 2007.

Hasan, Asma Gull. *American Muslims: The New Generation*, 2nd edition. New York: Bloomsbury, 2002.

Hauser, Thomas. *Muhammad Ali: His Life and Times*. New York: Simon & Schuster, 2006.

Hing, Bill Ong. "Vigilante Racism: The De-Americanization of Immigrant America." *Michigan Journal of Race and Law* 7/2 (2002): 441–56.

Hoffman, Shirl James. "Harvesting Souls in the Stadium: The Rise of Sports Evangelism." In *Sports and Christianity: Historical and Contemporary Perspectives*, edited by Nick J. Watson and Andrew Parker, 131–49. Hoboken: Taylor and Francis, 2012.

Howell, Sally. "Muslims as Moving Targets: External Security and Internal Critique in Detroit's Mosques." In *Arab Detroit 9/11: Life in the Terror Decade*, edited by Nabeel Abraham, Sally Howell, and Andrew Shryock, 151–85. Detroit: Wayne State University Press, 2011.

Huizinga, Johan. *Homo Ludens: A Study of the Play-Element in Culture*. Boston: Beacon Press, 1955.

Iorizzo, Luciano J., and Salvatore Mondello. *The Italian Americans*, revised edition. Boston: Twayne Publishers, 1980.

Isenberg, Michael T. *John L. Sullivan and His America*. Champaign: University of Illinois Press, 1994.

Jackson, Sherman A. *Islam and the Blackamerican: Looking toward the Third Resurrection*. New York: Oxford University Press, 2005.

Jay, Kathryn. *More than Just a Game: Sports in American Life Since 1945*. New York: Columbia University Press, 2004.

Joseph, Craig M., and Barnaby Riedel. "Islamic Schools, Assimilation, and the Concept of Muslim American Character." In *Being and Belonging: Muslims in the United States Since 9/11*, edited by Katherine Pratt Ewing, 156–77. New York: Russell Sage Foundation, 2008.

Kabir, Nahid Afrose. *Young American Muslims: Dynamics of Identity*. Edinburgh: Edinburgh University Press, 2012.

Kahan, David. "Islam and Physical Activity: Implications for American Sport and Physical Educators." *Journal of Physical Education, Recreation, & Dance* 74/3 (2003): 48–54.

Keyworth, Karen. "Islamic Schools of America: Data-Based Profiles." In *Educating the Muslims of America*, edited by Yvonne Y. Haddad, Farid Senzai, and Jane I. Smith, 21–37. New York: Oxford University Press, 2009.

Kibria, Nazli. *Muslims in Motion: Islam and National Identity in the Bangladeshi Diaspora*. New Brunswick NJ: Rutgers University Press, 2011.

Kimball, Richard Ian. *Sports in Zion: Mormon Recreation, 1890–1940*. Champaign: University of Illinois Press, 2003.

Kleindienst-Cachay, Christa. "'Balancing Between the Cultures...' Sports and Physical Activities of Muslim Girls and Women in Germany." In *Muslim Women and Sport*, edited by Tansin Benn, Gertrud Pfister, and Haifaa Jawad, 92–108. Abingdon: Routledge, 2011.

Kohn, Alfie. *No Contest: The Case Against Competition*, revised edition. Boston: Houghton Mifflin, 1992.

Lawrence, Bruce B. *New Faiths, Old Fears: Muslims and Other Asian Immigrants in American Religious Life*. New York: Columbia University Press, 2002.

Lee, Kangjae Jerry, Rudy Dunlap, and David Scott. "Korean American Males' Serious Leisure Experiences and Their Perceptions of Different Play Styles." *Leisure Sciences* 33 (2011): 290–308.

Levine, Peter. *Ellis Island to Ebbets Field: Sport and the American Jewish Experience*. New York: Oxford University Press, 1992.

Mahmood, Saba. *Politics of Piety: The Islamic Revival and the Feminist Subject*. Princeton: Princeton University Press, 2005.

Maira, Sunaina Marr. *Missing: Youth, Citizenship, and Empire after 9/11*. Durham NC: Duke University Press, 2009.

Mamdani, Mahmood. *Good Muslim, Bad Muslim: America, the Cold War, and the Roots of Terror*. New York: Pantheon, 2004.

Mandelbaum, Michael. *The Meaning of Sports: Why Americans Watch Baseball, Football, and Basketball, and What They See When They Do*. New York: Public Affairs, 2004.

Martin, Randy, and Toby Miller. "Fielding Sport: A Preface to Politics?" In *SportCult*, edited by Randy Martin and Toby Miller, 1–13. Minneapolis: University of Minnesota Press, 1999.

McCloud, Aminah Beverly. *Transnational Muslims in American Society*. Gainesville: University Press of Florida, 2006.

Merry, Michael S. *Culture, Identity, and Islamic Schooling: A Philosophical Approach*. New York: Palgrave Macmillan, 2007.

Mir, Shabana. *Muslim American Women on Campus: Undergraduate Social Life and Identity*. Chapel Hill: University of North Carolina Press, 2014.

Miracle, Jr., Andrew W., and C. Roger Rees. *Lessons of the Locker Room*. Amherst NY: Prometheus Books, 1994.

Moore, R. Laurence. *Religious Outsiders and the Making of Americans*. New York: Oxford University Press, 1986.

Mrozek, Donald J. *Sport and American Mentality, 1880–1910*. Knoxville: University of Tennessee Press, 1983.

Naber, Nadine. *Arab America: Gender, Cultural Politics, and Activism*. New York: New York University Press, 2012.

———. "'Look, Mohammed the Terrorist Is Coming!': Cultural Racism, Nation-Based Racism, and the Intersectionality of Oppressions after 9/11." In *Race and Arab Americans Before and After 9/11: From Invisible Citizens to Visible Subjects*, edited by Amaney Jamal and Nadine Naber, 276–304. Syracuse NY: Syracuse University Press, 2008.

Nasr, Seyyed Hossein. *The Garden of Truth: The Vision and Promise of Sufism, Islam's Mystical Tradition*. New York: HarperOne, 2007.

Novak, Michael. *The Joy of Sports: End Zones, Bases, Baskets, Balls, and the Conse-cration of the American Spirit.* New York: Basic Books, 1976.

Nussbaum, Martha C. *The New Religious Intolerance: Overcoming the Politics of Fear in an Anxious Age.* Cambridge MA: Belknap Press of Harvard University Press, 2012.

Oren, Michael B. *Power, Faith, and Fantasy: America in the Middle East 1776 to the Present.* New York: W.W. Norton & Co., 2008.

Overman, Steven J. *The Protestant Ethic and the Spirit of Sport: How Calvinism and Capitalism Shaped America's Games.* Macon GA: Mercer University Press, 2011.

Parker, Ian. *Qualitative Psychology: Introducing Radical Research.* New York: Open University Press, 2005.

Peterson, Richard F. "'Slide, Kelly, Slide': The Irish in American Baseball." In *The American Game: Baseball and Ethnicity,* edited by Lawrence Baldassaro and Richard A. Johnson, 55–67. Carbondale IL: Southern Illinois University Press, 2002.

Pope, S. W. *Patriotic Games: Sporting Traditions in the American Imagination, 1876–1926.* New York: Oxford University Press, 1997.

Quadri, Habeeb, and Sa'ad Quadri. *The War Within Our Hearts.* Leicestershire: Kube Publishing, 2009.

Radzi, Wirdati Mohammad. *Muslim Women and Sports in the Malay World: The Crossroads of Modernity and Faith.* Chiang Mai, Thailand: Silkworm, 2006.

Riess, Steven A. *City Games: The Evolution of American Urban Society and the Rise of Sports.* Urbana: University of Illinois Press, 1989.

———. "Sports and the American Jew: An Introduction." In *Sports and the American Jew,* edited by Steven A. Riess, 1–59. Syracuse NY: Syracuse University Press, 1998.

———. "Tough Jews: The Jewish American Boxing Experience, 1890–1950." In *Sports and the American Jew,* edited by Steven A. Riess, 60–104. Syracuse NY: Syracuse University Press, 1998.

Roediger, David R. *Working Toward Whiteness: How America's Immigrants Be-came White: The Strange Journey from Ellis Island to the Suburbs.* New York: Basic Books, 2005.

Rosen, Joel Nathan. *The Erosion of the American Sporting Ethos: Shifting Attitudes Toward Competition.* Jefferson NC: McFarland, 2007.

Rosengren, John. *Hank Greenberg: The Hero of Heroes.* New York: NAL Hard-cover, 2013.

Said, Edward W. *Covering Islam: How the Media and the Experts Determine How We See the Rest of the World,* revised edition. New York: Vintage Books, 1997.

Saldaña, Johnny. *Fundamentals of Qualitative Research.* New York: Oxford University Press, 2011.

Sarna, Jonathan D., editor. *The American Jewish Experience*. New York: Holmes & Meier, 1986.

Schmidt, Garbi. *Islam in Urban America: Sunni Muslims in Chicago*. Philadelphia: Temple University Press, 2004.

Schwalbe, Michael L. "A Humanist Conception of Competition in Sport." *Humanity & Society* 13 (1989): 43–60.

Seidel, Michael. *Streak: Joe DiMaggio and the Summer of '41*. Lincoln: University of Nebraska Press, 2002.

Shepherd, Gordon, and Gary Shepherd. *A Kingdom Transformed: Themes in the Development of Mormonism*. Salt Lake City: University of Utah Press, 1984.

Shields, David Lyle Light, and Brenda Jo Light Bredemeier. *Character Development and Physical Activity*. Champaign IL: Human Kinetics, 1995.

Shryock, Andrew. "The Moral Analogies of Race: Arab American Identity, Color Politics, and the Limits of Racialized Citizenship." In *Race and Arab Americans Before and After 9/11: From Invisible Citizens to Visible Subjects*, edited by Amaney Jamal and Nadine Naber, 81–111. Syracuse NY: Syracuse University Press, 2008.

Sirin, Selcuk R., and Michelle Fine. *Muslim American Youth: Understanding Hyphenated Identities through Multiple Methods*. New York: New York University Press, 2008.

Smith, Maureen. "*Muhammad Speaks* and Muhammad Ali: Intersections of the Nation of Islam and Sport in the 1960s." In *With God on Their Side: Sport in the Service of Religion*, edited by Tara Magdalinski and Timothy J. L. Chandler, 177–96. New York: Routledge, 2002.

Sorin, Gerald. *A Time for Building: The Third Migration 1880–1920*. Baltimore: Johns Hopkins University Press, 1992.

Sperber, Murray A. *Shake Down the Thunder: The Creation of Notre Dame Football*. Bloomington: University of Indiana Press, 2002.

Spinner-Halev, Jeff. "Extending Diversity: Religion in Public and Private Education." Paper presented at the Canadian Centre for Philosophy and Public Policy Conference "Citizenship in Diverse Societies," University of Toronto, Toronto, October 1997.

Stodolska, Monika, and Jennifer S. Livengood. "The Influence of Religion on the Leisure Behavior of Immigrant Muslims in the United States." *Journal of Leisure Research* 38/3 (2006): 293–320.

Thangaraj, Stanley. "Playing through Differences: Black-White Racial Logic and Interrogating South Asian American Identity." *Ethnic and Racial Studies* 35/6 (2012): 988–1006.

Treat, Roger L. *Bishop Sheil and the CYO*. New York: Messner, 1951.

Tucker, Todd. *Notre Dame vs. the Klan: How the Fighting Irish Defeated the Ku Klux Klan*. Chicago: Loyola Press, 2004.

Walseth, Kristin, and Kari Fasting. "Islam's View on Physical Activity and Sport: Egyptian Women Interpreting Islam." *International Review for the Sociology of Sport* 38/1 (2003): 45–60.

Whelan, Irene. "Religious Rivalry and the Making of Irish American Identity." In *Making the Irish American: History and Heritage of the Irish in the United States*, edited by J. J. Lee and Marion R. Casey, 271–85. New York: New York University Press, 2006.

Wilcox, Ralph. "Irish Americans in Sports: The Nineteenth Century." In *Making the Irish American: History and Heritage of the Irish in the United States*, edited by J. J. Lee and Marion R. Casey, 443–56. New York: New York University Press, 2006.

———"The Shamrock and the Eagle: Irish Americans and Sport in the Nineteenth Century." In *Ethnicity and Sport in North American History and Culture*, edited by George Eisen and David K. Wiggins, 55–74. Westport CT: Greenwood Press, 1995.

Zaman, Hasina. "Islam, Well-Being, and Physical Activity: Perceptions of Muslim Young Women." In *Researching Women and Sport*, edited by Gill Clarke and Barbara Humberstone, 50–67. Houndsmill: Macmillan, 1997.

Zine, Jasmin. "Safe Havens or Religious 'Ghettos'? Narratives of Islamic Schooling in Canada." In *Educating the Muslims of America*, edited by Yvonne Y. Haddad, Farid Senzai, and Jane I. Smith, 39–65. New York: Oxford University Press, 2009.

Internet Sources

"6th Annual Muslim Family Fun Day—Allentown USA." The World Federation of Khoja Shia Ithna-Asheri Muslim Communities, http://www.world-federation.org/Secretariat/Articles/Archive/6th_Annual_Muslim_Family_Fun_Day_Allentown_USA.htm. Posted 28 August 2013. Accessed 8 May 2014.

"70 Who Quit Over Prayer Time Return to Work." http://www.nbcnews.com/id/18869414/ns/us_news-life/t/who-quit-over-prayer-time-return-work/#.VQNFoLFOmM8. Published 25 May 2007. Accessed 13 March 2015.

"About An-Noor Academy." http://www.annooracademy.com/About/general-information. Accessed 21 April 2014.

"About ICNA." http://www.icna.org/about-icna. Accessed 14 March 2015.

"About MAS." http://www.massandiego.org/index.php?option=com_content&view=article&id=13&Itemid=69. Accessed 14 March 2015.

"About MPAC." http://www.mpac.org/about.php. Accessed 14 March 2015.

"About *UnMosqued*." http://www.unmosquedfilm.com/about/. Accessed 14 March 2015.

"Abu Saleh (CD) Arcade Game." http://www.islamicbookstore.com/abusalcdarga.html. Accessed 14 March 2015.

"ADAMS Youth." http://www.adamsyouth.net/. Accessed 28 April 2014.

"Al Bireh Society: About Us." http://albirehsociety.org. Accessed 11 March 2015.

Al-Kawthari, Shaykh Muhammad ibn Adam. "The Fiqh of Sports and Games." http://sunnahmuakada.com/2013/02/14/the-fiqh-of-sports-and-games/. Posted 14 February 2013. Accessed 23 April 2014.

"American Muslim Voters: A Demographic Profile and Survey of Attitudes." http://pa.cair.com/annreport/AmericanMuslimVoters.pdf. Released 24 October 2006. Accessed 14 March 2015.

Angevine, Eric. "U.S. Muslims Find 'Love and Camaraderie' on Court." http://www.nbcsports.com/other-sports/us-muslims-find-love-and-camaraderie-court#page=1. Posted 23 August 2012. Accessed 21 April 2014.

"Az Hakim Foundation: About Us." http://www.hakim4kids.com/about. Accessed 23 April 2014.

Banks, Sandy. "Mixing Girls' Sports and Muslim Tradition." http://articles.latimes.com/2001/aug/14/news/cl-33980. Published 14 August 2001. Accessed 21 April 2014.

Bashir, Shahina. "Muslim Women Develop Sisterhood Through Sports." http://www.examiner.com/article/muslim-women-develop-sisterhood-through-sports. Posted 18 April 2013. Accessed 21 April 2014.

"Basketball a Slam-Dunk for Area Muslims." http://uhdnews.uhd.edu/news/stories.aspx?articleid=302&zoneid=1. Published 4 June 2012. Accessed 22 April 2014.

"Bernard Hopkins: An American Muslim Boxing Success Story." *The Muslim Observer.* http://muslimmedianetwork.com/mmn/?p=6362. Posted 17 June 2010. Accessed 22 April 2014.

"B'nai B'rith International: About Us." http://www.bnaibrith.org/about-us.html. Accessed 14 March 2015.

"Bodykini Modest Sportswear." http://www.bodykini.com/. Accessed 11 March 2015.

"Boxing as a Sports [*sic*] in Islam." http://en.allexperts.com/q/Islam-947/2009/2/boxing-sports-islam.htm. Posted 22 February 2009. Accessed 23 April 2014.

"CAIR: Vision, Mission, Core Principles." http://www.cair.com/about-us/vision-mission-core-principles.html. Accessed 14 March 2015.

Cart, Julie, and Larry B. Stammer. "Kareem Rebuked Over Beer Ad." http://articles.latimes.com/1997-01-18/sports/sp-19764_1_kareem-abdul-jabbar. Published 18 January 1997. Accessed 23 April 2014.

"'The Deen Show': About." http://thedeenshow.com/page/about. Accessed 11 March 2015.

"Ephraim Salaam Represents Muslim Athletes at U.S. State Department." http://muslimjournal.net/?p=455. Posted 10 February 2012. Accessed 23 April 2014.

Fink, Steven. "For the Best of All Listeners: American Islamic Hip Hop as Reminder." *Journal of Religion and Society* 14 (2012). http://moses.creighton.edu/jrs/2012/2012-14.pdf. Accessed 13 March 2015.

"Florida Family Association: About Us." http://floridafamily.org/full_article.php?article_no=94. Accessed 14 March 2015.

"*Fordson: Faith, Fasting, Football* and the American Dream." http://www.fordsonthemovie.com. Accessed 24 April 2014.

"Future Foundation: About." http://future-foundation.com/about/. Accessed 22 April 2014.

Ghert-Zand, Renee. "First Palestinian-American in NFL." http://www.timesofisrael.com/first-palestinian-american-in-nfl/. Published 28 April 2013. Accessed 21 April 2014.

Glauber, Bob. "Debut of Jets' Wilkerson Falls on Sept. 11." http://www.newsday.com/sports/columnists/bob-glauber/debut-of-jets-wilkerson-falls-on-sept-11-1.3152791. Published 7 September 2011. Accessed 23 April 2014.

Goodstein, Laurie. "Stereotyping Rankles Silent, Secular Majority of American Muslims." http://www.nytimes.com/2001/12/23/us/stereotyping-rankles-silent-secular-majority-of-american-muslims.html. Published 23 December 2001. Accessed 14 March 2015.

Haddow, Joshua. "There's a Muslim Football Team at a High School in Michigan." http://www.vice.com/read/fordson-faith-fasting-football-rashid-ghazi. Posted 31 January 2012. Accessed 24 April 2014.

Hamiche, Abdelhak. "Sports in Islamic Perspective." http://thepeninsulaqatar.com/special-page/islam/225700/sports-in-islamic-perspective. Posted 15 February 2013. Accessed 23 April 2014.

Hanzus, Dan. "Abdullah Brothers Put NFL on Hold to Pursue Faith." http://www.nfl.com/news/story/09000d5d82a06d69/article/abdullah-brothers-put-nfl-on-hold-to-pursue-faith. Published 21 June 2012. Accessed 15 March 2015.

"Harvard Gym Accommodates Muslim Women."
http://usatoday30.usatoday.com/news/health/2008-03-04-muslim-gym_N.htm. Posted 4 March 2008. Accessed 8 May 2014.

Hendricks, Shaykh Seraj. "Sport and Islam."
http://mysite.mweb.co.za/residents/mfj1/sport.htm. Published 24 November 1998. Accessed 23 April 2014.

"History of the Khoja Shia Ithna-Asheries." http://www.world-federation.org/Misc/KSI+History/. Accessed 28 April 2014.

Hochman, Benjamin. "Nuggets' Power Forward Pick Faried Creates Buzz."
http://www.denverpost.com/ci_18400591. Posted 3 July 2011. Accessed 22 April 2014.

"IBall Academy: Basketball Training Overview." http://www.iballacademy.org. Accessed 8 May 2014.

"The Islamic Center of Southern California: About Us."
http://icsconline.org/aboutus. Accessed 25 April 2014.

"Islamic Games: About Us." http://www.islamic-games.com/. Accessed 24 April 2014.

"Islamic Society of Central Jersey Belief Statement."
http://www.iscj.org/AboutBeliefStatement.aspx. Accessed 28 April 2014.

Ismail, Hafez Afzal. *Islam and Sport.*
https://archive.org/stream/IslamAndSportsByHafezAfzalIsmail#page/n0/mode/2up. Accessed 31 January 2014.

"Jaguars' Owner Bought Team Undeterred by Racism."
http://www.cbsnews.com/news/jaguars-owner-bought-team-undeterred-by-racism/. Posted 25 October 2012. Accessed 15 March 2015.

"Kanoute Refuses to Wear Gambling Logo."
http://www.ummah.com/forum/showthread.php?96249-Kanoute-refuses-to-wear-gambling-logo. Accessed 14 March 2015.

Kaplan, Ron. "Jewish Athletes and the 'Yom Kippur Dilemma.'"
http://njjewishnews.com/njjn.com/092806/sptsJewishAthletesYomKippr.html. Published 28 September 2006. Accessed 14 March 2015.

Khan, Mas'ud Ahmed. "Islam and Boxing."
http://www.masud.co.uk/ISLAM/misc/boxing.htm. Accessed 23 April 2014.

Kugel, Allison. "Shaquille O'Neal Talks Kobe Bryant, Pat Riley, & NBA Politics: 'I Did It My Way.'" http://www.pr.com/article/1191. Posted 11 November 2011. Accessed 22 April 2014.

Lattin, Don. "Standoff Over the National Anthem/NBA Suspension of Muslim Stirs Free-Speech Debate." http://www.sfgate.com/news/article/PAGE-ONE-Standoff-Over-the-National-Anthem-2990682.php. Published 14 March 1996. Accessed 22 April 2014.

Lazuta, Jennifer. "American Female Muslim Athlete Inspires Girls in Dakar." http://www.voanews.com/content/first-american-female-muslim-athlete-inspires-girls-in-dakar/1846731.html. Posted 7 February 2014. Accessed 22 April 2014.

Leighton, Paul. "Muslim League Promotes Tolerance through Sports." http://www.salemnews.com/local/x546350755/Muslim-league-promotes-tolerance-through-sports. Published 29 December 2009. Accessed 24 April 2014.

Lewin, Tamar. "Some U.S. Universities Install Foot Baths for Muslim Students." http://www.nytimes.com/2007/08/07/world/americas/07iht-muslims.4.7022566.html?_r=0. Published 7 August 2007. Accessed 13 March 2015.

"Lifting Covered FAQ." http://www.liftingcovered.com. Accessed 24 April 2014.

MacFarquhar, Neil. "Muslim Player Thrives with Nourished Spirit." http://www.nytimes.com/2007/10/13/sports/football/13fasting.html?_r=1/. Published 13 October 2007. Accessed 21 April 2014.

"Many Muslim Athletes to Fast After London Olympics." http://sportsillustrated.cnn.com/2012/olympics/wires/07/20/2090.sp.oly.ramadan.olympics/index.html. Posted 20 July 2012. Accessed 22 April 2014.

"Marjaan: About Us." http://www.marjaan.org/about-us/. Accessed 29 April 2014.

"MAS Tampa MYathlon." http://www.mastampa.org/MYathlon/. Accessed 8 May 2014.

"MAS Youth." http://www.massandiego.org/index.php?option=com_content&view=article&id=16&Itemid=30. Accessed 13 March 2015.

"MCWS Campus Events Calendar." http://mcws.org/home. Accessed 28 April 2014.

"MIST: About." http://www.getmistified.com/about/. Accessed 8 May 2014.

Mohamed, Ahmed. "Michigan Hosts Large Muslim American Sports Event." http://iipdigital.usembassy.gov/st/english/article/2009/08/200908191642352sademahom4.323977e-02.html#axzz2t8TEsPfh. Posted 20 August 2009. Accessed 24 April 2014.

Mohammed, Aliyah. "Muslim NFL Players Fast During Ramadan." http://www.nbcbayarea.com/news/local/Muslim-NFL-Players-Come-to-Bay-163640676.html. Published 7 August 2012. Accessed 21 April 2014.

"MSA Showdown." http://www.msa-texas.org/#!msa-showdown-2015/c8mg. Accessed 13 March 2015.

Musaji, Sheila. "American Companies Accused of Joining the All-American Anti-Muslim Bandwagon."

http://theamericanmuslim.org/tam.php/features/articles/all-american-muslim/0018896. Posted 20 December 2011. Accessed 14 March 2015.

"Muslim Athletic League: About Us." http://malusa.org/about-us/. Accessed 8 May 2014.

"Muslim Basketball: About Us." http://muslimbasketball.org/about.asp. Accessed 12 March 2015.

Muslim Basketball League website. http:www.hometeamsonline.com/teams/?u= MBLEAGUE&s=basketball. Accessed 13 March 2015.

"Muslim NFL Players Hamza and Husain Abdullah '30 for 30' Ramadan Tour." http://www.salatomatic.com/cbe.php?id=127. Posted 29 June 2012. Accessed 15 March 2015.

"Muslim Sports Day: Rules." http://msd.icnanj.org/index.php?option=com_content&view =article&id=174&Itemid=2. Accessed 8 May 2014.

"Muslim Sports Tournament Expected to Draw 2,000 to Orlando in 2012." http://www.letsmove.gov/blog/2011/11/16/muslim-sports-tournament-expected-draw-2000-orlando-2012. Posted 16 November 2011. Accessed 21 April 2014.

"MYCC: About." http://www.myccnj.org/about/. Accessed 8 May 2014.

National Muslim Athletic Association website. http://www.nmaa-us.org. Accessed 8 May 2014.

"National Muslim Basketball Tour: About." http://www.nmbt.org/about. Accessed 8 May 2014.

"New Horizon School Pasadena: Mission & Goals." http://www.newhorizonschool.org/pages/about_us/missiongoals. Accessed 25 April 2014.

Norfleet, Nicole. "St. Paul YMCA and Police Start Somali Girls Swim Group." http://m.startribune.com/?id=232082231. Published 18 November 2013. Accessed 22 April 2014.

One! Athletics website. http://oneathletics.org/. Accessed 14 March 2015.

Pandith, Farah. "Eid Reception Recognizes American Muslims' Achievements in Athletics." http://blogs.state.gov/stories/2011/09/09/eid-reception-recognizes-american-muslims-achievements-athletics. Posted 9 September 2011. Accessed 21 April 2014.

"Physical Education for Saudi Girls Stirs Debate." http://muslimwomeninsports.blogspot.com. Posted 15 April 2014. Accessed 8 May 2014.

Pilon, Mary. "Before Games, Religious Questions." http://www.nytimes.com/2012/03/03/sports/in-texas-islamic-schools-face-tough-road-to-participation.html?_r=0. Published 2 March 2012. Accessed 21 April 2014.

Quick, Jason. "During Ramadan, Forward Fasts in the Daylight Hours, Reads the Quran, and Doesn't Complain." http://www.thecoli.com/threads/shareef-abdur-rahim-being-a-muslim-i-think-thankfullness-thread.70004/. Posted 9 November 2004. Accessed 22 April 2014.

Radia, Andy. "Rayane Benatti, 9-Year-Old Quebec Girl Banned from Soccer Game for Wearing Hijab." https://ca.news.yahoo.com/blogs/canada-politics/9-old-quebec-girl-banned-soccer-game-wearing-182157253.html. Posted 10 July 2012. Accessed 8 May 2014.

Remington, Alex. "Why Aren't There More Muslims in Baseball?" www.fangraphs.com/blogs/why-arent-there-more-muslims-in-baseball/. Posted 8 August 2013. Accessed 22 April 2014.

Robertson, Dale. "Ryan Harris Is Making the Most of His Opportunity." http://blog.chron.com/ultimatetexans/2013/07/ryan-harris-is-making-the-most-of-his-opportunity/. Posted 29 July 2013. Accessed 23 April 2014.

Sacirbey, Omar. "A Source of Pride and Hope." http://m.spokesman.com/stories/2007/feb/03/a-source-of-pride-and-hope/. Published 3 February 2007. Accessed 22 April 2014.

———. "Why Basketball Is Muslims' Favorite Sport." http://www.huffingtonpost.com/2012/05/21/basketball-muslim-favorite-sport_n_1528495.html. Posted 21 May 2012. Accessed 21 April 2014.

Schlussel, Debbie. "Buh-Bye: NBA Gravy Train Ends for Muslim Proselytizer Who Supports Cop Killers." http://www.debbieschlussel.com/4261/buh-bye-nba-gravy-train-ends-for-muslim-proselytizer-who-supports-cop-killers/comment-page-1/. Posted 23 September 2008. Accessed 22 April 2014.

Siddiqui, Samana. "Muslim Schools vs. Public Schools." http://www.icna.org/muslim-schools-vs-public-schools/. Posted 14 December 2009. Accessed 13 March 2015.

Stanmyre, Matthew. "New Jersey Islamic Students See Basketball League Taking Shape." http://www.nj.com/hssports/blog/boysbasketball/index.ssf/2013/04/new_jersey_islamic_students_see_basketball_league_taking_shape.html. Published 14 April 2013. Accessed 21 April 2014.

"Sunnah Sports: About." http://sunnahsports.com/about/. Accessed 8 May 2014.

T.E.A.M. 96 webite. http://www.mwteam96.com. Accessed 23 April 2014.

Toothnail, Buckus. "Has Kareem Abdul-Jabbar's Religion Affected His Legacy?" http://bleacherreport.com/articles/437893-has-kareem-abdul-jabbars-religion-affected-his-legacy. Posted 17 August 2010. Accessed 23 April 2014.

Traikos, Michael. "Muslim Nazem Kadri Is Emerging from the Background as One of the Best." http://www.thenational.ae/sport/north-american-sport/nhl-muslim-nazem-kadri-is-emerging-from-the-background-as-one-of-the-best. Published 5 April 2013. Accessed 23 April 2014.

"Umoja Games: About Us." http://www.umojagames.org/about-us/. Accessed 8 May 2014.

"Umoja Games: Academy." http://www.umojagames.org/academy/. Accessed 8 May 2014.

"UNC MSA Sportsfest." http://www.uncmsa.org/#!sportsfest/c17et. Accessed 14 March 2015.

"U.S. Muslims [*sic*] Love Story with Basketball." http://www.onislam.net/english/news/americas/457590-us-muslims-love-story-with-basketball.html. Posted 16 June 2012. Accessed 22 April 2014.

Waldron, Travis. "Fox News on Swim Class for Muslim Girls: 'Sharia Law Is Changing Everything.'" http://thinkprogress.org/sports/2013/12/02/3009111/fox-news-fond-muslims-participating-sports/. Posted 2 December 2013. Accessed 22 April 2014.

Waszak, Jr., Dennis. "Oday Aboushi, Jets' Palestinian-American Rookie, Defends Against 'Muslim Extremist' Claim." http://www.huffingtonpost.com/2013/07/12/oday-aboushi-jets-palestinian_n_3588928.html. Posted 12 July 2013. Accessed 21 April 2014.

Welsh-Huggins, Andrew. "Ohio Removes Pork from Prison Menus in Nod to Muslim Inmates." http://cnsnews.com/news/article/ohio-removes-pork-prison-menus-nod-muslim-inmates. Published 5 October 2011. Accessed 13 March 2015.

Wilkinson, Paul. "Islam, Sport, & Terrorism." http://chersonandmolschky.com/2014/01/23/islam-sport-terrorism/. Posted 23 January 2014. Accessed 23 April 2014.

"World Values Survey." http://www.worldvaluessurvey.org/wvs.jsp. Accessed 15 March 2015.

Zirin, Dave. "Not a Game: How the NYPD Uses Sports for Surveillance." http://www.thenation.com/blog/176082/not-game-how-nypd-uses-sports-surveillance. Posted 10 September 13. Accessed 21 April 2014.

Index

Baer, Max 54
Bagby, Ihsan 67
Baker, William 16, 17 (fn12), 19
  (fn16,17), 30, 47, 136, 145
Baldassaro, Lawrence 40, 41
Ballard, Melvin 12
Baltimore Orioles 39, 40
Barrett, Paul 4 (fn6)
baseball
  Catholics in Major League Base-
    ball 39-43
  Jews in Major League Baseball 32,
    55-59
  Mormon recreation movement
    baseball activities 22
  Muslims in Major League Base-
    ball 128-129
  Protestant church baseball activi-
    ties 20
  YMCA baseball activities 18
basketball
  Asian Americans in the National
    Basketball Association 106
  Catholic Youth Organization bas-
    ketball activities 29, 30
  Islamic school basketball activities
    113, 191-193, 230-231, 234,
    235, 236, 239, 240, 242
  Jewish basketball leagues 53
  Jewish semiprofessional teams 53
  Jews in college basketball 52
  Mormon recreation movement
    basketball activities 22-23
  mosque basketball activities 200,
    203, 205, 208, 209, 210-211,
    212, 214, 216, 220, 221
  Muslim basketball leagues 96-97,
    156, 160-176
  Muslim high school basketball
    players 100, 105, 109, 191-
    193, 194-196, 230-231
  Muslims in college basketball 92
  Muslims in the National Basket-
    ball Association 102, 126-127,
    137-148

  pick-up basketball among Mus-
    lims 107, 159-160
  popularity of basketball among
    Muslim Americans 156-159;
    Protestant church basketball
    activities 20
  revivalist organization basketball
    activities 1, 180-181, 182, 184,
    185, 186, 187-188, 189, 191-
    193, 194-196
  YMCA basketball activities 18
Bazzano, Carmelo 36 (fn11), 111
Beecher, Lyman 35
Billy Graham crusades 27 (fn34)
Blauvelt, Chris 148, 152, 160, 181
B'nai B'rith 53
Boas, Franz 247 (fn3)
Bodykini 121
Boko Haram 249
bonding, explanation of term 2
Borish, Linda 114 (fn24)
Boston Celtics 138, 201
Boston Red Sox 55 (fn66), 58
Boulmerka, Hassiba 82, 118
bowling
  Catholic Youth Organization bowling
    activities 29, 30
  Protestant church bowling activities 20
boxing
  Catholic professional boxers 37-39
  Catholic Youth Organization box-
    ing activities 29, 30-31
  Jewish professional boxers 53-55
  mosque boxing activities 205
  Muslim professional boxers 130-
    137
  Muslim views regarding violence
    in boxing 94-95
Boyd, Todd 157 (fn6)
Brady, Tom 153
Bredemeier, Brenda 98 (fn50)
bridging, explanation of term 2
Bright Ascension 229
Brinkmann, Svend 6 (fn13)
Brisbane, Arthur 55

Index

CPSIA information can be obtained
at www.ICGtesting.com
Printed in the USA
LVOW12s0845090916

503740LV00002B/2/P